USING THE "Z" WORD

Smith hushed the buzzing in the room, and said, "Dr. Curry, can you explain your statement regarding 'erratic and confusing but not lethal' symptoms? Do you mean that the patients are uncooperative?"

"That would be an understatement," Curry said. "And the disease appears to be highly communicable. There are several cases where all but airborne transmission appear to be ruled out. We *are* confident that the disease is droplet borne and transmissible via bites."

This time Paul spoke over the chatter around the table. "Doctor, when you say 'transmissible via bites,' are you referring to family pets and the like?"

"No. I mean transmissible via bites from people." Curry looked over the top of his glasses at the intel specialist. "As in, if a symptomatic victim bites a nurse, then that nurse may develop symptoms within hours, which as far as we can tell is much faster than other vectors. In known bite cases, the second set of symptoms took anywhere from hours to days to manifest, but it skipped the flu component entirely."

A voice from down the table said it for everyone. "Like zombie bites? Are we talking about zombies?"

Curry winced, then nudged his glasses upwards so that he could rub the bridge of his nose.

"Yes. Ah mean just like 'zombies.'"

This time it took Smith much longer to quell the hubbub.

THE VALLEY OF
SHADOWS

JOHN RINGO
& MIKE MASSA

THE VALLEY OF SHADOWS

A Baen Books Original

Baen Publishing Enterprises
P.O. Box 1403
Riverdale, NY 10471
www.baen.com

ISBN: 978-1-9821-2419-9

Cover art by Kurt Miller

First printing, November 2018
First mass market printing, November 2019

Library of Congress Control Number: 2018032981

Distributed by Simon & Schuster
1230 Avenue of the Americas
New York, NY 10020

Pages by Joy Freeman (www.pagesbyjoy.com)
Printed in the United States of America

10 9 8 7 6 5 4 3 2 1

ACKNOWLEDGEMENTS

First and foremost, I'd like to publicly thank John Ringo for allowing me to not only participate in a world of his making, but actually play a bit with one of the most beloved characters of all time in the Ringoverse. Additionally, I genuinely appreciate your patience and tuition as we argued the fine details—like why contractions are a "good thing"! Like hundreds of thousands of others, I've loved your books from the first read and now I've been allowed to help build one. John, thank you for inviting me to come along on a hell of a ride.

I owe a debt of thanks to Toni Weisskopf for taking a leap of faith on a new guy—her investments in people and willingness to take a chance make this possible. Seriously, I'm just glad that when I received her message out of the blue inquiring when I might be submitting a book proposal there were no witnesses on hand to observe the manly and top secret Navy SEAL "tippy-toes dance of surprised joy" that accompanied my fifteenth reread of her communication.

Thank you to the many folks who made themselves available to assist us with details of the National Guard, police procedure, virology, anesthesiology, rotary wing aviation and general encouragement—too

John Ringo & Mike Massa

many to name, but most certainly Mike Gantz, Jamie Ibson, Aaron Mays, John Holmes, Josh Barnett, Kevin Tucker, Kevin Partridge, Tamar Newberry, Frankie Terzoli, Kelly Lockhart and of course the indomitable quartet of Griff, Speaker, KC and Chris!

—MM

FOREWORD

The decline of our shared cultural literacy means that we live with many sayings whose origins aren't widely remembered, even where documentation is easy to find. Good examples are legion—especially with regard to sayings rooted in the British maritime tradition. Some sayings go further back, far enough that even in the original Greek or Latin, there are disagreements on the finer points as to what the ancients really meant.

One such saying revolved around the rarity of salt.

For all that early civilizations often bordered salt water, pure concentrated mineral salt was rare. Prior to the advent of canning and refrigeration, salt was also critical for food preparation and preservation. Poorly preserved food meant poisoning or death. The inability to safely store food could mean famine. Salt was so valuable that during the Phoenician period it was accepted as currency, alongside gold and silver, remaining precious into the Roman era. Moving this salt required good roads and reliable soldiers. A network of special roads was built to secure and rapidly move salt into the Roman Empire. Guarded and often built by Roman soldiers, the Via Salarium drew its name from the trade it carried: salt. Pliny the Elder recorded in his work *The Natural History* that Roman soldiers were often paid in salt, giving rise to the term that we use today, "salary." The financial resources used by a commander to operate his military forces in a given theater of operations, whether he was garrisoning or expanding territory, were known as Salarium. They included both specie and salt, and these were used to pay for the business costs of the units under the general's control.

As with any business venture (and war was Rome's most profitable business), there were always problems. Sometimes soldiers found that they were serving under a dishonest, politically optimistic or just plain idiot of a general (See: The Battle of Cannae). But whether legionnaire, centurion or tribune, once you joined the legion, you agreed to follow all orders and remain loyal to your commanders for the duration of the campaign, whether successful or disastrous. You were being paid to do the job to the best of your ability even unto death. Soldiers might rationalize their desire to be somewhere else, or working for someone else, but if you "took the salt," you were committed, come hell or high water.

A legionnaire who stood by his commitment and honored the bargain was said to be "worth his salt." That legionnaire placed his honor, in the form of his commitment to his word, above all other considerations.

Today, soldiers who transition to civilian life bring with them concepts about personal honor and commitment which, though not unknown outside the ranks, are not as common as they are inside the military. They tend to take the matter of promises to their employer and to themselves very seriously. Accepting "the salt" is still a thing, and seeing a veteran "stick" with a firm even when things start to slide is pretty common.

What does it take to make him reconsider?

PROLOGUE

They took care to periodically lock a school child's bicycle to a post along the executive's predictable commute route. After a while, the careful security sweep along the route simply noted it as an expected, unremarkable part of the environment. Then the attackers hid the bomb in a knapsack hung on the back of the bike.

The explosively formed projectile was triggered by an infrared detection beam that counted past the lead security car, which in response to threats had been added to the detail a week earlier. The charge calculation took into account the armor placement on the hardened Mercedes sedan and successfully penetrated just below the thickest protective belt, perfectly breaching the rear passenger compartment. The blast threw the car off course, starting a fire that would eventually consume the vehicle. Not that it mattered.

The terrorists knew their target. They calculated the timing to a hair. Their patient, thorough intelligence knew all about the escort vehicles and the Mercedes's armor. Alfred Herrhausen, then the Chief Executive of Deutsche Bank A.G., died on the scene from blast and fragmentation wounds created by a bomb exquisitely tailored just for him.

1

It didn't matter whether the bomb belonged to the last active terror cell of the Red Army Faction striking against a hated symbol of capitalism or to the East German Stasi trying to delay national reunification or to some other attacker. The shockwaves that Herrhausen's death sent not just throughout Germany, but through the banking industry in general, were severe. Banks had long known that everybody wanted what they held—but a sophisticated bomb attack using infrared trigger beams and explosively formed penetrators and backed by painstaking research was beyond their ken. Rather suddenly, the traditional answer to filling banking security leadership roles with retired cops didn't seem like quite enough. The 1989 attack that killed Herrhausen had another victim. The old school of financial services security died that day too. Its death just took a little while longer to register.

Bankers have money and brains, and can apply both in their own self-interest when appropriately motivated. The best bankers learn to make their decisions ahead of any curve. So it was that, upon learning that the chairman of one of the largest banks had been killed despite the strongest precautions then in existence, the boards of the top investment banks considered alternatives in security. Shortly afterward, their recruiters received new orders.

Options weren't deep, but only a few years before, the British Special Air Service, or SAS, commandos had made the professional acquaintance of some uninvited Iranian guests during a "dinner party" at the Iranian Embassy in London. Not long thereafter, the SAS led the recapture of the Falkland Islands. Soon after that, Special Operations units were getting publicity in Operations Urgent Fury, Just Cause and a little dustup called Desert Storm.

The time seemed right to do a little poaching, banker style.

They didn't know just how well it was going to pay off.

CHAPTER 1

"Bulls, Bears, and Bioterror: Preparing the Financial Industry for a Pandemic was a two-day symposium on avian influenza for business leaders and influencers from the financial sector, focusing on corporate security, business continuity, crisis management and resilience. This event brought together industry experts and biologists to discuss . . ."

—*Journal for Business Risk Management,*
Vol. 1 no. 3 (2010)

May 15th
Bank of the Americas Global Headquarters
Manhattan, New York

"How the *hell* did you not see anything until now?"

Tom Smith was pissed.

The managing director for Security and Emergency Response at Bank of the Americas, and late of the Australian Special Air Service Regiment, had been recruited as a straight-up protective-detail agent by Barclays in the Sydney office. Despite the cultural hindrance of a profile fit enough to prompt the secretary pool at the bank to joke that Clark Kent worked for the Bank, not the paper, he leveraged his ability to rapidly adapt to new and potentially hostile cultures, like those found in parts of the third world or *really competitive* banks. His attention to detail and discretion had caught the eye of the local managing director and he found himself bumped into the occasional broader duties. After some seasoning in Singapore, he was poached by BotA and eventually promoted into his current role—and his current headache.

His job was a lot less glamorous than most imagined. The number one role of the BotA Security and Emergency Response (SER) team was to keep the bank trading as long as the market stayed open. The nightmare scenario for any bank wasn't a robbery, or a kidnapping, or even a bombing. Though unpleasant, those sorts of events were, if not routine, at least well understood. No, true horror would be to be excluded from the market while everyone else was still in it. One of the banks in the World Trade Center had been a leading clearance house for euro-based trades and temporarily ceded the position to another bank as it relocated its operations to a new building after 9/11. It never regained the market and died, not because it lost physical infrastructure and staff to terrorists, but because the competitors scented blood and made a meal of their injured peer.

Sharks are like that. Banks are smart sharks, the scariest of them all.

To that end, Tom's current employer didn't just set up the traditional doormen and access control, or "Guards and Cards," security division. Tom oversaw the usual Executive Protection and Building Security, but also directed a bigger team. The Anti-Fraud division fought wire fraud and protected high-value digital payments, Disaster Recovery and Business Continuity operated redundant, hardened trading floors and data centers, and the Protective Intelligence, or PI, team, looked deep into their crystal ball to predict what might be coming next.

They didn't seem to be doing a very good job.

"*We* set up the Vietnamese wet market network," Tom continued somewhat more mildly. "We have hooks into the CDC and the WHO, and you convinced me to fund permanent networks in North Africa and equatorial America. So, tell me, Paul, why has exactly none of this *expensive* early warning paid off?"

Tom looked up from the Daily Intel Brief that PI released before the market opened every day.

No one likes to be on the carpet and Paul Rune was no exception. As ambitious as he was intelligent, the fit and aspiring VP ran the PI team, having left a senior analyst position at the National Geospatial Intelligence Agency to give investment banking a go. It paid much better, but like a lot of intel types, he was an information junky. Bank of the Americas funded information access nearly as well as his old job, so he never regretted the move to industry. Usually.

At the moment he was explaining a possible intel failure in front of his direct report whose nickname was "Thomas the Train Engine," in part due to his drive to get things done. Also, he was quite large. And at the moment just a tad scary.

Swallowing, Paul made his case.

"Boss, we watched all the leading indicators," Paul said. "I have been tracking the overnight swings in live poultry, not just in Vietnam and Korea, but anywhere there is a wet market for the last thirty-six months."

"Wet market," referring to the "buy it live, take it home butchered" approach, was still the way of shopping for food in much of the world. Also, a really good way to spread disease.

"We have been getting ready for the monsoon season in Asia, so we have a special watch right now,"

Paul continued. "No way is this an avian flu variant that hopped the species barrier somewhere in Asia. No way in hell. We would have seen prices fall off a cliff as local farmers start dumping their birds. The network functions as advertised."

"Apparently not this time," Tom said, crossing his arms. "The first warning—*nonexclusive,* mind you— that we have is that there are active cases of," he consulted the brief, "'potentially fatal, nonspecific flu with similarities to avian influenza' and *that* comes from outside the bank. Six cases, including one fatality in Shanghai. Unconfirmed reports of more in three other cities in Asia. Anything else in Asia from last night?"

"Nothing yet," Paul said, squaring his shoulders. "I already sent the order to the Asia-Pacific center to disperse the Tamiflu to avoid local government seizure. The Tokyo and Shanghai bourses closed normally. The LSE has been open for three hours and nothing has twitched. We have a good network in the Gulf and eastern Europe, but nothing so far. And, Boss, we wouldn't have even this much warning if I hadn't recruited that analyst in Taiwan last year."

"Duly noted," Tom said drily, "that you were *doing your job.* But good job on getting the antivirals out right away. Let's assume that this is just an isolated incident. If there is more, update me ASAP. I'm going to let the chief risk officer know right away. He can decide if this is worth the CEO's time or not."

"Boss, another thing." Paul wasn't done, yet. "If we know, you can bet CDC, NIH, USAMRIID and the rest of the usual suspects are already on it. If any release a statement, it could become too late to exercise the first steps for Plan Zeus."

Plan Zeus was the bank's Catastrophic Market Suspension Response Plan. Tom privately thought of it as the "If It Gets This Bad We Are All Likely Dead Anyway So Open The Good Bourbon" plan.

It was so sensitive that few even inside BotA were aware of its existence. Among those, the possibility was just so unlikely that even fewer took it seriously. It was so ridiculously expensive that it couldn't be rehearsed. But "Train" Smith had made preparedness his hobby. Okay, his obsession. He was delighted that his job let him play "What if?" with other peoples' money.

Plan Zeus was his baby.

Tom rubbed his chin, which was marked by a thin white scar obtained in a most educational way.

"Can't call Zeus unless we brief the CEO. Can't do that yet. Stay in your lane for now, Paul, but keep me posted. At least every two hours, got it?"

"Got it."

Tom called past Paul's receding back for his administrative assistant, or "admin."

"Gizelle!"

"Yeah, Boss?"

"Ring Rich's office—see if he can take a high-pri right now."

"On it."

Richard Bateman—Rich to his inner circle—was the chairman and CEO of BotA. As a rule, Tom didn't take problems to him straightaway, usually working directly with the regional chairmen who ran the five top offices globally. However, Tom had worked enough emergencies for the Board that he had a feel for when to go directly to the top. When the Pakistani terrorists had attacked Mumbai and overrun a hotel where BotA was wooing investors at a swanky dinner, he jumped levels in command and activated bank assets that had saved lives and left the firm sitting pretty. It hadn't hurt Tom's bonus either.

A potentially global issue such as a pandemic was a case where Bateman would expect to exercise his "Right of First Refusal"—electing to learn first and monitor closely. He would also react "unhelpfully" if he was being disturbed for something below his pay grade.

That was the understood cost of access at the highest levels.

"Train—sort of early, isn't it?" the CEO joked. "Where do I send the lawyers and how much cash do you need?"

"Sorry to disturb you, Rich—but remember the swine flu in Mexico City?"

"Oh Christ, another bug hunt?"

Bateman was also a secret science fiction geek. It made him easier to work for.

"The intel team handed me a hot one." Tom paused almost imperceptibly. "We're not sure—but the reports suggest an avian flu variant, only a handful of cases, some fatal, unknown parameters—first reports in Shanghai, maybe two more cities. Nothing publicly released yet, but I've authorized antiviral dispersion throughout the Asia Pacific offices. I'm monitoring closely, but if it ticks up even a little bit, we'll need to move to a Gold response. This will be in the morning papers before the markets open in Tokyo and Hong Kong."

BotA had elected to copy the framework for emergency response management originated by Scotland Yard and later adopted by the U.K.'s Metropolitan

Police Department. "Gold-Silver-Bronze," or GSB, corresponded to the levels of authority and control that an organization delegated during a crisis. Tom's team could run local, minor issues to ground by invoking the Bronze team, confining issues to a single city and local management. If the calamity escalated up to Gold, Tom would integrate the executive board of the bank and all regional managing directors and would set the most alert posture for all Security and Emergency Response related staff. The board would choose when to integrate law enforcement and other governmental agencies. Initiating the GSB process officially acknowledged that there was an "issue." The existence of Plan Zeus was only known to a subset of bank staff—not even the entire security team was aware, but all the players on a Gold call would be.

Bateman understood risk—but he also understood markets.

"The reference to avian flu is going to make headlines." The CEO's tone was serious. "If you get anything solid, start the Gold call straightaway and don't wait for my approval. Before we get to that I'll send a note to Global Markets. They can turn a buck on anything. Also, if you get an inkling that this is going bigger—let me know right away. I'll tell my admin to let you break in."

"Thanks Rich—more as I get it."

The bank usually over air conditioned its offices to the point where many of the female staff routinely complained. Ordinarily, Paul was sympathetic; he hated being unnecessarily cold too. However, as he liked to helpfully point out, they could always add a sweater but anyone who was too warm was constrained from taking off their shirt.

The cool air wasn't helping. Paul was sweating through his expensive, formerly crisp dress shirt. Once his PI staff knew what to look for, the count of "potential" cases of the new flu strain had increased, and the number of affected cities grew. There were reports of an anomalous, unseasonal flu and…unusual symptoms. His second report to Smith included two more cities, both in Asia. Within another hour, the news became alarming.

There were three more "possibles," all in Europe or the Mediterranean by the next time he reached Smith on the phone. His boss picked up before the end of the first ring.

"Smith."

"It's Paul." The head of intel kept his tone level, but it took effort. "I've got six more cities with possibles: Tokyo and Freemantle make sense since they're both Pacific Rim cities, but now we also have Athens, Cairo, Barcelona and maybe L.A. If these originate from the same pathogen, it's less than likely this is a natural event. And by 'less,' I mean no damned way."

"Shit." Paul's deadpan delivery didn't fool Smith.

"Tom, another thing," Paul added. "We've done some digging, and some medical staff are reporting that the families of the sick people report a severe flu preceding the current symptoms by as much as a week or so. The onset of the second set of symptoms includes"—Tom could hear the rustling of paper from Paul's end of the line—"spontaneous sociopathy, severe anhedonia, aggression and instantaneous aphasia."

"'Aggression' I got." Smith was in no mood for

biotech-babble. "As for the rest, congratulations on winning this round of 'stumping your boss,' Paul. English please."

The intel chief paused, and then took the plunge. His boss wasn't noted for asking twice.

"In a word, zombies."

"Bloody hell, Paul," Tom said wearily. "Are you tired of working for me?"

"I swear I'm not making this up," Paul replied. "The people that aren't dying straightaway from the disease stop talking and start trying to *bite* everyone else."

"Right," Tom said. It came out as *"Royt,"* the boss's normally unnoticeable Australian accent kicking in a bit. There was a brief pause as his boss digested the analysis. "I am initiating the Gold call right now. Pull a short deck together with the confirmed and potentials plotted on a map, and get me the historical summaries for both H5N1 and the swine flu. Also, get the first three people on our bio-attack and pandemic expert list here, yesterday."

Tom hung up, externally as calm as his intel manager had sounded. His left hand hurt a little and he looked down to see that he was gripping the chair arm hard enough to stretch the thick leather to the point of tearing. With a deliberate effort, he relaxed his hand, but he couldn't fight off the queasy feeling in his gut.

Zombies? There was no way that he could initiate a Gold call with a zombie warning. The number of cities with the virus was bad enough. Also, an artificial event?

Shit.

He reached over to his second desk phone, hard-wired only to interior numbers, took a breath and for only the second time in his career pressed the Executive Committee call line for a Gold call.

The line was reserved exclusively for emergencies that required the immediate attention of the executive board and all five regional chairs. Upon activation, a specialized ring tone and text message would sound on every device belonging to each committee member, beginning with their personal devices, escalating through their immediate staff and ending with their private residences.

Tom pressed the speaker phone button and leaned back in his seat. He had a moment until the seniormost people in his bank joined the call and demanded just what the hell was important enough to disrupt all of the schedules for the bank's top executives.

The last time that he had employed this line he'd used the brief wait to rehearse his answers in order to have quick, confident replies on tap explaining the need to interrupt their routine.

This time he had not a bloody clue what to say.

CHAPTER 2

⎯⎯⎯❧❧⎯⎯⎯

"Three years after the near collapse of international banking during the 2008 liquidity crisis, and nothing has changed! The defensive plays that banks and individuals make in order to protect themselves from downside have a tendency to take cash out of the market exactly at the time when the smooth functioning of the system requires not only cash but confidence. If something affects both . . ."

—Financial analysis explaining the record swings
in the stock market, early May 2011

All banks, and for that matter major companies of every stripe, as well as government organizations the world over, prepare for a variety of possible crises of varying severity. Localized environmental events, regional wars, massive global inflation, multiregion wars between major nations—all of these will interrupt "normal" life for a time. Post 9/11, national regulatory agencies required market makers—major actors on the exchanges whose activity facilitated the daily movement of cash money throughout the economy—to have plans to cope with these "mundane" catastrophes. Even the recent Paris scenario or the "nuclear event in the Caribbean" that the PI team strongly suspected *hadn't* been a hoax represented manageable events, for values of the word manageable.

To comply with their "market maker" status, BotA

and all its peers had the ability to shift trading activity between widely separated and redundant physical trading floors, complete with identical work stations, data feeds and trading turrets. These facilities were located at radii of increasing values from the "main facilities," which always resided in very large cities: London, New York, Tokyo, etc. During a truly major event that might cause trading to be temporarily suspended for a day or three, the banks could "pass the book" to other regional offices located on other continents, allowing trades actually in progress to be completed. The financial sector practiced these routine sorts of emergencies every year.

However, a few entities, mostly nation states and very large multinationals, extended their planning further.

How does one preserve civilization in the event of a *smallish* planetary comet strike? What if the Yellowstone supercaldera lets loose just enough to stop the next growing season? How do you cope with the use of several major EMPs detonated in near Earth orbit? These events wouldn't merely perturb markets for a short while. Globally integrated economic activity could cease for an indefinite period. Without the ability to finance fuel, fertilizer, spare parts and transport, the system that fed, clothed and healed the world would degrade very rapidly and even perhaps shut down across entire regions.

Thus, Plan Zeus.

In the event that market activity was projected to be suspended for a significant period, and the reopening could not be accurately forecasted, BotA had a "Go To Hell" strategy. In a nutshell, it would rapidly exercise long-term options on certain properties and stocks of materials. It would dispatch personnel for long-term duty at hardened data centers in order to preserve an image of global financial activity and capital reserves, to the level of individual retail transactions, enabling a restart at some future point. Certain high-value private banking customers would be notified and offered *personal* options. In short, the bank would function as a parachute for such of its staff and customers that could either afford the cost, were senior enough to negotiate this as a perk or possessed an indispensable skill needed to execute the plan.

Although Tom had actually enjoyed working through the minutia needed to fill out Plan Zeus, he knew that refreshing the basic concept for the decision makers would require carefully reviewing and then explaining the rationale for the project. Once he had called the meeting, most NYC staff filtered into the secure conference room. A larger number were Skyping from London, Singapore and Zurich.

However, the agenda that he had envisioned for the Gold call hadn't survived two minutes. First, the meeting had been relocated to a large, bright executive briefing room with a multibillion dollar view of Manhattan, blowing his careful information security plans out of the water. Second, the first objection appeared before Tom finished his basic brief.

"I'm not saying that this is a paranoid distraction that we don't need on a Friday, but chrissakes, Rich!"

Herbert Elliott, the regional chair of the Americas wasn't raising his voice, much. However, his whining tone grated on Smith's nerves. Titularly junior to the CEO, Elliott controlled a region that punched above its weight in revenue and that bought him quite a lot of leeway.

Bateman smiled as though he didn't take any offense at the outburst. He kept his tone mild, which his staff knew was Step One on the way to getting angry. Bateman trusted Smith, but he needed to get a sense for how his Board and Operating Committee were going to react.

"Herb, maybe you could unpack that a little more helpfully." The CEO replied smoothly. "Fill in the blanks."

Elliott moderated his tone a little and readdressed Smith. His angry squint didn't change, however.

"Rich, Tom, look—I understand. No, let me finish!" Elliott said, raising one hand though Tom hadn't made any move to interrupt. "I understand that we need to accept the possible financial and morale costs of distributing our *expensive* antivirals on a global basis, even in places where we aren't supposed to have them—and that is going to raise hell in Mexico City, I can tell you. I can even accept that we start with social distancing and send half of our non-business-critical staff to work from home."

Herb warmed up, sounding more confident.

"I can even understand that we need to open the recovery sites in case we elect to send staff there." The tubby executive gestured magnanimously. "I'll stretch as far as a sign off on the approval for the charge strings for this *unbudgeted* exercise, just in case there is something to it. What I can't wrap my head around is that Tom wants to activate this insane, paranoid plan to exercise options for the haven sites at a cost of..." he consulted the briefing slides in front of him "...a hundred forty-five million dollars. Christ, that is our entire profit margin for the first quarter! And that's just for the *Americas* region."

Tom carefully watched all the players without being obvious. Bateman kept his peace as well, but glanced at Smith. Clearly, he was reserving his personal capital and allowing some in the group to let off steam before he weighed in. Besides, Tom suspected that he enjoyed watching the gladiatorial style politics play out among the sharks on his staff.

That's how you bred better sharks, after all.

Rolling his shoulders to relieve the tension, Tom abused his suit jacket seams and answered.

"Herb, first, thank you, sincerely, for supporting the initial steps." Tom's polite smile was precise. "To your question though—this will rapidly become a 'use-it-or-lose-it' proposition. If we don't exercise the options soon, and by that I mean before the information that we have becomes public knowledge, the cost will jump substantially. If the assets remain available at all. We're on the cusp of the weekend and rumors are going to have three days to build fear and uncertainty."

"Tom, pardon me, but that is bullshit speculation," Elliott retorted angrily. "How many people died in the avian flu? Under a hundred? How much business disruption did we see from swine flu? Barely any. Why do we need to stampede to an expensive decision now?"

"Herb, if I may?" Another voice cut in.

Bradley Depine III, another managing director and the senior acquisitions officer for the Americas happened to be visiting from his L.A. office.

"I want to congratulate Tom on being on top of this situation," Depine said, his blotchy jowls jiggling as he spoke up. "The first new reports are only now becoming public—so we beat the news cycle again.

We took a position on some pharma indexes which look to pay off nicely. Well done to the Security and Emergency Response Team."

He paused before he slipped the knife in. It never hurt to keep the regional chairs sweet—you never knew when you would need a favor and he *knew* Herb would remember this one.

"However, I agree with Herb that we have the entire weekend ahead to monitor the situation and gather more information."

He affected a neutral pause before continuing unctuously.

"Tom, this seems like an overreaction. How do we know that this situation is so different from what we have seen and weathered before?"

Tom stayed cool. He knew that he was being played. What he wanted to do was roll his stapled brief into a rigid cylinder and then shove it down the visitor's wobbly throat, where it could cohabitate with the Delmonico's twenty-ounce sirloin and the half bottle of claret that Depine had likely inhaled during lunch. But, politics aside, these were smart people after all—he just needed to explain carefully.

"I have to drop in to lecture mode for a bit—sorry."

Tom drank some water and composed his reply.

"I was running security and risk operations during both outbreaks," Tom said. "So let me address the comparisons to the avian flu from 2003 and the swine flu in 2009. Yes, it's true that only about sixty people died in 2003 from H5N1—and actually about six hundred more since then. What made, hell, still makes H5N1 so scary is that it has a sixty percent mortality rate—but it isn't terribly communicable as these diseases go. That's a bit of luck. Swine flu, or H1N1, was much more communicable and therefore widespread but it had a very low mortality rate. Estimates are that more than a billion people have developed a strain of H1N1, and that it killed as many as two hundred thousand people over the course of fix or six years—but the geological and chronological distribution of deaths, as well as the booming global birth rate, made them nearly a global nonevent."

Blank stares.

"One was deadly, but hard to catch," Tom said, standing to make his point. His heels sank into the soft carpet so he braced himself by leaning upon the smooth, polished tabletop. "The other sort was really easy to catch, but it was merely a bad head cold for most of the afflicted. One *or* the other isn't too bad. As of the start of this meeting, I've had about two and half hours to gather as much information on this disease as I can. What I know is that it's damn scary. It looks like a flu at first—and simple flu is something that we know how to deal with. However, this seems to be different in a few critical ways: it appears to have a broad distribution, like swine flu."

Smith paused, and glanced around the room, reading his audience. There was a surfeit of skepticism, anxiousness and a bit of hostility. What he didn't feel was a receptive vibe that might make it worth it to introduce a discussion of *zombie*like symptoms.

"It also appears to have a very high mortality rate, like avian flu." On the fly, he elected to omit the Z-word and resumed. "It may be a two part disease where extreme symptoms occur later. Finally, the timing on the simultaneous emergence of a previously unknown pathogen with a high mortality rate in several places is strongly suggestive of an artificial event. In my opinion, and that of our intelligence staff, the likelihood that this disease arose purely due to natural causes is precisely zero."

There was a brief pause as the audience looked at him and one another.

Bateman spoke up.

"Tom, are you saying this is a man-made disease?"

Smith looked his boss in the eye, and then scanned the room.

"Rich, I've exercised our options for the services of a few epidemiologists and virologists, and the first is due in the office soon," the tall security chief replied, his voice confident. "I'll be speaking to him shortly. I expect to be able to answer your question more definitively then. However, at this time, with the information and analysis we have *right now*, what I'm saying is that this very strongly appears to be an artificial event. A bio-attack by a previously unknown pathogen which has been spread worldwide."

He took another deep breath because he could already sense that he wasn't reaching this audience, and that made him angry.

"But that doesn't matter. As we have seen before, there are three predictors for success for organizations that weather or even thrive during a crisis. One—have a plan. Two—access to intelligence. Three—move first. We've already expended capital to complete the first two. What we're discussing now is whether or not we want to invest in the final step."

"It's a pretty expensive *final step* that you're proposing, Tom," Depine said. "As you say, we don't have complete information yet, and the government isn't saying anything. There's barely any mention online or in the news."

"Look Brad—here's the bottom line," Tom replied. "Ensuring that we're the first mover *is* Plan Zeus. Access to assets will rely upon exercising the options early in the news cycle. We can get them now, if we work fast and spend the weekend closing deals. I can't guarantee that we can get them next week. If we wait till we have one hundred percent confirmation, we won't get these assets at all and we'll need another plan."

Bateman cut the exchange short, shooting a quelling look at the fat accountant and his tall head of security.

"Thanks, Tom."

Surveying the room in turn, Bateman addressed the entire group.

"We've both a quorum of the Operating Committee and most of the executive board in the room or on the call. Can I get a sense of how many in either group feel that they have enough information to exercise Plan Zeus options now?"

Tom looked around as well. There were a few hands up, but nothing like a majority, despite a few affirmative comments on the phone speaker.

"Thank you," Bateman said. He turned to his right and addressed the Chief Risk Officer, a Swiss national and former armor officer known for his calculating nature and casual association with morals.

"Otto, I'd like your global team, including Tom, to warm up alternate trading floors in all regions and stress test all the data pipes within the next day. Overtime for contractors is authorized."

He looked at the VTC camera and continued.

"Right—two things: internal and external," Bateman said. "Internally, everyone prep their teams to work the weekend. Monday, I'm directing that we establish readiness to move fifty percent of our trading operations to the alternate sites on one hour notice. That means bringing luggage to work and it means we'll need to have thousands of hotel beds for an indefinite period. On Monday, we'll also brief the possibility of social distancing rules for all staff. Purell stations on every floor of our towers and refresh all employees in your divisions on the 'work-from-home' protocols. Externally, I want Global Markets to recheck their existing workup on industries potentially affected by a pandemic so we'll be ready to adjust our market position at start of business Monday. I also want the heavy industrials, metals and cereals teams reading what Markets and the business intel team put out on an ongoing basis."

He looked directly at Tom.

"Tom, excellent brief. Tell your team that they did good work. Please keep all us updated and call me personally if there are critical developments. We can reconvene if there is new *solid* data, so everyone keep your phones with you and your admins aware of your location. Meeting adjourned."

Dr. Dave Curry was normally unflappable when it came to disease. He particularly enjoyed competing with his equally bloody-minded fellow virologists. There was a rotating award held by the scientist who could think up the most unlikely and fatal disease with the most ridiculous imaginary symptoms while still remaining epidemiologically possible. His personal favorite was the hunchbacked duck plague that would compel sufferers to crouch-walk everywhere while honking and quacking before dying of stroke. After showing that it lay within the realm of medical possibility, Curry had been the proud holder of the award, a gray plush neuron doll.

No one even tried to joke about a straight-up zombie plague. It was just too cliché to be competitive.

The chartered G6 that picked him up from Mexico City had in-flight Internet, so he was able to stay hooked into the exploding dialogue among the global community of scientists. They had woken up this Friday to the ultimate cliché.

Zombie plague it was.

One of the nice things about his consulting contract with BotA was that they respected his ability enough not to screw around with commercial travel. As a result, instead of fighting the traffic at Kennedy, the G6 greased the runway at the northern New Jersey Fixed Base of Operations, or FBO, where billionaires made their entry and exits from Manhattan.

The black Mercedes that collected him from the FBO also had Internet.

The information stream kept worsening.

Twenty-five minutes later the car pulled through the chicanes and antivehicle barriers into the BotA lot under the Wall Street tower. He still hadn't found any good news to share.

Whisked upstairs in a private elevator car, he was asked to leave his electronics behind and was offered a wall locker for his mobile phone and notebook PC. Finished, he found some very intent people waiting in a conference room equipped with anechoic tiles on the walls and a peculiarly thick door. Smith, and a few others he recognized from a previous investigation on a biotech startup, rose from their chairs.

Tom Smith shook Curry's hand.

"Dr. Curry, thank you for coming so rapidly."

"Well, you do ask the most interesting questions," drawled Curry. "This one is a doozy." He looked around.

"Nice room."

"This get together, all subsequent meetings and any data that we generate is being held very closely at this time," Tom said, smiling faintly. "So, I'm taking advantage of one of our 'deal' rooms. Harder to snoop and fewer distractions. You're the first of our experts to make it here, so let me introduce you to the team."

After the usual impossible to memorize exchange of names around the room, Tom led off. Though they had already spoken a few times, Smith started at the beginning, mostly for the benefit of his staff in the room who were hearing information for the first time.

"Dr. Curry, you know that we're monitoring the emergence of a potentially new pathogen that appears to have manifested on three continents within a single day. We're seeing conflicting reports in some places. What can you tell us?"

"Right off, let me apologize for mah accent." Curry had anticipated the easy questions. "Grew up in the South, and it's never rubbed off. But, to your state-ment, this disease isn't on three continents. Between Wednesday morning, when some of the international labs upgraded their level of concern for what appeared to be a nasty, but still manageable seasonal flu, and this moment, I have read credible reports that there are cases with congruent symptoms on every continent save Antarctica."

Murmurs spread around the room.

"We have been aware of the unusual symptom pattern for about a week," Curry continued. "Nationally, UCLA had led the way in gathering preliminary information, largely due to their information hooks into Asia and Oceania. However, the amount of educated guesswork is still pretty high. The disease appears to have at least two stages, the first of which includes traditional, and in some cases lethal flu symptoms, and a second set, which are erratic and very confusing but so far, not directly lethal to the actual infected persons."

Everyone was taking notes and several members of the audience were quietly exchanging asides.

"Next, and please note that the following figures involve a lot of speculation and extrapolation from scarce data, but it seems that about five percent of the cases result in death during the early stages of the disease." The virologist held up one finger. "As you no doubt recognize, that's a high mortality rate, but I need to emphasize that this is based on a relatively small case count, which can badly skew analysis. My immediate circle of professional contacts, as well as nearly every other specialist in the field, are working to refine the numbers."

Smith hushed the buzzing in the room.

"Dr. Curry, can you explain your statement regarding 'erratic and confusing but not lethal' symptoms? Do you mean that the patients are uncooperative?"

"That would be an understatement," Curry replied. "Where we can document symptoms, now that there are a few videos available, the second stage features a completely dissociative, violent sociopathy, rendering patients untreatable and unmanageable unless they are completely immobilized. This occurs in at least half the suspected cases."

Tom looked over at Paul and raised his eyebrows.

". . . severe anhedonia, aggression and instantaneous aphasia," Paul said aloud.

"Well yes, exactly," Curry said, appearing startled at Paul's ready grasp of the lingo. "But remember, the law of small numbers applies. A few cases can appear to dramatically change the curve. These statistics are very, very preliminary."

Tom grimaced.

"What can you tell us about communicability?" he asked.

"The disease appears to be highly communicable," replied the academic. "We don't know with certainty, but there are several cases where all forms of transmission appear to be ruled out except for airborne spread. We *are* confident that the disease is droplet borne and transmissible via bites."

This time Paul spoke over the chatter around the table.

"Doctor, when you say 'transmissible via bites' are you referring to family pets and the like?"

"No. I mean transmissible via bites from people." Curry looked over the top of his glasses at the intel specialist. "As in, if a symptomatic victim bites a nurse, then that nurse may develop symptoms within hours, which as far as we can tell is much faster than other vectors. In known bite cases, the second set of symptoms took anywhere from hours to days to manifest, but it skipped the flu component entirely."

A voice from down the table said it for everyone.

"Like zombie bites? Are we talking about fucking zombies?"

Curry winced, then nudged his glasses upwards so that he could rub the bridge of his nose.

"Yes. Ah mean just like 'fucking zombies.'"

This time it took Smith longer to quell the hubbub.

CHAPTER 3

"Look, check for obvious flu symptoms. Next, what you do is look 'em real close in the eyes and the hands. The fine motor control in the small muscles starts to go, even 'fore they get that itchy feeling all over. 'Course, you keep your gun handy, because they can turn lickity split..."

From: *Collected Radio Transmissions of the Fall*
University of the South Press 2053

Tom Smith did enjoy the panorama. One of his perks was a corner office view from the fortieth floor. In clear weather it afforded him a view from Governor's Island to the Verrazano-Narrows Bridge and across to North Jersey. The air was clear enough that green mountains were visible in the distant Hudson Valley.

The new, creepy sensation crawling up Smith's spine had him mortally convinced that any view of the city was best taken from a great distance.

Orbital distance sounded about right.

The meeting with their tame virologist had broken up in order to allow Curry to try to weasel some more information out of the Centers for Disease Control, the Army Medical Research Institute of Infectious Diseases and the other usual suspects.

Smith looked down at the data accumulating on the disease, which still lacked a name. The number of suspected cases was growing. He was still a little shaken from Curry's preliminary report on the spread of the disease.

He tried to remind himself that initial reports during a crisis are rarely as bad or as good as they are first reported.

There is an exception to every rule. His gut was telling him that this might be the one.

Throughout Friday, he had updated Bateman on the new estimates for the spread of the disease, but the CEO was unwilling to make any profound moves prior to an official announcement from the government.

At which time the bank would be in "reaction mode" and not out in front of the market.

Tom looked over at the flat screen on his notebook PC where he had paused the Thursday night video from Osaka. In the HD security cam image, the emergency room staff was lying across a gurney to restrain a naked man, who had his teeth buried in the arm of one of the paramedics, judging by the uniform.

Blood spatter was visible on the pale floor.

Everything that he did, all the information that his organization generated, from daily intelligence and security briefs for the management group to the annual risk assessment that was included in the firm's stock filings for the SEC, was covered by an iron-clad nondisclosure agreement. Legions of hungry attorneys had battled over that NDA across the years, resulting in a strong, refined and in legal terms, lethal document.

Getting caught sharing "inside" or nonpublic information wouldn't merely be a Career Limiting Decision, or as the street liked to joke, a CLD. It could rapidly lead to a lawsuit that pitched him against the bank, or worse.

Usually, worse.

Tom well understood his obligation to the bank. Like any of the former military who were sprinkled around the financial services industry, he still held strongly to the concepts of loyalty and personal honor. He "got it"—that in return for a hefty check he had sold his best efforts and pledged his personal word. He'd stand by that. If he were inclined to make an exception, well, he knew the penalties for violating the employment NDA with BotA, and he would accept the consequences.

After all, he valued the team that he had built, and currently led, and wasn't about to walk away from them, even if things went for a ball of chalk.

But damnit . . . there was family to consider.

He numbered among his "chosen" family a few very close friends, mostly from his service days with the international special operations community, including a few Ami friends from the 'Stans. In addition to this group, there was the regular sort of family too.

His brother Steve, a former Aussie paratrooper, had "married into America." Now he was a pleasantly domesticated, naturalized U.S. citizen teaching high school history, of all things. Stacey, his brilliant American wife, had tutored Tom as he "upped his game" in the banking world, coaching him on the mysteries of the bespoke suit and the designer ties from houses like Zegna and Armani. With their daughters, they lived in Richmond.

A highly communicable, airborne pandemic would sweep through the heavily populated cities like a flame through tinder. The I-95 corridor where the Smiths lived would go up like a powder train.

He and his brother, and others in their circle, didn't

live for the end of the world despite the negative connotations about preppers in what passed for Western pop culture. All things considered, Tom Smith rather enjoyed living with the "rule of law." It made available much of what made life worth living.

The occasional kite surfing trip out to Sandy Hook, driving up to wine country, the alternative club scene in the City and the women he met there, all of it was made possible by a very complex system whose rules were understood and largely backed by an overwhelming proportion of the population.

No rules? No system.

But the system worked. Always had.

Still, that hadn't kept the Smith brothers and their friends from playing a slow motion game of "what if?" over the years, often fueled by beer. All right, and some really decent bourbon, the quintessential American whiskey.

Even sober, buying a little insurance for emergencies had made sense. To that end, a small circle of like-minded friends had invested in a generous but remotely situated parcel of land in the Appalachian Mountains, balancing the need for distance with a decent growing season and accessibility from their metro lifestyles, given enough warning time.

Tom couldn't live there year-round, but he paid into the share system every quarter. His background was intrinsically useful and his money was welcome, but his global network of information was an order of magnitude more important. The families took turns staffing the property to keep it up, letting the capital improvements accumulate without the perils of renting the property to outsiders. In a few more years there was even a chance that the property, which now included a walnut orchard, some hay fields and an increasingly productive truck garden, might begin to meaningfully contribute to the mortgage.

The real intent had been to have a fallback location to ride out periods of civil unrest, if such became likely. An economic collapse would do for that. However, it was also a great place for large-scale weekend BBQs and unregulated fireworks. Nice shooting range too.

The circle of friends had even rehearsed a small list of codes for passing information across unsecure networks, even though Smith always felt more than a bit melodramatic when he participated.

He brought a small file up on his personal notebook PC, and decrypted it. A list of contingencies and corresponding codes scrolled down his page.

If he sent this and he was wrong, he was going to fuck up a lot of lives. His red-headed sister-in-law would kill him, for one. His nieces would help. Teenage girls and their tempers.

Tom winced.

On the other hand, if he didn't send it and the pandemic was as lethal and fast moving as they believed, the big cities could become impossible to escape very, very quickly. If he waited until there were publicly confirmed reports in the east coast mega cities, it might be too late to avoid infection.

Unconsciously, he rolled his shoulder. The rotator cuff had been rebuilt after a last-second canopy collapse on a HALO jump, but it still seemed to be the first place that he could feel stress building up.

In the end, it amounted to this: how much potentially lethal risk to his family was he prepared accept

as the price of waiting for more information in order
to "play it safe"? If he was wrong, it would cost
money, in fact, a *lot* of money. However, money was
a resource that one could renew. If his gut feeling
was right, then earlier was better, and he would save
lives—things of infinite, unreplaceable value.

He picked up his cell, and consulting the list of
brevity codes on the screen, tapped out a text message.

"Alas Babylon, Q4E9."

If it all came apart at high speed, at least someone
was going to get out. Hell, he might even be one of
them.

He chuckled once, mirthlessly.

Royyyt.

He turned back to his e-mail and prepped a weekend schedule for his global team.

Dave Curry plugged himself into Bank of the Americas' intelligence department. He supposed that he was
naive to continue to be surprised at the extent of the
banking intelligence network that spanned the world.
Telecommunications, foreign affairs, manufacturing,
agronomy...the bank had its fingers in everything,
nearly everywhere.

Over an early Saturday morning breakfast in the
bank's canteen he complimented Smith.

"I knew that you bankers were connected, but *ah've*
to give it to your man Rune." Even through his thicker
than average Southern accent, Curry's tone was equal
parts admiration and wonder.

A newly pressed suit and fresh haircut struggled
to mask Smith's fatigue as he squinted across his first
coffee of the day, eyeing the medico.

"Thanks," Tom said without inflection. "Let's keep that to ourselves for the time being. I need him hungry just now. Speaking of which, what new info—if any—have you heard on the lashup?"

Smith referred to the continuous global conference call that had grown out of an international circle of Curry's peers. It hadn't been cheap, exactly, to buy a way into the conference, but information on the disease was literally priceless at this point. Results would justify the expenditure of hard cash that was beginning to add up, even by bank standards.

The scientists had been on the phone since the crisis was recognized, alternating between being glued to the emerging analysis and the resulting reports on one hand and mercilessly whipping their research and lab teams to greater efforts on the other. Late on Friday night, or maybe it was Saturday morning, someone had a rush of blood to the head and suggested that they securely combine all of the similar calls then underway between big pharma companies, within the European version of the CDC and most especially across the universities in Asia and the Pacific. Members of the intelligence community also sat in, albeit very discreetly.

That's when Bank of the Americas bought in, courtesy of a heads up from a niche biotech in which they had a controlling interest. Once the disparate teams started talking to each other in a structured way, the spread of the infection had become apparent.

The virus was pretty much everywhere. Including on the Internet, which was just starting to go nuts, mostly over handheld shaky phonecam video of crazy, naked bloody people fighting, biting and being restrained.

Practically effervescent, the virologist was happily submerged in his element.

"Well, we have a name—for now," Curry said, burbling contentedly. "We're calling it the Pacific flu. CDC and USAMRIID isolated it first, but their work has already been duplicated. Looks like a variation on the influenza type A virus subtype. Think of the H in avian influenza, thus H5N1. Confirmed to be highly pathogenic, which we already strongly suspected. Affects multiple organs in the body. So far symptoms only manifest in people, but we are still checking if animals, birds in particular, can be carriers."

"Christ," Smith said, staring balefully into his mug. "That is all we need—birds carrying this around even faster."

"Any additional carriers would actually be redundant, at this point," Curry replied. "The disease is actually quite elegant."

Smith's eyes snapped back.

"Elegant how, *exactly*?"

"Well, a few places are still sequencing the complete genome and we'll have that data shortly," Curry explained patiently. "But it's apparent that this H7 variant is engineered. Ah'll start with the flu piece. It's pretty straightforward and very aggressive. Carriers are infectious at least four days prior to developing stage one symptoms, might be as much as a week."

He glanced around and sobered, noting that several members of Smith's team had drifted into range.

"Do y'all want to go to that fancy room of yours?"

"Horse, barn door," Smith said with a shake of his head. "If the information that you have is already out to the participants of your call, there isn't a point in compartmentalizing. We'll confine use of the deal rooms to our internal preparations. Please continue."

"Well, like I said, up to a week-long window of communicability before you know that you are sick." Curry took a bite of coffeecake and washed it down with coffee. "And this thing is transmissible as hell. Air borne, droplet borne and blood borne. Trying to narrow down if it can be transmitted purely by sexual contact, but that is harder to prove, since any, uh, romantic contact usually includes the exchange of, uh, more than..."

Curry looked helplessly around at the growing crowd, including many women, that now entirely surrounded their table.

"We get it, Doc," Smith was in no mood to spare Curry's southern sensibilities now. "People kiss when they root. Keep it moving."

"Root?" Curry asked, confused.

"Australian for 'have intimate relations,'" Rune offered helpfully as Smith slightly narrowed his eyes.

"Right," the virologist said nervously. "Well, then there are up to three days of misery as the flu tears you up—worse than the seasonal, but not nearly as hard hitting as SARS. The prompt mortality rate from the flu symptoms is at least five percent—might go as high as ten. We are still firming that up."

Someone in the ad hoc audience exhaled audibly.

Rune was listening in.

"How about the Tamiflu?"

"This critter laughs at every antiviral we have tried so far," Curry said dismissing the query. "Tamiflu doesn't really 'kill' viruses, you understand. It binds to the neuraminidase receptors that virii use to dissolve the coatings on uninfected cells. No neuraminidase, no way to infiltrate a healthy cell and hijack its genetic machinery. We still don't know which protein the new virus is using, so no antiviral remedy is even on the radar. But if I may..." Curry said, vaguely waving at the intel leader.

Smith looked over at Rune.

"Let him get to the end, then we'll get a proper brief upstairs ASAP. Cut to the last bit, Doctor. Tell me about zombie part."

"Ah yes, well that is one of the elegant bits, really, if it is intentional," Curry smiled again, back in his element. "I rather think it is."

"Intentional. You mean that you have confirmation that someone made this...virus?"

"It's definitely a virus and I don't have any doubt that it's a synthetic pathogen. The virus is behaving strangely, for a virus that is. Let me stress that this is a very preliminary opinion, and not everyone agrees, but its behavior, the actual virus's behavior is atypical. Somehow, it's creating dual symptoms, and further, symptoms are varying by transmission method. This is a first, in my experience."

Smith stared at him for a moment, and then made little "go on" hand motions.

"Recall that the reports state that most afflicted patients often strip off their clothes?" Curry continued. "Well, a few days after the flu symptoms wear off, the virus starts Act Two. Patients remain infectious as hell, by the way, but the virus generates neurological symptoms, starting with paresthesia..."

Smith's eyes narrowed.

The academic went on hurriedly. "...which is to

say, the feeling of itching or tingling, like there are ants under your clothes, you understand? It's perfectly hideous, actually. One of the big problems with the zombie plague myth is that a mindless human predator wouldn't bother with the social niceties of removing and replacing clothing to eliminate waste. Shortly, they would suffer from impaction, infection and death. In my opinion, this is a little bit of deliberate forethought which sidesteps that issue. The infected persons react to the itching by stripping off their garments. Problem solved."

Curry beamed at his attentive, if horrified, audience.

"There is more, too. The initial presentation of neurological symptoms also features palsy, confusion, dizziness, reduced vision and, as I said, that itchy feeling of bugs under your clothes, *formication*. Speech centers and behavioral regulation are profoundly affected. As these symptoms intensify, the patients become wildly aggressive. If they survive the onset of the second symptom set, and now we're finding that most don't, they'll attack anyone and anything on sight—including each other."

Smith rapped out, "Mortality rate on the second stage?"

"Well, we have lots of reports of infected patients now, but none that document the progression of the disease while under constant surveillance from start to finish. Say, of the twenty-plus confirmed cases in Asia Pacific so far, maybe sixty percent went to stage two. Of those, perhaps another fifteen percent died intra-stage. That is a very rough estimate. Law of small statistical populations, you know. However, we are getting more data all the time."

Tom stood.

"Doctor, I expect that we'll be extending your retainer indefinitely." He glanced around the table.

"Everyone upstairs," Tom gestured sharply to his team. "Paul, set up an updated brief for thirty minutes from now. Doctor, you are going to brief the CEO, *personally*. We might have time for Zeus, after all. I am going to try to squeeze a couple calls in first."

Officially named the City of New York Police Department, the NYPD was the largest municipal police force in the United States. The actual number of employees exceeded fifty thousand, though perhaps only two thirds of that number were sworn officers. Organized into more than a hundred precincts, it served all five boroughs of the City and included the waterways that had originally made New York a port hub long before banking, marketing or fashion began to contend as the driving heart of the city. Most precincts were referred to by the rank and file cops by their number—thus the Fifty-First Precinct became the "Five-One." However, no precinct was more prestigious or had greater visibility to the police brass than the one that housed the headquarters and spanned downtown Manhattan from Battery Park to the Brooklyn Bridge and west to Greenwich.

Rafe Dominguez ran "One" with a quiet authority and a certain elegance that belied his origins as a patrol officer in Flushing. You didn't survive years of grinding work "in the trenches" if you stuck to the rules of the Marquess of Queensbury. One of his arrests had culminated in a court case downtown, and Dominguez had seen another side of policing. While most cops eschewed proximity to the flagpole, the wiry cop was inherently drawn to a different world, where power lay closer to the surface, within reach of someone who could bring street smarts into play, and still "clean up" right.

Street smarts Dominguez had in plenty, and from that point forward he had shaped his ambition with an eye to becoming a Precinct commander, then an Inspector and ultimately the Chief of Department, if not in NYC then in another large metro area. His determination never wavered. His peers, who had hung the handle "Ding" on him, ribbed him when he spent extra time studying. They quieted a bit when he passed the exam for sergeant with the highest score ever recorded.

One malcontent cop who thought Ding was aiming a little too high talked behind his back, attempting to tarnish Dominguez's halo with lurid tales of his ruthless treatment of arrestees. As special treat, he described a lucky punch from a gang banger that had connected, briefly ringing Dominguez's bell, and started calling him "Ding Dong." Ding restrained his first impulse, which was to collapse the greasy vice detective's trachea on the spot. He smiled a bit thinking about watching the loudmouth's face turn purple as he choked to death. Using that smile, he just nodded and grinned for the audience of chuckling detectives, *Good one, you got me!* Big grin. Big.

Not even six months later that cop was fighting a losing battle against Internal Affairs charges for extorting "personal favors" from suspects in a prostitution bust—one that had gone down in Dominguez's last precinct.

Purest coincidence. Check.

Don't cross Ding.

When he dug in and completed a night school bachelor's degree in Criminology, no one raised an eyebrow. His carefully selected wife, the daughter of a deputy commissioner, coached him on protocol among the higher ups. Approving nods were registered as the new "comer" made all the right moves. He carefully didn't try to parlay his minority status into advantage, which appealed to the mostly white NYPD leadership even more. When he sat his lieutenant exam with results like unto the earlier tests, there was respectful applause.

In short, he was utterly committed. His hard work, insider horse trading and strategic moves shaped the arc of his career steeply upwards. A chance to relax was a rare commodity.

Saturday was typically a quiet time for a Manhattan cop, even a precinct captain. Nearing the top of his profession, Rafe Dominguez could actually get up at a reasonable hour and enjoy his coffee with his family before heading out the door for Rafe Jr's Little League. Commanding the prestigious First Precinct was the highlight of his career to date and he understood that one didn't risk the work invested to achieve that career merely in order to satisfy a passing urge.

Which was why he didn't quite snarl into his personal cell phone when he answered it at 10:30 am that morning. You never knew if the commissioner was checking up on his star players.

"Captain Dominguez."

"Captain, this is Tom Smith at Bank of the Americas." Smith's tone was polite, but firm. "I am very sorry to disturb you on a weekend. Believe me, I really wouldn't waste your time unless it was an emerging issue. One that you are going to want to know about."

Dominguez knew Smith. He kept tabs on all the major players in his precinct. His principal connections to the multi-trillion-dollar banks that were in his precinct were through their various heads of security. A little quid pro quo here and there kept valuable bank employees from having arrest records, while the occasional bad apple was tossed over the transom for the police to publicly charge in high-profile fraud and drug cases. Everyone benefited.

Mrs. Dominguez also enjoyed the mysteriously inexpensive tickets to popular Broadway shows, and advance invitations to sample sales at Michael Kors.

"Emerging issue" was usually a code word for some serious banking faux pas, such as a senior bank officer getting caught with a dead hooker or a live boy. Neither of which was going to be a good enough justification for calling his personal cell on a Saturday, banking influence be damned.

"Tom, I'm happy to pass you to the duty officer at the pre—"

Ding's voice didn't betray his annoyance, but Smith didn't need to hear it to know that it was there. His tone was brisk and all business.

"Captain, I'm in receipt of nonpublic information that you *need*," the banker cut in smoothly. "First reports are going to start hitting cable news right about now. I anticipate that you're going to be getting a call very soon about an announcement from the Centers for Disease Control regarding a new virus. They aren't going to tell you how bad it is yet.

I most strongly recommend that you find a way to protect your officers from what are going to appear to be EDPs who are going to be incoherent, aggressive and try to bite them."

Emotionally Disturbed Persons, or EDPs in law enforcement-speak, were the most common of the calls that the NYPD dealt with. Ranging from a depressed trader considering a long fall via a short step off a tall building to the classic paranoid meth user, EDPs came in many flavors, few of which were the sort of dangerous that warranted a weekend interruption.

Saturday beckoned.

"Tom, I appreciate the heads up, but—wait." Dominguez registered the words. "Did you say *'bite them'*?"

When bankers talked about disclosing "nonpublic" information, they were telling you that they were committing career suicide. It was very nearly an automatic SEC investigation and license suspension. Bankers never gave that kind of information away.

Never.

Not unless they were a lot more concerned about something else besides their careers and their money.

Dominguez blinked.

All that bankers cared about were their careers and their money.

"Bite them," Smith replied. "Like a dog. Exactly like a rabid dog. The pathogen can be spread by vapor droplets, aerosolized blood and may even be airborne. Looks like a flu. Highly lethal. And it comes in two stages—after the flu symptoms, EDPs start stripping, fighting and attacking anyone they see."

Ding stood, knocking his hip against the kitchen

table sharply enough that his wife looked up in equal parts reproof and alarm.

"That sounds a lot like—"

"Yeah. I know," Tom said. "I know the word you're going to use. I think that if you move quickly, you can brief your officers and start getting some Kevlar gloves and spray shields before they run out. And they *are* going to run out. I'm already stocked and now I'm buying all the extras that I can."

"Are you sure about this, Tom?" the captain worried. "It seems over the top. It's not even good enough to be a bad joke. Remember when synthetic Cathinone was all the rage?"

Dominguez recalled the initial impact of cheap designer meth substitutes which created... memorable overdose symptoms. A few high-profile "bath salts" cases had been caught on film, capturing the overdose victims practicing cannibalism.

Dominguez could hear Smith clear his throat.

One of the police captain's former cop friends had gone civilian and ran the physical security side for BotA under Smith, so Dominguez had heard a few stories and knew Smith's professional bona fides. Clearing his throat was the equivalent of the former spec ops troop yelling at the top of his lungs in order to get attention. And he was sharing nonpublic data...

Smith's intel on the precinct captain was as good as Dominguez's on his opposite numbers in the banks.

"Ding, I tell you three times." He deliberately used Dominguez's handle in order to make his point. "This is legit. Were I in your shoes I would get it to your boss ASAP, but I would appreciate it if you didn't attribute the source. The faster you move on this the better. Everything I'm seeing suggests that it's going to be big."

"You got it." Dominguez added it up. "And Tom?"

"Yes?"

"Thanks for the heads up."

"Scratch my back sometime, Captain."

CHAPTER 4

"The regional petroleum storage capacity for the American northeast exceeds seventy million barrels, sufficient for weeks of feedstock. The real bottleneck is refining capacity, which generates gasoline and other fuels at a rate barely above replacement levels, and which, ironically, itself depends upon fossil fuel for critical operations."

—Summary: U.S. Department of Energy
after action report for Hurricane Irene, 2011

Tom reminded himself that politics in the bank were the art of the possible. You got a little of what you wanted, you resigned yourself to getting the rest when you could and you smiled as though you liked it.

You also remembered who you needed to bury in the future.

If the bank didn't sort itself out, it could come to that, literally.

The next Gold call had gone better than the first. Bateman took control early, and apart from some preliminary questions right at the start, the meeting had been limited to an update on the disease, led by Dr. Curry.

Plan Zeus wasn't going to happen, not yet. At least no one had objected to the implementation of full social distancing rules, including deployment of some of the work force to the nearest alternate trading sites, as well as IT preparing for a work-from-home regime for fifty percent of those who stayed. The executives were nervous enough that they also approved the Executive and Special Personnel Evacuation exercise, or ESP-E. A subset of Zeus, it was better than nothing, but still amounted to half measures.

Smiling wryly, Smith could see the typical banker logic at work. *I'll hedge my bets just enough to cover myself, but let us see if someone else makes a mistake first . . .*

Still, with a little luck, he could pad the preparations here and there and buy a little more time.

He enjoyed watching Fat-Ass Depine start to sweat. That one was already thinking evacuation. Bateman and Smith still saw eye to eye on that. It was much too premature for a full-blown evacuation, so they would keep playing this by ear.

After the meeting, he waved Rune over to huddle with Curry.

"Paul, Dr. Curry will be working with us for the duration," Tom said. "He is going to need the ongoing full support of your team. Executive hires, travel security research, regional intelligence updates—everything is secondary. Move people as necessary to access what he says he needs. That includes someone to type his notes and provide updates to me every six hours, or more often as the doctor recommends."

Rune was scribbling notes.

"Boss, what about the deal books we have underway now?"

Deal books were large projects for the intel team. Drawing their name from the traditional oversize folios used to organize all the papers associated with a major acquisition, the "books" now digitally stored and indexed all the critical information for large-scale bond issues. More to the point, the bank made a lot of its profit on large deals that provided exclusive underwriting access to companies about to go public.

A successful stock launch for a firm like Twitter could be worth billions. Reducing effort there would paint a neon target on his back. Smith knew that the success of his plans would depend on retaining a measure of support among the influential managing directors who held those deals close.

"Nope, keep those moving, but slow roll 'em," Smith said, flexing his shoulder. "Carefully, mind you. Retask half the staff to cover this virus. I'll contact M and A to explain. I think that the bottom is about to drop out of all our pricing confidence, anyhow."

He turned to Curry.

"I know that you need to get back on the CDC call," Tom said. "Anything you need, anything at all—tell Paul."

Curry nodded thoughtfully as Smith strode off.

Rune spoke up.

"Okay, Doc. What's first?"

"Popcorn," Curry said. "Microwave popcorn. None of the weird flavored stuff either. Just butter."

"No problem, Doc." Rune scribbled in his ever present notepad. "How much?"

"All of it."

Dominguez knew about favors. Second only to information, favors were the currency of the bureaucratic tangle that was City Hall. The size of the city and scope of the financial activities that it hosted conferred power upon the mayor and his staff far out of proportion to what most expected of a major U.S. metroplex or even a small country. The staff that ostensibly served the city was thousands strong, and numbered among them were a first deputy mayor, several additional deputy mayors, assorted directors and commissioners and even a chancellor. Of course, these were all before one counted the city council and its staff.

However, Orwell had the right of it. Some animals *were* more equal than others. One such was the director of the Office of Emergency Management.

Doing a favor for the director of OEM rarely failed to pay dividends, eventually. Juicing her with a little nonpublic information might pay off sooner.

Joanna Philip Kohn—"That's Ms. Kohn to you"—had moved into city government after a brief flirtation with the financial services sector. In her early twenties the financial analyst had stood in lower Manhattan the day that the towers fell, and she never forgot her feeling at the sight. Not rage. Not anger.

Wonder.

Then she had remained frozen as the sensation washed over her, and her mind raced at the possibilities.

The implications.

The cloud that obscured the skyline somehow opened a new vista for her.

Her coworkers had walked her stiffly back indoors, presuming a case of shock. Instead, she was still thinking through all of the new ideas.

Prior years of expensive therapy, courtesy of her parents' financial wherewithal to meet the terms of the juvenile parole board, equipped her with mannerisms that she could employ to rapidly simulate a profound spiritual injury. She instinctively knew that she had an opportunity to dramatically change her strategy. She wouldn't participate in the banking lottery in order to earn the financial freedom to act and remake her world. That was too uncertain, would take too long.

Unacceptable.

Instead, she would use the City's response to the changed world to catapult ahead. It would help if she appeared to respond to the "grief" that had consumed her by dedicating herself to public service. She crafted a narrative that she slowly revealed to a few colleagues. She told them that sooner or later she would have her revenge, if not upon the dead already beyond her reach, then upon a system that had made the attack possible.

They said that they understood.

The first step is often simply finding an activity to fit your narrative. The Vassar graduate turned her hand to serving her city. Emergency Management, a city function long underfunded but suddenly thrust into the limelight, fit her mood. Even as the city survived further bomb attacks, Nor'easters and catastrophic hurricanes, she realized how broken the system was. It continued to fail, not just once, but in a string of catastrophes and policy disasters. Where bureaucratic incompetence and laziness was the norm, even a modicum of intelligent hard work is a distinguishing feature.

Kohn worked hard.

It was a good start, but rapid advancement and accumulating real power required more. Over several years she had risen far and fast, promoted over superiors a decade older. Her secret was neither an

IQ a couple of standard deviations to the right of the mean, nor dedication and cunning.

Those were the ante.

It wasn't even her wide and still growing network of the rich, the semifamous and her fellow travelers in power. She had built her foundation by judiciously and selectively prioritizing information, critical assistance and recovery funding to ensure that those possessed of valuable resources were first put at the head of the queue and then made aware of her help and planning. Oh, everyone got assistance, eventually. She just chose who received it first.

That, however, was just the strategy.

Kohn's secret was her resentment at being anywhere but the very top, in control. Deep inside, where she hid her heart, she knew that she was destined to bring . . . a change. Her first effort at change, long since past, had been childishly premature. She didn't quite know what final form the change would take, but she would know it when she saw it.

In the meantime, she fed her network and looked to the future.

Her staff had brought her the CDC precis on the virus on Friday morning. Heavily redacted, it was still alarming. Still, the city was practically a nation state in its own right, and in short order NYC OEM staff epidemiologists were participating in what amounted to a global conference call attended by experts who then briefed the policy makers. Considerable resources were being marshaled to meet the still unknown challenge.

Saturday found her, like many in New York, working from the office. Her assistant buzzed in that she had a call from NYPD and Joanna picked up.

"Ms. Kohn, this is Captain Dominguez at One." Dominguez's tone was respectful. "Sorry to disturb you on a Saturday."

Kohn tapped her fingers on her desk in a staccato rhythm. The silly self-reference to what was clearly the First Police Precinct of the NYPD was a typical affectation of the sort that cops, soldiers and other members of the patriarchy used to show their status. Yet, Dominguez was one of her more useful contacts in the police department. Best to see what he had to offer.

"Hello, Captain, it is always nice to hear from you, even on a Saturday," she said, tapping her fingers on the desktop expectantly. "What can the OEM do for you?"

Intelligence was just one important part of his organization. Smith called a department head meeting spanning all the components of his Security and Emergency Response team.

One by one he received the updates from his lead sled dogs. Anti-Fraud was quiet. Per Bateman's early direction, the Disaster Recovery plan for all trading operations had been flexed and critical connectivity double-checked. Crisis Management had updated all the nontrading communications information and run a test that measured the response time of every member of the bank to a simulated emergency message. Special Projects was tracking the costs of properties and assets comparable to the ones that comprised Plan Zeus. As expected, there was a significant uptick. The meeting moved along briskly until the last team reported in. The Physical Security and Executive Protection director had a lengthy report to deliver. Phil Skorpio was another former military officer who had turned his hand to commercial security. After a few years as a military policeman, he transitioned to civilian law enforcement with the NYPD, and then into financial services. His groups were split between visitor management and building-perimeter security, as well as controlling access to sensitive internal rooms like the high-value asset vault.

Skyscraper office buildings are *big*. Even a medium sized building of fifty or fewer floors might still hold twenty thousand people. A really big office building, like the One World Trade building still under construction, might hold three or four times that number. In normal operation the bank's security had to screen and pass those thousands through a perimeter security system at the rate of under one per second per entry and yet filter out one hundred percent of potential nonemployees. This was normally a simple matter of scanning bank issued credentials and maintaining a guard presence at the entry halls. Following the discovery of flu virus, that was clearly insufficient.

"Tom, it's pretty straightforward," Skorpio said. "Even if we keep half the staff at home, we've got to be up and running at the start of the market. That means screening twelve thousand people an hour, two hundred a minute and maintaining a zero error rate. My team is good, but they're not doctors. Apart from obvious zombie symptoms, what do we look for?"

"Doctor, what does it take to develop a test or some sort?" Tom turned to Curry. "What does your conference hive mind have to say?"

Curry had been on the conference call nearly

continuously since the emergency began. The bright conference room lights weren't doing Curry's now sallow complexion any favors.

"We've already established an initial RNA fingerprint for the virus, but it isn't stable," Curry replied thickly. "There is a fair bit of disagreement on why we can't perform what should be an established procedure. However, eventually we'll have it, and we can use a polymerase chain reaction to detect the viral DNA. Under ideal circumstances, that test can require hours, not minutes or seconds. Likewise, culturing a sample of possible virus would confirm its presence, but that method requires days. The best we can hope for is rapid antigen detection, but it will detect all of the members of the H7 family, not just our prime suspect. Since that would detect many ordinary flus, you are just as well off if you simply look for cold symptoms."

"What about a thermal testing system?" one of the junior aides asked. "They used that for SARS."

"This ain't SARS, kid," Curry said grumpily. "SARS was thermal specific from first period of infectivity. A-series influenza is asymptomatic infective for nearly a week, as I *already* told you ..."

"Got it, Doc," Smith said, sending a quelling look down the table. "But thermal will pick up those who are potentially infectious. That have gone beyond the asymptomatic period, right?"

"Yeah," Curry said. "It will. Also it will tell you who in your building has been exposed to *something* that gives you a *fever*. Which amounts to just about *every* condition on earth including bacterial infections, nonepidemiological viral infections, autoimmune conditions, strep throat, the common cold and *cancer*.

But go set up your thermal cameras if it makes you feel better."

"When can we hope for an antigen-specific test, then?" Smith said delicately.

"I don't know," the virologist admitted tiredly. "We could just start testing for simple flu, but even though we can use a nasal swab for each specimen, each test requires a few moments. You aren't going to get it to under a minute per person."

The head of security for the bank glanced at his head of intel, sitting behind the virologist. Rune met his eyes but didn't add anything. Tom looked back to Curry.

"Doctor, a lot of people have colds. Give me some options."

"There isn't anything yet," the doctor responded. "I can start working on an antigen test right away, if you have the equipment. Might need help, though."

"Everything stays in house." Tom insisted. "Give Paul a list of what you need. We need a test as soon as possible." Smith turned his attention back to Skorpio.

"Phil, in the meantime, anyone with obvious cold symptoms doesn't come inside." Tom went on firmly. "Anyone who recovers from flu symptoms stays at home for two weeks. If you need more people, tell me. We can temporarily move people from other teams."

Smith held up a hand to forestall a caw of protest from his chief of Anti-Fraud.

"Keep going, Phil."

"What about weapons, Tom?" Skorpio wasn't done. "I saw the videos and I don't want to tell my team that they have to arm wrestle with insensate cannibals who also have a high pain tolerance."

The entire team had been watching videos drawn from security cam footage and bystanders at several dozen attacks. There was a real lack of enthusiasm to handle zombies hand-to-hand.

"Tasers, impact weapons, then pistols," Smith said firmly. "Prep doubled up flex cuffs and some kind of antibiting masks and have them at the entry halls. In fact, you get to draft a proposed Rules of Engagement and a protocol for how we are going to deal with zombies. Bring me a draft by close of business. I'm staying late."

Tom noted the skeptical look on Skorpio's face but couldn't muster any managerial outrage at the minor show of recalcitrance.

"Anything else? Right. Let's get to work."

Smith's next call was to his brother. Reaching his sister-in-law Stacey, he confirmed that they were executing a complete bug-out from Richmond to the Virginia coast and were attempting to purchase a motor-sailer. Remaining at sea would decrease the level of social interaction which could potentially expose the family to the as yet dimly understood but absurdly virulent disease.

Tom Smith had established a convenient and perfectly legal shell corporation. Based in the Caymans, the corporation was the parent of several smaller firms, including one that invested and managed real estate, another that brokered farm equipment and fertilizer and a third that ran a curio and relic firearms business. Provided that the firearms in question met certain age limits, they weren't even legally classified as arms and could be imported and sold with no more documentation than furniture.

The partnership also had set up "throw-away" or single use storefronts for future use. One such was the Aurelius Corporation. Smith planned to use it now to facilitate the acquisition of the boat. In the long run, say six months, it might prove sticky considering that they weren't really in a cash position to buy a boat outright.

Still it got his brother's family in the clear. What was it that his old sailing master Tris used to say, back when they were banging charter boats around the Solomons?

"Once the boat clears the dock, all debts are paid."

Paul Rune was back in the zone. The upside of a zombie apocalypse was that his boss, the entirely "too fast to be that big, and too smart to be that intimidating" "Train" Smith appeared to be dwelling on matters other than the short notice that Rune's expensive intelligence team provided on what was shaping up to be the crisis of the year.

After getting a starter pack of popcorn for their resident virologist he had called an intel team meeting to share the new information priorities.

He looked around at his small local team clustered in his office, and mentally counted the dial-in participants. Twelve wasn't really too many to provide the geographic coverage for which government agencies hired hundreds. His acting deputy was another refugee from what was obliquely referred to as the IC, or Intelligence Community. Kendra Jones, or Jonesy to her friends, was an athletic late twenties something blonde who had been hired as part of last year's intel team overhaul.

When Smith promoted Rune, he'd offered carte blanche to build the team that Rune thought was best suited to the mission. The quid pro quo to that complete authority was complete responsibility for any failure. Since the bank mostly targeted economic, business and political data and since those data were in fields largely dominated by men, Rune hired the smartest, hungriest and most attractive women that he could, easing out some of the traditional and longer-in-the-tooth hires.

Fair? Not particularly.

But sweet Jesus did the new analysts deliver.

The combination of mostly female talent was absolutely shredding the backlog of traders' requests for essential elements of information. Rune had fueled the fierce internal competition by holding open the deputy position. A few burned out, uncomfortable with the work pace. Some wanted a better work-life balance.

Paul Rune loved his job, and expected his team to feel the same way. Complaints were addressed by Rune with one of Smith's favorite sayings: "This is an investment bank, not a 'lifestyle' bank. You want a life? Get a different job—there are ten hungry applicants for every seat on the Street."

And there were. Wall Street still offered a path to accumulating wealth and extinguishing student debt in a few short years and everyone wanted a piece. But no one came to the Street for the relaxed lifestyle.

His new team composition continued to prove its worth externally, using a combination of intelligence, drive and guile that befuddled male counterparts and intelligence sources equally. The benefits inside the bank were useful too. Most banks skewed hiring towards men, and the emphasis on female hires in this team bought the Security and Emergency Response team some respite from the periodic EEO Human Resource inquisitions.

Jones was aware of that, and Rune could sense that she resented it. However, like him she could also look at the productivity stats, which had climbed sharply in every category. Yes, the intel team was predominantly women. However, they happened to be damned good at their jobs. It wasn't her fault that most men seemed to lose about fifteen percent of their functional IQ when dealing with her and her attractive female teammates.

That was on them.

However, the entire team was caught on the back foot by the current emergency, and the small team of analysts and collectors was still in scramble mode. Rune couldn't be everywhere, and Jones was going to have to fill that gap as well as cover her own "beat." By keeping her hand in nearly everything, she avoided surprises.

After Rune wrapped up the meeting, he had a surprise for her.

"We're going to be working with Dr. Curry for the duration of this crisis," Paul said. "We need to understand the business and operational impact of every detail that he notes. Nothing is too small to be relevant. Since he isn't a banking expert, he may not recognize the impact of a datum which is trivial in his world, but deadly in ours."

He paused, but Jones wasn't drawn in. She waited for the other shoe.

"To that end, I am detailing you to accompany him

everywhere short of the bathroom," Rune continued. "Every phone call, every internal meeting, every e-mail exchange—you are to be his 'finance' translator and 'go-fer,' not to mention ensuring all data stays internal. Whatever he needs, he gets. You have direct access to the 'Overhead' charge string up to a hundred large, anything larger than that ping me personally."

"The rest of my work?" she asked angrily. "We have to finish…"

"Kendra, this is the number one issue for the fore-seeable future," Rune said, cutting her off. "If I wasn't filling in for the boss at some events, I would take this and have you run the rest of the team. However, I don't have that luxury. I need someone that I don't have to babysit to, well, babysit this guy."

If working for the bank had taught her anything, it was to negotiate.

"And afterward?" Jones eyed him evenly. "How does this stack up for bonus season? And for that matter, what does Curry think about this?"

Rune was already looking down at his smartphone, scrolling through messages. He squinted at the screen.

"Well, *that* is interesting." He looked up. "But since you asked, if there is an 'afterward,' I'll take care of you. For now, you share the same risks and uncertainties that I do, but I need you glued to Curry, and now I have to take this."

He dialed a number on the phone as he waved Jones out of the office.

In order to balance risks with opportunities, Smith relied on information and relationships with other play-ers that touched the financial services world: insurance underwriters, other banks, local law enforcement, city government, the local field office of the FBI and some "other governmental agencies" who found it convenient to maintain offices in New York City. However, the bank did have to maintain a certain distance, or at least deniability, from having direct relationships with... extralegal entities. His reporting chain was direct to the chairman, on occasion, so there were limits to how close to the gray zone of legality he could tread.

Paul Rune had his own sources of information and coordination. Some of the best information didn't come from places where the street lights shone brightly.

The text that he received was from a former personal friend, an MBA school acquaintance in fact. Joey Tradittore was a good-looking, smooth-talking, morally flexible man with a grudge and a grad school degree.

Tradittore had left the government during a purge following some sticky Congressional testimony. Just prior to 9/11, the Bush administration had sold advanced weapons systems to the Kingdom of Saudi Arabia and other Middle Eastern governments. Israel squawked, AIPAC yanked the leashes on their pet congresspersons and suddenly most of the intermediate level "worker bees" who had made the deals happen operationally were persona non grata anywhere in government service or contracting. The suddenly unemployable intelligence staffer and "fixer" initially scraped by on some under-the-table consulting jobs. Since he retained his basic competence, albeit leavened with a heavy dose of cynicism, he ended up where the money was—New York—working for a large import-export firm.

The "firm" was mostly a cash business, but the volume of money, the popularity of its "goods and services" and the increasing sophistication of what was, let's face it, a more modern version of the Mob, benefited from his logistics know-how and foreign contacts.

A resurgence of the traditional Sicilian-led "firm" was underway, mostly in New Jersey. When Paul moved from northern Virginia to Manhattan, Tradittore had gotten back in touch. He worked both sides of the Hudson River, and had started sharing information with Rune on a limited basis. If you wanted to know how things sat in the city, and you needed information from the dark corners where even cops didn't go in groups of fewer than four, then you needed to talk to the people who worked "in the dark."

And now Tradittore's boss wanted a meet.

Soon.

CHAPTER 5

*"Sir, I am very sorry, but the parts for your air conditioner
are not made here. They're from China and at the moment,
the shipping situation from China is very confused. Yes,
I understand that you're very hot, yes sir, yes . . ."*

—Customer Service Representative, U.S. AirCo, June 2012

Phil Skorpio stood outside Bank of the Americas' Wall
Street tower and craned backwards to look as high
up the building face as he could. He smiled at the
perfectly reflective glass that sheathed the huge tower,
ignoring the crick in his neck. His team protected
the largest trading floor in Bank of the Americas'
considerable portfolio. That didn't even take into
account the bullion repository and the third of the
board that operated from this location. In the years
that he had run the New York City Building Security
and Executive Protection team for BotA, there had
never been a security failure.

The wind whipped along the street, channeled by
the tall buildings that lined every block, like canyons
of man-made stone. Skorpio laid a proprietary hand on
the building wall for balance as he straightened, then
checked to make certain that his jacket wasn't hiked up
over his concealed pistol. Selected staff were trained

and city licensed to carry firearms as a product of the increase in threat to banking operations. But only a small handful. New York was generally death on guns.

He hadn't left work since the Friday brief called by his boss. While they waited for some kind of screening test, Skorpio had doubled up on the number of security staff in order to visually check each employee for flulike symptoms. Sniffles, red eyes, sneezing—any of that was enough of a reason to peremptorily deny employees entrance and send them to work from home instead. In addition to the white N95 breathing masks and dark, biteproof gloves, each team member was equipped with a Taser. Each entry hall included at least one person with a discreetly carried hand gun as well.

The sounds of a scuffle caught his attention.

A food cart piled high with bananas, breakfast pastries and coffee served hungry commuters their last-minute breakfasts. However, one of the customers, a BotA employee judging from logos on his colorful badge lanyard, was having a fit and tearing at his suit. He had managed to knock over a display.

Skorpio yelled for his team, and drew his Taser as he closed the distance. The wild-eyed man had kicked off his shoes, pants and was tearing his shirt off, revealing a well-muscled physique.

"Sir!" Skorpio yelled. "SIR! Hey you!"

The panting man, surrounded by a circle of onlookers who were jostling as they snapped photos with smart-phones, lunged clumsily and fell, provoking nervous laughter. A few of the more thoughtful onlookers rapidly moved away as their coworker writhed, pulling at his remaining clothes.

Skorpio's shift lead and several BotA guards began

shoving the gawking crowd farther back as the man, now fully nude, swayed unsteadily back to his feet.

"Jenkins and Cordova, get ready to tase this guy," Skorpio ordered. Without taking his eyes from the rapidly steadying man he added, "The rest of you watch the crowd in case there is another one." He addressed the growling man.

"Sir, last chance. Get down, stay down!"

The new zombie looked straight at Skorpio and, faster than Skorpio anticipated, dove into him, covering the ten feet between them in an eyeblink.

Even as the afflicted man moved, Skorpio and two others fired their Tasers, hitting their target but once. The zombie's muscles immediately spasmed, but his momentum knocked Skorpio down. The Taser's electrical charge transmitted to the chief, leaving Skorpio and the infected shuddering on the ground. The guard who had hit the zombie immediately let up on the juice, leaving the security chief to try to shove the shuddering zombie off himself.

"Get this asshole off me!" Skorpio was as disturbed by the idea of a naked man lying on top of him as he was by danger from the virus. "NOW!"

The zombie immediately began to revive, and clutched at Skorpio as it started snapping. A wrestling match ensued as the zombie rapidly regained strength. Skorpio kicked and fought in an effort to open the distance and rammed a forearm under the zombie's chin until he could raise his legs and kick the zombie away. However, the zombie grabbed his trouser leg in a painful grip. Another Taser fired, causing the zombie to lock up again.

Ignoring screams from the crowd, Skorpio yanked his leg away.

"Jenkins, keep the goddamn Taser on this time," Skorpio yelled. "Cordova, stop spectating and get some flex cuffs on this guy. As soon as the flex cuffs are on his hands and feet, Jenkins gets a bite sack over his head and then we can cut the current."

Additional staff came forward and helped in the procedure. As soon as the zombie's head was covered, it quieted considerably, but the keening and growling kept the attention of the now respectfully distant crowd.

"Why didn't you shoot this guy, Phil?" asked the shift lead.

Panting, Skorpio looked at his subordinate with a *Really?* expression on his face.

"Like I briefed *all* of you," Skorpio said, still trying to shake off the Taser's effect, "NYC hasn't authorized deadly force unless everything else fails to stop an infected person. You want a manslaughter charge ... I'd say go for it but be ready to enjoy your trip downtown."

He gestured around the busy street, where foot traffic was still flowing around the cordon of security staff and gawking smartphone wielders.

"Also, not exactly an opportune backstop anywhere, right? Once you shoot, the bullets tend to keep going until they find something to hit."

He make a circle gesture over his head, a forefinger extended.

"Okay, show's over," Skorpio said. "Cordova and Jenkins, get a tarp over this guy and sit on him till the cops come." He looked ruefully at his torn suit leg. "Goddamnit, this is a new suit!"

He didn't notice the minor scrapes on his shin.

∞ ⊖ ∞

Paul accepted the restaurant recommendation from Tradittore, but eating in a darkened Italian trattoria was nearly too cliché to be borne. Officially, they were just on a lunch break, but their table at Fattore's was covered with a checkered red and white cloth set for four. At this boss's insistence, they arrived several minutes early to find Mr. Fattore himself waiting at the door to greet them.

"Ah, Mr. Smith!" The short, swarthy, dark-haired and rounded owner waved them into the restaurant. "Iva been expecting you, itsa so nice-a to meet you, please to follow me!"

The interior was dimly lit but nearly full of diners, most of which were dark suited men. Many glanced up to register the new arrivals. Most of those tracked them all the way to their table. It was a long walk to the back of the narrow, but deep restaurant.

Tom had read the intel team's file on the Cosa Nova backwards and forwards. The Sicilian mob had slowly declined in significance into the new millennium while the Triads, the Central American narco gangs like Mara Salvatrucha Trece and a new Afro-Caribbean organization had supplanted them in all five of the boroughs.

There is a saying "Demographics is destiny." While not always the case in the general populace, it certainly was the case in organized crime. The original Sicilian mobs had made their bones during Prohibition, a time when large numbers of Sicilians and Italians were emigrating to the United States. It was this continuous flow of immigrants, and large Catholic families, a trait shared with their primary competitors the Irish, which allowed the casualty attrition rates necessary to take over their somewhat violent business interests.

Many causes had been attributed to the downfall of the traditional Mob. But the reality was that when the Cubans and Colombians started flooding in during the 1980s the Sicilians, who by then were second and third generation, were either already living a mostly middle to upper class lifestyle or had suffered the loss of most of their leadership. Constantly surveilled by the FBI over the years, the Sicilians simply did not have the sheer mass of desperate soldiers willing to fight for their territory.

Thus, they dwindled in influence, got out of the most lucrative criminal enterprise, drugs, and generally faded into the background.

However, Frank Matricardi had methodically built an import business by leveraging key contacts at Port Elizabeth in New Jersey. Anything that he could buy cheaply and wholesale dearly inside the U.S. would do. Bulk marijuana and generic oxycodone were a staple, and there were enormous margins in "unsexy" materials such as nonquota seafood, counterfeit luxury goods and even counterfeit super cars. His growing team, styling themselves the "New Thing," was interested in anything illegal that would turn sufficient profit. And the profits were good.

The New Jersey Sicilian community is quite close, and Matricardi's business wasn't exactly secret, even though proving something would be a challenge. His sons once chafed at being ribbed by their friends that their dad was a "fishmonger." Before being sent off to college, they were allowed to see *some* of the books and realized that up to a third of the nearly five-billion-dollar-a-year U.S. seafood market was illegally imported goods, much of that controlled by dear old dad. It helped them settle right down.

It didn't hurt that they eventually got around to remonstrating with anyone foolish enough to persist in grade school name calling.

Like any successful businessman, Matricardi took the long view. You do what you can with what you have and you don't lie to yourself. He never tried to kid himself that he was anything other than a criminal businessman, but along the way he reveled in opportunities to *retire* some of the animals that sold heroin to kids, or traded kids. Yeah, he made a shady buck here and there. And yeah, he wasn't going to change the world. Killing truly evil men was just a personally satisfying sideline.

A zombie plague was a real problem though. Bad for business. Banks were an important component of his business supply chain, even though their counter money-laundering efforts were stringent and effective. Frank didn't take it personally; he was a pragmatist. He regarded the antilaundering operations as another way to weed out the less fit competitors. However, the information that he had on the plague really bothered him. His family advisers included economists, politicians and smart lads like Tradittore. They all said, effectively, the same thing.

"Find out what the really big money is doing, and copy that."

When Matricardi strolled into Fattore's, he was effusively greeted by the owner. From the back of the restaurant, Tom Smith noted that the trim Sicilian was wearing what seemed to be the de rigueur uniform: a very traditional dark suit, wing tips and a nice tie. A bright white carnation sat on his lapel. He was accompanied by Tradittore and a third person, a woman. She stole the show all by herself. The black Helmut Lang dress that the brunette wore was styled in anything but a conservative manner. Its form-fitting cut hugged her curves and accentuated all of her body's subtle movements. Men surreptitiously watched her pass.

She watched everything but them.

The party strode directly to the table where Smith and Rune rose to greet them.

"Mr. Smith, Mr. Rune, please accept my thanks for meeting us today," Matricardi said, offering a firm handshake. "I believe you are acquainted with Mr. Tradittore." The suave aide nodded and shook hands with the two bankers.

"I also asked my companion, Ms. Oldryskya Khabayeva, to join us. I hope that you don't mind."

"Delighted to meet your associates, Mr. Matricardi." Tom nodded at the companion. "How do you do, Ms. Khabayeva?"

"Quite well, thank you," the woman replied coolly.

"Please, everyone sit." The head of the Cosa Nova waited as the others sat in the chairs helpfully pulled out by the wait staff. "I'm delighted that we can all meet as friends and enjoy this restaurant. It's one of my favorites."

As the group seated itself, Matricardi snapped his fingers like a rifle shot. Before the sound had faded, Fattore led a short squad of tray bearers to the table. It rapidly filled with wine, rolls, antipasti, frutti di mare and some very small crescent pastries. Rune saw that his boss hadn't reached for anything, and copied his example.

"Please, the appetizers are excellent," Matricardi

said, shoveling calamari onto his plate. "Talking goes better with eating, believe me."

"Perhaps I would be a little more comfortable if you asked your security, who is doing a bad job of ignoring me, to either join us or leave," Smith said, smiling slightly. "Their watchfulness is ruining my appetite."

Rune controlled a start. He hadn't noticed any surveillance. Matricardi smiled thinly and nodded to Tradittore, who tapped on his smartphone. Moments later two pairs of men rose from different tables and quietly exited the restaurant.

Smith reached over and spooned some antipasti onto his plate and added a roll. He nodded to the door.

"Thank you."

The charcoal-suited businessman shrugged and took a bite of his squid.

"It's a normal precaution," he said. "But here, as I said, perhaps we can all be friends.

"This zombie plague is scary stuff," Matricardi continued. "At first a lot of people left the city, but then nothing happened. Every day some people turn zombie, maybe they bite some people, and then the cops snatch them up. My sources tell me that the hospitals are already nearly full. My sources also tell me that this might be some kind of biological weapon attack. They say that the government, the military, the banks and the biotech companies are all trying to make a cure. I notice that you banks are still running your operations in Manhattan, so maybe things aren't so bad yet. Am I right?"

He emptied a partial bottle of red into his own glass and motioned for more wine.

"I am, at the heart of the matter, a businessman."

He gestured around the restaurant. "This disease is bad for business. More than that, even though my businesses may be unconventional, they fulfill a need and a purpose. Otherwise, why would I even exist?"

"No argument here," Smith said with a nod. He took another bite and tucked the bite into his cheek as he talked. "Here's what I am ready to share now, here. One: the disease *is* synthetic. We think it's a weapon, but we don't know who made it or why. There appears to be no specific motive."

His audience was rapt.

"Two: even though we are catching and isolating victims, the infection curve is still accelerating. We've started to get a feel for the natural resistance rate and it's not good. Whereas with something like smallpox you've got a high enough natural resistance rate that society can continue to function even in a major outbreak, the natural resistance rate to this is low enough . . . so, very not good. Barring a cure or at least a vaccine, it will eventually reach a take-off point from which there is no recovery."

Tradittore laid down his silverware. Khabayeva hadn't picked hers up.

"Last: in order to have the best chance to find the vaccine and manufacture it in amounts sufficient to dose the entire population, we need the engines of the economy to keep turning." Matricardi seemed unperturbed while Smith spoke. The mob boss chewed and swallowed and followed that with wine.

"My business is a part of that engine, right?" Matricardi made a little open palmed gesture towards his side of the table.

"Yes," Smith agreed equably. "Businesses of all

kinds preserve the feeling in all people that things are 'normal,' for values of the word normal. I understand that you sell a lot of tuna and swordfish." He sipped some of the wine and nodded in appreciation. "This needs some of that prosciutto." He forked prosciutto and green honeydew melon onto his plate.

The Sicilian rotated one hand a few times, flipping it first palm up and them palm down.

"Tuna, swordfish, orange roughy, seabass, cod, abalone, lobster..." Matricardi grinned. "Yeah, I import a bit of seafood."

"Let's say that you supply something like fifty percent of illegally caught wild seafood on the East Coast," Smith continued. "Round numbers. Looking at just one sector, let's pretend you had to stop bringing flash-frozen swordfish into New Bedford, Port Elizabeth and Pompano Beach. That would cut the annual supply by a wholesale value upwards of a hundred million dollars or conservatively, what, thirty percent? There would be places that couldn't keep it on the menu. Ditto other seasonal items. Ditto a number of other, lets call them consumer goods, including some truly impressive volumes of oxycodone."

Tradittore involuntarily grimaced. Matricardi's genial expression didn't change at all.

"We all know that the price of unleaded changes overnight every time some Saudi prince breaks wind," Tom said. His tone was light, even if his eyes were hard. "Food prices move almost as fast. If consumer prices for everyday expected goods spike or worse, the products are simply not available, then the man on the street assigns the responsibility for that missing item to the zombie plague. If he reflects on how his 'normal' is being changed, then he might be a little more susceptible to fear. He may start thinking about his participation in doing his 'normal' job. The absence of an expected good or service can prompt further inventory shortfalls, if you see what I mean."

While Smith talked, silverware clinked lightly and waiters poured more wine. Matricardi swirled the deep red liquid around in his glass as he listened. Tradittore and Rune ate but Khabayeva still hadn't touched the food since Smith began sharing details.

"So, you see..." He looked at each person in the party in turn. "...it isn't just in my interest to keep the bank running...and the financial engine that fuels this city, this country and by derivation the laboratories and scientists searching for a cure to the Pacific flu. It's in *everyone's* interest."

Rune was attentive, Tradittore was blandly pleasant, but Khabayeva was unsettled. Or unsettling. Smith wasn't certain. Her slightly tilted violet eyes were cool and intelligent, not appraising like the moll that he had expected.

Something deeper was there.

"Mr. Matricardi's businesses are considerable." Old-ryskya spoke in clear, if slightly accented English, filling the brief pause. "But they are not comprehensive. Does your information cover the...other businessmen in the area?"

Tradittore shot her a surprised look, almost shocked. One doesn't expect a pet, no matter how beautiful, to participate in a meeting. Matricardi held up his hand to forestall an interruption and looked at Smith instead.

Tom addressed her in a Slavic tongue.

"No, not Volograd, farther south actually," the

woman replied. "But your accent is quite good. Still, the question is for you."

"The real currency in banking isn't money," Smith said, smiling a little crookedly. "We deal in information. Mr. Matricardi may not be the largest in all the markets where he...competes. But the Cosa Nova's interests aren't so different from Wall Street's interests."

Matricardi didn't quite frown, but his glance appeared to quell Khabayeva from saying more.

"And yes"—Smith looked back to Matricardi—"the economic activity in your, pardon, in these sectors are as much a part of the economic engine as any other."

"Your information is quite good." Matricardi thought a moment, then took a final bite of calamari. "I won't pretend that I don't know what you are talking about. As for the rest, that's a lot to think about. This take-off point for the disease. You got a date?"

Smith grimaced, showing his first real emotion of the meeting.

"That's the million, sorry, trillion dollar question." He dabbed his mouth with a brilliant white linen napkin. "I'm trying to get the best estimates for designing and mass producing a vaccine to our market modeling analysts. Other teams are working on a therapy for the already infected. A number of factors are driving the infection rate, and we don't yet know them all. An additional number of factors are complicating the vaccine design, and the best virologists are fighting over the desperately important details, which are not yet all finalized."

Matricardi gestured impatiently.

"Other countries are not uniformly reporting their infection rate," Smith continued. "And they aren't aggressively using measures that we know work such as isolating *anyone* who has any flu symptoms and screening travelers, as well as protecting critical transportation and security personnel. These factors and more prevent me, with great regret, from having a precise answer."

"But . . . ?" Matricardi slapped a palm on the table this time.

"Best case?" Smith asked with a shrug. "We find a really cheap way to vaccinate and we make it past Labor Day and reach an equilibrium. We still take a big hit, deaths in the millions. But the general national framework holds mostly together."

Smith looked around the restaurant, then worked his shoulders and met the gangster's eyes steadily.

"Worst case: sixty days. Turn the lights out, shut the door, civilization is closed for the night, however long that night be. Very little chance anyone sitting at this table survives. At least with a functioning brain."

Matricardi grunted and glanced around the table at a very quiet group.

"Two months, eh?" Matricardi said with a grunt. "Two months to doomsday. Just when I was getting the family business back on its feet. Wouldn't you know?"

He thought about that for a moment, then smiled broadly, revealing very white teeth.

"So . . . who wants the calzone, eh?" he said, smacking his hands together and rubbing them. "They make it really good here!"

CHAPTER 6

"Unsurprisingly, kids are a major driver. Parents are keeping their children home in record numbers. In a home with two wage earners, that means that one parent is at home, cutting the economic productivity of that home in half. Multiplied by millions of instances, it's starting to affect our economy."

—Atlanta Business News (WZED) analysis
on the unexpected U.S. GDP contraction
in the second quarter of 2012.

From: *Collected Radio Transmissions of the Fall*
University of the South Press 2053

In the days since Skorpio had wrestled the zombie in front of Bank of the Americas, the legend of his physical prowess had grown among his staff. Even some of the more experienced staff had given him the calm approval that amounted to the best reward that any security specialist could hope for. He had even gotten a "good job, Boss" from two of his key people that were the *special* hires that Smith had personally brought into the bank. Unlike the traditional former cop or straightforward veteran background that most of the financial services security community shared, these two were . . . different.

Jim "the Kapman" Kaplan was former Special Forces, former Triple Canopy. His appearance was surprisingly unremarkable, neither especially tall nor particularly muscular. On close observation his wrists and forearms seemed unusually thick, and his hands were heavily scarred, like those of a mechanic. Kaplan wasn't especially talkative but Skorpio noted that he had a quality that cops labeled "cop sense," a sort of *feeling* for things that didn't belong. After he successfully blocked an Occupy activist's effort to glitter bomb their chairman by somehow seeming to teleport between the target and the security cordon, Skorpio had asked him how he had known that an attack was coming.

"Just a feeling," Kaplan said with a shrug. After getting the raised "eyebrow" from the security chief Kaplan provided a better explanation. He clearly didn't like talking about his "skill set." Or talking at all for that matter.

"His shoes weren't right and he was carrying his weight on the balls of his feet. Most of the protesters were wearing Chuck Taylors, sneakers or cheap hiking boots. I even saw a pair of green Crocs. The crowds was either dancing around on their toes in order to see over us, or just standing flat footed and shouting. This guy was wearing Salomons, staying on the balls of his feet, leaning forward and panning his head back and forth. So, I tagged him as a potential. There were seven in the crowd. This one had a bag that never left his left hand. Since most people are right handed, it figures that he was going to need to reach into it in order to do something. If he had pulled a gun or a bomb he would have been a tango."

And wouldn't that have gone over well if his detail

killed an ordinary protester? However, Kaplan had been right and exercised good judgement. No one was shot, and if the glitter bomber had accumulated a painful collection of bruises and abrasions when Kaplan plowed him into the cement, well then fuck him if he couldn't take a joke.

On that much, Skorpio could agree.

About the same time that Kaplan had been hired, Smith had found another former special operations veteran. Smith had handled this particular hire personally, and apart from a functionally detailed resume that included not one *named* employer, Skorpio didn't know much about the second new guy. Usually, bank background checks were more comprehensive than military Top Secret clearances.

Dave "Gravy" Durante's background came down to "REDACTED. REDACTED. REDACTED..." He graduated from high school in Ohio. No drugs, no priors, lettered in soccer, president of the school computer club. Joined the Army as a communications and computer specialist. Ten years later he was suddenly available for hire. Nothing in between.

Durante was a physically intimidating presence, as tall and broad as Smith, but with unusually long arms, sandy blond hair and a perpetual calm smile. The "new hire" was a physical security specialist. What he didn't know about breaking and entering a building, including the electronic defenses thereof, wasn't worth knowing. For all that he was phlegmatic, he also was a surprisingly good writer. The drafts of the Bank's Physical Security plan were auditable items and Durante's rough draft had been good enough to pass on the initial round of review—the first time that had happened with any Security and Emergency Response governance documents since Skorpio had been working.

Even though he wasn't particularly tight with most of the Executive Protection detail, Durante was more than good enough for Skorpio, who made him his deputy for all details in New York.

This morning Skorpio woke up with a mild sore throat and a runny nose. By the time he had his second coffee, he was powering through Nasonex in order to keep his sinuses open. A few ibuprofen dealt with his joint aches, because let's face it, getting old sucks. Visine for the eyes—gotta keep those peepers bright.

After he cleared the morning e-mail it was time for the department head meeting with Smith. The walk to the conference room was blurry. He paused and grabbed a double espresso from the coffee station outside the boardroom and dropped into his seat in one of the bank's secure conference rooms.

The meeting started and he methodically scribbled some notes, absentmindedly scratching his arm.

Damn psoriasis.

As he prepared to kick off the brief, Smith noticed that a faint, buttery movie theater smell hung about the bank's virologist.

"Dr. Curry has just delivered an urgent report to the CEO." Tom wrinkled his nose at the stale odor. "I should note that while Mr. Bateman is aware there is now some source of vaccine, he is . . . too busy trying to keep everything running to worry about the details."

Tom looked at the group carefully, waiting for them to process what he'd just said. He'd officially distanced the CEO and the Board from the following discussion. Since it was about how they were going to start murdering people en masse, it was at best a fig leaf but it was a legal fig leaf.

"The basic information is going to be covered here so that the team is clear on our operational situation. I'll summarize the basics. We understand how the virus is creating two different sets of symptoms, and we have a plan to produce a vaccine. Dr. Curry, go ahead."

Smith motioned to the lab-coated virologist, who stood. Clearing his throat, Curry launched into his remarks.

"There are two salient points that I have to cover right away." He cleared his throat again. "The first thing is that we have a better understanding of why the disease symptoms presents in two ways.

"The disease, which now has its own classification code, is called H7D3. The H refers to a key protein on the surface of the virus called hemagglutinin. Recall when I described how the virus ignored antivirals such as Tamiflu? This is because those antivirals are designed to block the receptor sites on a cell's surface and deny the virus any way to access the interior of the cell and then reproduce. The hemagglutinin protein in H7D3 has been engineered with a different geometric configuration. An antiviral designed for the old configuration literally can't bond to its target. The next piece is the D in the name. It stands for *Dual Expression*. Well, when H7D3 does access a cell and compromises the synthesis process, it does something utterly new."

"Expand," Tom said pointedly.

"It makes two *types* of virii, a previously unknown mechanism called dual expression," Curry said with a little side-eye to Tom. He didn't like to be interrupted in one of his spiels. "The first packet is just another H7D3 virus, which carries on the process, looking for another cell to compromise and spread the disease further, behaving like a seasonal flu virus. The second packet is the one that attacks the victim's brain and creates the zombie symptoms. It's also an engineered component, based largely on rabies. It attacks the central nervous system, especially the brain stem and specific brain components, including the frontal lobe and parts of the parietal lobe. These areas are responsible for critical thought, speech, pattern recognition, etc."

Murmurs greeted this extended explanation. In the Security and Emergency Response team, researching the fundamentals of virology had become even more popular than checking stock prices during working hours. Staff might not have Ph.D.s, but "rabies" was a term they could understand.

Curry paused and took a bite of popcorn from the bowl on the table and then drained his coffee cup. Behind him, Jones passed him a bottle of water.

"Any questions on that bit, because it isn't the most important part."

"Assume some sort of cure," Rune said. "Does the . . . afflicted have a chance of regaining . . ."

"No," Tom replied curtly. "There have been some people who have naturally thrown off the virus after going through all the symptoms. They're . . . pretty much the same. Sometimes with slightly higher or lower levels of aggression but always nonsentient. Once you're a zombie you stay a violent zombie or remain in a vegetative state. No take backs."

Tom had planted that question with Rune because

it was important to the rest of the discussion. There was no murmur this time, just brief glances.

"The second and most important new bit of data is confirmation of what you all suspected: the rate of the spread of the disease is accelerating," the virologist continued tightly. "If we can't begin manufacturing a vaccine in industrial amounts very soon we'll have no hope of getting in front of the disease. We don't have long, not very long at all."

Curry stopped, swallowed, then closed his eyes for a moment before proceeding.

"The good news, for values of good, is that we have been given a green light to proceed with a plan to start making a vaccine. It won't be a cure, but it should block further spread of the virus. The virus concentrates in the afflicted nerve tissue of its victims, which so far are limited to higher order primates. What we need is to harvest the nerve tissue of higher order primates saturated with the virus."

"Does that mean we need to start sourcing rhesus monkeys, chimpanzees and so forth?" Rune perked up. He hadn't been told the reason for the planted question. "Can't be too many of those in the city. We'll probably have to look international—"

Curry looked unhappy, but replied.

"The amount of raw materials needed rules out zoo animals and imports," Curry said, shaking his head. "You get, maybe, one dose of vaccine from a green monkey, the most available primate. And they're being swept up in Africa in job lots for research. Very few are available on the market and the price is staggering. Being absolutely blunt: There is only *one* large-scale source of higher order primates currently available."

Faces around the table looked puzzled. Slowly comprehension dawned. Tom watched the team work through the obvious. Jones's face was stone.

Someone knocked their chair against the table, loudly. About to speak, Curry looked up, irritated. Down the table, Skorpio's chair knocked against the conference table again, as he scratched his ribs vigorously.

"Hey, Phil," Smith said, looking down the table. "PHIL!"

Someone was calling his name. Kept calling his name.

Irritated, and feeling itchier by the second, Skorpio looked up.

What the fuck was under his suit? Goddamn...

Tom cursed himself.

The existing bank protocols were entirely inadequate. From the time that his trusted security deputy had screamed, then roared and started tearing at his clothes, to the moment when Smith had drawn his bank-issued SIG Sauer P226 and staged the trigger, only two seconds passed. Fully aimed, Tom waited until others had moved away from Skorpio. He'd waited a further fifteen seconds until it became obvious that there was neither a Taser in the room nor time for a security detail to make it to their floor, high in the Bank of the Americas' tower. Then he floated five empty casings, putting every round into the newly turned zombie's center of mass.

Instantly two things happened.

Skorpio dropped, flailing, to the carpeted floor and writhed, screaming all the while. And Tom's hearing was overlain with the siren song of damaged cochlear cells—tinnitus—which provided a semipermanent ringing sound that contributed to the unreality of the scene: Tom shooting another employee in his own fortieth-floor conference room.

His shots must have struck the zombie's spine while avoiding the heart, because Skorpio had begun very slowly crawling across the floor towards the cluster of people now scuttling behind Smith, including Rune, Curry and others. With single-minded, predatorlike determination, the mostly naked zombie buried its fingers in the plush carpet and pulled itself by main force towards its intended quarry.

Tom sidestepped away from the group and put his back to the conference room glass wall, which looked out over a dirty brown East River. He kept his pistol at a low ready and scanned the rest of the group, who looked back at him uncomprehendingly.

"Everyone stand up straight, show me your face." This from their resident mad scientist. Unsurprisingly, Curry mentally got there first. "Show me your eyes!" he commanded.

"Do what he says," Smith added. "New rules, is anyone feeling sneezy or itchy? Everyone look left, look right—examine them like your life depended on it."

Comprehension dawned on the group, and they began looking at each other and back at the zombie. It was still several feet away, slowly working its way across the plush carpet, leaving a broad and slippery red trail.

"No visible symptoms, Mr. Smith," Curry said. "I just got focused on the business problem and didn't *see* his." He gestured to the zombie, which was within ten feet.

Smith looked at the group one more time and coldly barked: "Security rounds!"

He fired once more, striking Skorpio in the head. The zombie dropped, motionless, yellow brain matter visible from the exit wound.

Smith decocked and reholstered; his face was drawn with anger.

"This simply won't do."

He looked over at the door, which had just been flung open, and where Durante had just skidded to a halt, pistol drawn. Kaplan bumped into him from behind, having run from the elevator with a few others.

"Congratulations, Dr. Curry," Tom said. One side of his mouth twitched a bit in what might, charitably, be called a smile. "You now have some live virus with which to proceed."

"You are officially insane," the city attorney said, quietly addressing the head of the OEM. If his statement bothered her, it wasn't obvious to the audience.

Kohn had been making her case to manufacture the attenuated vaccine since she had co-opted the status report and update being delivered by the deputy mayor for Health and Human Services.

You could see the individual beads of sweat across the brows of some city administrators, even though they were miles away. This unhelpfully clear detail was usually a positive feature of the high-definition telepresence display that covered the entire wall of the underground conference facility beneath city hall. Each participant was rendered in life-size scale, enhancing the feeling that all of the attendees were actually there in person. This time though, the details didn't inspire confidence.

The visible underarm stains and sweaty collars were there for all to see. Grim looks or blank faces predominated.

Kohn was smiling on the inside, where no one could see. Fear was to her advantage.

The city of New York enjoyed excellent communications infrastructure, especially for the channels serving critical disaster response and crisis management functions. After 9/11, a combination of federal funding and fees collected from the financial services sector had built a large integrated surveillance and communications system.

Initially dubbed the Lower Manhattan Security Initiative, it first focused on protecting the city's life blood, the bankers and insurers clustered in lower Manhattan from which location they generated the revenue that made the entire city possible. Later, the system had grown to cover most of the island and the important areas of the adjoining boroughs. Supported by major technology companies, the effort eventually grew into the integrated City of New York Domain Awareness System, and now it could connect NYC officials by video anywhere in the city, as well as control tens of thousands of cameras, street barriers, traffic lights and special sensors.

The distributed secure video capability was a good thing because the mayor had decamped from downtown early in the crisis and was ensconced in an undisclosed location, funded in part by the licensing of his successful business systems and media brands. Naturally, he had empowered the first deputy mayor and other commissioners to make routine decisions. However, Kohn knew that a decision of this magnitude would need his personal approval.

"Mr. Mayor, the biochemistry and technology to make an attenuated vaccine is a known quantity," Kohn said, ignoring the city attorney. "*If* we begin prototyping the process now, and *if* we can assure a large supply of live virus, we may be able to vaccinate not only the remaining emergency services personnel and critical city staff, but their families."

Say what you will about the mayor's physical courage, he didn't shy away from the core issue.

"Joanna, I want to be perfectly clear," he said in clipped tones. "What you are talking about is euthanizing the surviving infected people that we are now confining and using them to gather the 'live' virus. Do you know how many laws that would break?"

Angry faces stared back at Kohn from both the video teleconference monitors and from around the conference table. She ignored them all. Only the mayor could approve her plan. Or kill it.

She reached backwards with one open hand and Schweizer placed a blue binder in it. Kohn plunked it onto the table.

"*All* of them, Your Honor," she said, tapping the binder with one finger. Her tone wasn't insubordinate, exactly. "However, ask HHS if they think that there is an alternative. Ask them how much we know about the virus. Especially, ask how much *time* we have left to act."

She waved to her right, signaling the Health and Human Services official. He had remained standing during her interruption, and was poised in front of the large polished conference table that fronted the wall of virtual meeting attendees.

Wearing a deer-in-the-headlights expression that

failed to inspire confidence, HHS continued where he had left off.

"To recap, Mr. Mayor, the Pacific flu is a complex, manufactured biological agent," he said. The HHS rep apparently noted the slight quaver in his voice and took a breath. "The disease has been artificially spread using air fresheners placed in public bathrooms all along the eastern and western seaboards, the length of the Mississippi and most major international airports in the United States. This dispersion pattern has been replicated globally and Asia is especially hard hit. There's as yet no cure and no clear path to any therapy. Further, there's no practical way to rapidly manufacture vaccine using conventional processes. The infection rate is accelerating and, well, it's bad. It's really, really bad."

The mayor asked the question on everyone's mind.

"How long do we have before the disease spreads so far that we can't stop it?"

"Physical containment measures are already being introduced, with OEM's help," the sweating man said, with a deferential nod to Kohn. "We are trying to firewall locations where infection clusters occur, rapidly segregating anyone that's been exposed. The efficacy of this isn't yet known, in a practical sense."

"Practical sense?" asked the city attorney.

"I mean we haven't been doing it long enough to know if the changes in the infection rate, the rhythm if you will, is due to our response, or if the natural incubation rate is creating populations of infected persons who will reach stage two of infection as a group, each time jumping the perceived infection rate." The HHS man paused for a breath.

"But, bottom line, if we can't slow the infection we won't be able to provide city wide basic services such as transportation and law enforcement in something like six weeks, perhaps eight," he said, consulting his notes. "Fresh water isn't a problem, and primary power generation retains ample margin, but a lot depends on how long we can keep refined fuels flowing. Fuels are critical to keeping basic requirements like food, health care and security functioning. The fuels industry relies utterly on intra-bank liquidity. If we lose that, the total collapse of the refined fuel sector follows in less than a week. Once we lose fuels, we lose everything else in days. If we don't restart the energy sector within forty-eight hours then the cascade failure becomes effectively irreversible on a regional basis."

A staffer spoke up. "We have Indian Point, it can supply a large part of the critical energy requirement, probably for years."

Indian Point, a very old but still operating nuclear power plant, was located up the Hudson River, only a short distance from the City.

"Commercial nuclear power plants actually need some electricity from off site to function." Kohn spoke impatiently. She was aware that the newest plants could actually self-generate, but Indian Point was nearly thirty years old and there was no point in polluting the limited technical comprehension of her audience with precise details.

"If they perceive that there is going to be a loss of load, they will start slowing the reactors, and if they have to, they will use their onsite diesel to run the cooling systems until the reactors can be safely shut all the way down. Even if they did not shut down, you can not power trucks, trains and cars with Indian Point."

She nodded her head at the HHS officer, who resumed his seat. It was evident who was in charge. She looked back at the mayor.

"Our experts on the global pandemic all agree, to a point," she said, leaning over and tapping the tabletop in front of her. "As you just heard, there is no routine, available and *accepted* process to mass produce a vaccine in time to fight this plague. But...

"But," she continued, looking around at the audience, "we *can* make an attenuated vaccine. With a little luck, we might be able to vaccinate all of the critical city staff and their families. If we do that, we can then vaccinate enough of the citizen base that we can prevent the complete collapse of city services, the logistics infrastructure that we all depend upon and the economy that provides the cash flow that keeps everything running."

The City public affairs officer tried to interject but Joanna's words hammered over top of the feeble effort.

"If we keep businesses running long enough, we can keep at least the regional economy moving at a pace sufficient to buy the pharma industry, FEMA and CDC the time needed to begin a large-scale traditional vaccination program based on less...fraught manufacturing techniques. We can even start to reverse the disease trend lines—we can *beat* this."

Before she could proceed, the chief counsel to the mayor cut her off.

"Can you even feel remorse?" he yelled. "Do you know how many tens or even hundreds of thousands of doses that is? How many murders do you propose that the mayor authorize?"

Joanna drew upon the core of her belief in change. She had to convince the mayor and he had to take the critical step. This arrogant puffball of a city attorney could not see the entire picture. He could be dealt with later.

"Unacceptable." She struck the tabletop with a closed fist. "What this is, *is* life or death. If we do not stop the infection, This Is The End. All capital letters. There is no plan coming from Washington. The military has its own problems—we'll be lucky if we can hold onto the local National Guard. We have failed to get in front of *every* crisis that has hit this city in the past. If we had improved the emergency response after the '93 bombing, we might have gotten more people out of World Trade on 9/11. If we had built the floodwalls before Irene and Sandy, we would not have had to rebuild Rockaway and pump out lower Manhattan. Now we are faced with another decision. A harder decision. You are worried about the political damage to the mayor—I am worried about keeping the City *alive*. We could even save the country, and you want to *argue*."

She turned to squarely face the mayor's image.

"Sir, you have to sign the emergency finding that I drafted." Without so much as a glance at the attorney, she held a palm up to silence his exasperated objection before he could even begin. "With that authority, I can organize emergency services, the PD, and begin a coordination effort with the major city players. We can use the already afflicted and recover something from their loss by harvesting their infected tissue to make vaccine. Every day we wait takes us closer to a precipice beyond which lies eternal night."

The mayor squinted, chewing his lip. Her absolute conviction could not be doubted. He looked around the room, and the face of each person in the meeting revealed that everyone was visibly evaluating one of mankind's oldest compromises.

Maybe the ends justify the means...

However, the mayor also understood liability. Early in his career a mentor had cautioned him to praise publicly and criticize privately. The converse was true of taking on a liability, even one with a huge payoff.

"We aren't going to start murdering sick people to save our own skins," he said, forcefully and authoritatively. The mayor looked directly at his head of OEM.

"Joanna, your plan isn't acceptable. Our citizens are not 'harvestable.' Call me direct," he continued, then looked off-screen. "Break this down."

Joanna smiled inwardly.

She was a fan of theater. And she already knew that she was going to get whatever she needed.

The audience of senior police officers was already restive, chafing at the unaccustomed security precautions mandated before they could file into the large city conference hall. Only the seniormost NYC cops, down to the precinct captain and lieutenant level and who were also personally vetted by Dominguez, had been allowed in. No support staff had been permitted to accompany anyone.

The preliminaries had been uncharacteristically brief.

"The following is not for release outside this room." The deputy chief got to the heart of the matter. "During the two weeks since the infection was initially recognized and reported by the CDC, we have recorded thirty-two sworn officers and fourteen additional police department personnel who have been infected and already exhibit stage two H7D3 symptoms. Of these only three remain alive, the remainder having died during efforts to restrain them.

"Despite the adoption of more liberal rules of engagement for confirmed and suspected cases of H7D3, a further three hundred and sixty-eight department personnel—of which two hundred and fifteen are sworn officers—have been exposed. All appear to have stage one symptoms and are in isolation. Of particular note, when the disease is transmitted into an open wound, the onset of symptoms can progress atypically and very rapidly. Several officers have developed stage two symptoms without first presenting flu characteristics and have attacked and infected additional officers and emergency workers."

Murmurs greeted the summary. Dominguez glanced around the gathered senior officers. More than a few faces were pale contrasts to the dark navy uniforms they wore. However, he was ready for his role.

"Further, we have a large number of officers taking sick leave," the official continued. "Despite injunctions and penalties, the percentage of officers taking sick leave and not returning to duty is over eight percent. This figure, added to the known and suspected cases, approaches ten percent of our total officer corps. Since most of the absences and losses are from patrol officers in active precincts, the impact on patrol density and call service interval is significantly greater than the raw numbers suggest."

"When do we get the promised equipment?" an anonymous voice in the back called out. "Our guys are dying, or worse, because we don't have biteproof equipment!"

Several more voices, safely anonymous in the large auditorium, rose above the hubbub, expressing violent agreement. One hard case, a Brooklyn accented speaker, added what was on everyone's mind.

"When are we gonna get a vaccine! No vaccine, no cops!"

Even louder yells, clearly in agreement, greeted this sentiment. And this, from senior leadership.

The deputy chief tried to quell the group, holding his hands up and trying to talk over the crowd. Another figure stepped up to the microphone, and placed a keyed megaphone in front of the mic.

Loud, painful squeals of feedback overrode even the most determined protest, and the room quickly subsided enough that the next speaker could make herself heard.

Joanna Kohn gestured to the deputy chief, the "may I?" intent quite clear. He ceded the podium, mixture of annoyance and relief visibly warring on his face.

She wore a dove gray suit, the severely cut trousers sporting creases sharp enough to shave a police recruit. The matching but plain top was without ornamentation, save for small gold OEM flashes winking from each side of the high Mandarin jacket collar.

Despite the audible undercurrent of side conversations, Kohn began.

"Gentlemen, ladies, officers—my name is Director Kohn," she said. "For those who are not acquainted with me, I run the New York City Office of Emergency Management. I have the beginnings of a solution to procure a vaccine and protect all *critical* city staff. Do. I. Have. Your. Attention?"

By the time she had reached the word "critical," the conference hall was nearly still enough that you could hear a pin drop.

"I'll take that as a 'yes,'" Kohn said, smiling faintly. "I have information that you need in order to understand and commit to the next steps. First, I worked with Deputy Chief of Police Hammond to ensure that this meeting was tiled. Second, the chief himself is conducting a public press conference to divert attention from this assembly. Finally, I am in possession of an emergency finding, signed by the mayor, granting the OEM executive and controlling authority to take such measures as are required to expedite the fight against the virus. Therefore I shall speak plainly. We can make our own vaccine and protect first ourselves, and then our city."

Questions rose from the audience thickly enough to make comprehension a challenge, but the feeling in the room had shifted, subtly.

"I cannot quite make out individual speakers," Kohn said. "I will endeavor to answer your questions, if you can put them to me professionally."

That was his prearranged cue. Dominguez quickly rose to his feet and stepped into the aisle, so he would be recognizable both to the audience and to Kohn.

"My name is Dominguez," Ding called out sharply. "I run One and I'll ask the question that I think we all have, Director. What's your plan and just how are we going to make vaccine?"

He looked around the room, which was full of other senior cops craning their necks to see who had asked what they were all thinking.

"Christ on a crutch knows that we need it, and now."

He remained standing among loud murmurs of assent.

"Captain Dominguez, thank you," Kohn said, smiling calmly. She laid her hands on the side of the podium. One index finger began to tap, beating out rhythm of her words. "I will summarize my plan and explain the steps: As some of you might know, there are multiple ways to create vaccine..."

Kohn outlined the various scenarios including the attenuated vaccine methods without specifically referring to where to find the materials.

"We have a process," Kohn concluded, "that can eventually mass produce radiologically attenuated H7D3 vaccine with an optimally incidental exposure rate of under one percent of the inoculated adult population. Therefore, my plan is for the Office of Emergency Management, in cooperation with select staff from the police department and other city agencies, to recruit the necessary talent, lease the necessary hardware and facilities and collect the raw material needed to immediately prototype a vaccine."

Joanna paused and glanced around the room, stopping when her eyes rested on Dominguez.

"And where are we going to get live virus in quantity, Madam Director?" Ding asked.

"There is only one readily available source of higher order primates in the City, Captain," Kohn replied, dropping her hands. "Fortunately, a large number of them are available at the Afflicted Care Centers."

Now you could hear a pin drop.

CHAPTER 7

*"And on tonight's Early Edition, Cheryl will give us an
early look at Fashion Week's hottest looks! Cheryl?"*

*"Um, we'll see some daring I— Ah, I mean, sorry, I must
be having an allergic reaction to something from lunch, I,
I, ah, I, something . . . on me . . . Get it off, get it off!"*

*"Sorry, for that, we'll just move on while Cheryl
reco— Oh my god! Cheryl! CHERYL!"*

<camera shakes, falls>

<growling, screams>

—Recovered video clip, Fox News
Fashion Week report, July 1, 2012

Tom Smith strode into the CEO's office, barely preceded by the startled admin's announcement.

Bateman looked up from his desk and then did a double take. The bright morning sunlight streaming through the windows didn't do Smith's features any favors. He was clearly fatigued. Something else played across Smith's face, as well.

"Well, you are already here, or I'd invite you in, Tom. Why don't you take a seat?" The CEO's tone was wry.

Smith nodded, and sat. He leaned forward in his seat and placed a small glass vial on the large desk.

"Is that what I think it is?" Bateman asked.

"The pure quill," Tom said, exhaling. "Ten doses of primer. The vaccine is administered in a two-part series. First, the primer, which dramatically increases resistance to the neurological pathogen. That's followed by the booster, two weeks later. This is a quarter of our first production run. We acquired the raw materials yesterday afternoon."

Bateman picked up the vial, turning it over in his hands. "Does it work?"

"I'll know soon enough," Smith said. "I had the primer already during a delightful session with our now resident mad scientist. I've also authorized the first course for the other two members of my asset acquisition team and for our physical security details that are maintaining perimeter security. But we're going to need more. A lot more, I should think."

Bateman carefully set the vial down, making a slight tapping sound.

"Is it safe?"

"Again, I'll know soon enough," Tom said with a shrug. "Curry's already inoculated me. There are various possible side effects. Autoimmune reactions, immunological reactions including allergic reactions . . . all unknown. The live attenuated vaccine made by the big pharmaceutical companies under ideal and controlled conditions has an incidental infection rate well under one percent. You can't, well, shouldn't give it to kids, though."

"Why not?" The CEO looked up. "Dependent children are on the evac plan."

"Attenuated virus vaccines aren't approved for kids; different vaccines have different age limits," Tom explained. "HPV vaccine is limited to nine-year-olds and up, for example. WHO and CDC recommend that kids under ten get inactivated virus vaccines until their immune systems are challenged enough to have a robust, adult style response. Curry also has the idea that since H7D3 attacks brain tissue, the fact that younger children and even young adults are still increasing the density of the myelin coat on their neurons is a risk factor. If or when the CDC gets inactivated virus vaccine to use we can protect the youngest evacuees. But as for adults, it's safe. Mostly. It isn't like we are spoiled for choice, Rich."

Tom's level look communicated fatalism, determination, but there was still something else.

"Who are you working with to get this?" It was plain that Bateman was thinking though the actual process.

"I've some trusted teammates," Tom stated flatly. "Besides Curry, only two others who perform the actual collection are all the way in the know. They get vaccine and two seats out, plus hazardous duty pay. I hope that you're comfortable with this arrangement because we're behind the curve, and we're going to need more help, soon."

Smith wouldn't ordinarily present his CEO with that many details in something like this, but Bateman didn't seem offended. Just...tired. Tom felt the same way. He knew exactly what he was doing and did not care for it one bit. Needs must when the devil drives.

"I know that we didn't move on Plan Zeus right away," Bateman said. "However, in order to assure the number of staff that we must have to evacuate to even a single refuge, the early estimates on evacuees quintupled. I won't be surprised if they go up again, which means more vaccine."

"I know, Rich," Smith said. He rolled his shoulder and grimaced. "I ran the numbers myself. How do you trust a pilot with an expensive and scarce helicopter if he's worrying about his family? Even harder, how do you trust any critical staff person who has no familial anchor and effectively has nothing to lose? What keeps him from taking a better offer? We need support staff with something to live for—which means locating that 'perfect pilot' with a small family. We'll host the dependents in the refuge and make the pilot's best option the one where they keep flying in order to guarantee their share of vaccine. And...we very subtly keep the family under our thumb by 'ensuring their protection.'"

He looked out the window.

"A little polite extortion isn't new to this job," Tom said. "But just because it works, doesn't mean I have to *like* it any more than I have to like stripping spines out of infected people. But, we all took the money."

Bateman tried to reassure Smith.

"Tom, I know tha—"

"No," Smith said, cutting him off. "You don't know, Boss. You can't know. You've never even taken a life much less cut the head off of some poor woman just to strip out her spine. It's horrific. And it's necessary. Our only chance to survive is to dramatically accelerate collection and endure the horror now. It's the only way we can avoid an even worse outcome. I'll do it, and I'll push the security staff to do it—and it will get done. Which brings me to why I am here."

"Anything you need, we'll get for you Tom—you know that."

"Glad to hear it, sir," Tom said, turning back to his

boss with a slight, humorless grin. "The first thing is that Curry is going to need an assistant. For obvious reasons, it needs to be someone that we trust, can control, needs the vaccine and ultimately will agree with what we are doing."

"I leave it to you, just make damned sure it's someone we can trust," Bateman replied.

Smith grinned for what felt like the first time in days. It felt good.

"Oh, I think I can promise that much," Tom said. "We are also going to need more and heavier armament. I have a way to procure it, deniably. However, I'll be breaking several state and fed—"

"Didn't hear that one," Bateman said, interrupting and waving his hands. "Keep it on a cash basis."

Smith nodded again, this time with the ghost of a smile. New York had notoriously over the top antigun laws, at least for those below the millionaire class.

"The next thing is harder," Tom said. He inclined his head at the shining vial that Bateman had set back on his desk. "That's the most valuable substance in the city, maybe the entire country. We're going to have to look ahead on how we organize and regulate the collection, processing and distribution or we are going to have anarchy. Every organization that hasn't figured it out yet will do so in short order and start competing for, well, let's call them, *viral assets*. Anarchy equals less time to make the vaccine, and maybe a cure. We are going to need help and regulation."

"Who would have thought it—a banker calling for oversight and cooperation?" The CEO looked thoughtful. "Who do you have in mind to bring in?"

"We start with a few other banks," Smith said. He

smiled again, but this time it didn't warm him. Quite. "Then we're going to get unconventional."

Tradittore looked composed. The unfiltered Camel that he smoked irritated Paul Rune.

"Joey, do you really have to blow that in my face?"

Tradittore, unruffled, turned his head and exhaled in the opposite direction, sending the smoke across Washington Square Park. An organic fruit vendor jerked his head up, annoyed.

"Sorry man. But it's your dime. What do you need?"

Rune passed over a paper list, which Tradittore began to read.

"You guys certainly love your acronyms," the Sicilian said, tapping his ash. "Okay, most of this I recognize and we can get pretty quickly. Rifles, shotguns and pistols are easy. Ammunition, same thing. The explosives and the suppressors are quite a bit harder, as you know. That kind of merchandise attracts an entirely different level of heat."

He kept reading.

"Pneumatic auto-injector, reuseable?" he said, looking up. "What do you want that f— never mind. Don't want to know. Let's see. You also want eight sets of something called an A/N GP-NVG-18? That's a new one."

"NODs," Paul replied. "Sorry, night observation device. My boss says that this model preserves depth perception. Currently Mil/Law enforcement only. We've tried to get them through our own channels. No dice. If you can't get those, we'll consider other models, at a reduced cost of course. Probably going to end up buying even more."

Tradittore whistled.

"Well, in addition to your love of acronyms, you banks also don't appear to be scared of big numbers, which is what this is going to cost. I can set up a demo and a pickup for all of it in a week, maybe three." He refolded the list and tucked it away. "How are you going to pay?"

"Cash, naturally." Paul was confident on how the conversation would go next.

"No can do, roomie," Joey replied instantly. "Cash isn't what it used to be. Nope—you are going to have to do better."

The banker smiled.

"Bullion."

"Keep talking," Tradittore answered, with a wave of one hand.

"Figured as much," Paul said. He pulled a small rubber-topped vial from his own pocket. He carefully did *not* hand it over, but turned it back and forth in his hand, the sun striking highlights from the glass.

"Vaccine. First part of a two part series. We'll add ten complete series of vaccine to sweeten the vig."

Matricardi's man looked . . . amenable. But he was the mobster's man, after all. You never took the first offer, or the second.

"And?"

"And we'll teach you how to make more."

"How much more can you tell us about Smith, Ms. Kohn?" asked Sarissa Gauge.

"He's hardly remarkable," replied Joanna, giving Gauge's outfit a critical glance. The female half of her personal staff was wearing a severely cut suit close enough in style and color to Joanna's that it constituted a uniform. Gauge had deferentially chosen heeled ankle boots from Yves St. Laurent that were just one notch less fashionable than those of her director.

Joanna approved. Detail-oriented subordinates were less likely to make an error when it counted.

She resumed.

"Average intelligence, a conventional thinker, the physical type," Joanna said, continuing to tick off points. "In short, a typical example of the former military banker club, with all the downside that entails."

"Downside, ma'am?" asked Ken Schweizer. The formerly junior OEM analyst had taken a chance and hitched his star to Kohn during the 2010 hurricane season and had jumped several levels as a result. His attempt at a neatly trimmed beard, intended to convey maturity, was defeated by his narrow features, reducing the effect to that of a rat with patchy fur.

"He will be predictably loyal to Bank of the Americas," she replied. "He will be singularly focused on a clear mission and therefore easy to manipulate. By now, like some of the other banks, insurers and multinationals that are headquartered in the City, he is weighing the likelihood that this disease is an inflection point. He will be planning on how to keep the bank operating while being ready to respond if the disease has more impact than expected."

"Can we use that?" asked Gauge.

"Smith and his bank, as well as a few others, not to mention the NYPD, will be important components of the City's response to this crisis. Now that we have vaccine production underway, the next step will be to consolidate production. The problem is that the projected vaccine demand exceeds the source of raw materials."

"We have a fairly broad mandate," offered Schweizer. "And the continued absence of the mayor means that we can continue to work through the first deputy mayor's staff—"

"The secret finding gives us near carte blanche, Ken," interrupted Gauge. "And we control the daily brief to the mayor, the deputy and the council. What we need is to adjust the crisis further in our favor."

Joanna favored Gauge with another look before turning to Schweizer.

"We may need to accelerate the processes," she said. "I am aware that Smith is developing contacts in Cosa Nova. I want you to do the same, and also consider some of the other organized crime factions."

Joanna watched Gauge hiding her disappointment, resuming her customary businesslike mask.

"Sarissa, I am keenly aware of your contribution, but your efforts to deepen our network in the city council are vital," she stated, narrowing her eyes. "Further, I want you closer to the district attorney. We must deter premature reconsideration of our new powers until the situation is sufficiently dire that the evolution of OEM can not be rolled back. We need the City to sample a little of Hell."

This is what Hell must sound like, Dominguez had thought to himself upon entering the Afflicted Temporary Holding Facility for the first time. Initially the building had been labeled "Secure Infected Temporary Holding" by some dim bulb that hadn't ever seen the movies, so Dominguez had rapidly changed the name from SITH to its current title.

The volume of the screaming, howling and moaning

from the infected rendered normal speech impossible. Efforts had been taken to visually isolate the infected from each other, which seemed to reduce the amount of sound that each zombie made, but the overall volume remained shocking. Worse was the reek—the smell of rot and excrement was a palpable miasma that saturated one's clothing, even if a visitor didn't touch *anything*.

The top cop in One was fairly inured to the aroma now, but the noise level was still stunning. At least it wasn't feeding time. Ding didn't like to think about their source of zombie-chow.

One of two facilities, the large Queens warehouse had a small set of offices that was segregated from the honeycomb of hundreds of small chain-link mini cells, each intended to hold one infected. Two of the offices retained ad hoc VISITING FAMILY ROOM signs from a more optimistic time. There was even a small children's play area, filled with bright plastic furniture in cheerful primary colors. Those rooms had remained unused for their original purpose, nearly from the start.

The days when a cure was merely a statistical improbability instead of a forlorn hope were already far behind them. Initially, the number of infected held in the ATHF had been low, but once hospitals filled up, there was nowhere else to hold them. Moving the infected was a traumatic and potentially dangerous process. In the interest of simplicity, Ding had decided that rather than move the infected to another location, it was simpler to "process" the vaccine materials onsite.

Therefore, one of the visitor rooms had been adapted into a processing center. Another was a training room.

At the moment, senior police officers were attending mandatory training. That, in and of itself, wasn't unusual. However, even during a lethal pandemic, Ding still noted the bizarre situation that he found himself in. To be specific, helping to teach Zombie Spine Stripping 101 was still damned disturbing, and the subject matter mandated extreme safety precautions.

Despite the discomfort of their current rig, Dominguez and his students would have happily traded up to the even more uncomfortable environmental suits, but they could no longer be had for love or money.

Dominguez wasn't particularly unacquainted with human blood. He was not, however, accustomed to seeing so much of it. The hooded 3M exposure suit he wore was liberally dappled with red above the waist, and completely red below the knee. The floor wasn't just tacky with blood; the plastic sheeting lining the warehouse office floor was half a centimeter deep in carmine for a meter in all directions outwards from his feet.

"Easy, easy, just tug steadily." Another suited figure spoke, the voice somewhat muffled. "If you pull too hard the cord tears and then we can't get it out."

The senior cop listened to their trainer, another suited figure. The third participant was his deputy precinct commander, who was struggling to gently pull on the shoulders of the naked corpse of their "subject." Despite the hip-high gurney that had been placed in the center of the space, the cops struggled to manipulate the uncooperative corpse. Blood and lymph made a firm grip impossible, and the dead weight of the body worked against the team. Ding had recruited, well, extorted a compromised medical examiner to teach his cadre how to strip the spine from a dead zombie. Ding firmly believed that rank had its privileges, including going first and setting the example for the more junior officers whom he had selected.

However, cleanly severing a human neck while keeping the spinal cord intact and connected to the brainstem was surprisingly difficult. They had wasted one "asset" already and their co-opted medical examiner was getting frustrated.

Just getting this far was a technical process that could not be approached in a slapdash fashion. The human neck is packed with a remarkable amount of gristly connective tissue, and it had to be carefully dissected without damaging the all important trophy.

"Look, if you yank too sharply, you'll just shear the cord—it doesn't have shit for tensile strength," the shanghaied medical examiner said, irritated. "Do that and you waste the sample—might as well start over with the next one. What you want to do is sever the connective tissue between the head and the trunk just above the shoulders, leaving a few cervical vertebrae as an anchor point. Once you have it all separated, you can carefully slide the tissue out of the spinal column."

When the deputy returned to probing the gaping neck wound on the corpse with a large serrated knife, one of the cops watching the demonstration turned his head, his stomach spasming.

"For chrissakes, don't puke on the assets!" the medical examiner said, scolding the cop who had moved too close to the four additional corpses stacked in pairs on the side tables.

Noting the watchers' discomfort, Dominguez added to the instructor's comments.

"Also, the other thing is that once you are in this suit, you really, *really* don't want to upchuck." He spoke slowly for clarity and emphasis. "These masks will protect you from the droplet borne virus, but you have to maintain a perfect seal. Puke will clog the intake, it will almost certainly make you choke and it could cause a suit failure if you tear at your own protective equipment in order to try to catch a breath."

The NIOSH-certified full face respirators had been a godsend. When he tried to procure the necessary amount via the department there were already none to be had, but the bank had stockpiled an impressive amount. Now, he owed Smith a rather large favor. These even had two-stage filters, which added only incrementally to the protection but looked impressive as hell and bolstered the confidence of his harvest team.

"As soon as we have the first batch of effective vaccine, you'll all get the primer," Dominguez said, trying to reassure his team of students by repeating the terms of their additional duty. "That'll give you some protection. But for now, you must be very, very careful!"

Ding continued to maintain his hold on the shaggy black hair of the corpse as his partner finished cutting the last bit of connective tissue holding the head to the trunk. His gloves prevented him feeling the hair itself, which was probably for the best. Judging from the condition and smell of the body, this zombie had been a homeless man before H7D3 turned him into another lethal carnivore.

The spinal cord finally slid smoothly free in a rush of fluid, the yellow tissue visibly flecked with red.

"That's the stuff!" the examiner said, pointing with one gloved finger at the just barely visible red flecks on the neural tissue. "That discoloration is the pay dirt. Handle it carefully to avoid contaminating the specimen."

"Or yourself," Ding added. As he stepped to one side to afford the audience a better view, his booted feet squelched. "Lose your breathing protection seal around this much aerosolized blood and you'll contaminate yourself, earning a one way ticket to becoming the next contestant in a game of..."

The police captain held up the severed head, trailing the all important viral sample.

"...'Organ Donor Card Bingo!'"

While the examiner watched, Ding gestured to his assistant who picked up a specimen bag into which Dominguez slowly lowered the sample, finally snipping the cord free at the base of the skull. He casually dropped the head onto the chest of the corpse while the assistant carefully placed the sealed bag on a bed of ice inside a cooler.

"Good job," Ding said. His grim smile was plainly visible through the faceplate of his mask. "Got it done. First two volunteers, jock up. Don't forget the Kevlar gloves—you will want maximum sharps protection. Second pair, move these processed remains into that bin."

He gestured to a large open wheeled stainless steel bin labeled RECYCLING. "Then we'll work through the next four stiffs, one per student pair, and then go wrangle some more."

"Yes, even during a slow-moving zombie apocalypse, we still have meetings."

A few tired smiles appeared around the table.

Most of the North American security managers for the bank, as well as some additional hand picked staff, were back in the high-security conference room and the door was closed. One of the fluorescent bulbs flickered distractingly.

Tom Smith was already standing at the head of the table.

"This team, the people actually inside this room, represent the core of the bank security team that will continue to implement Plan Zeus. For those of you unaware of Zeus, we'll unpack more details during this meeting as well as during subsequent get togethers. Most of you know each other already. As for the rest..."

Tom indicated Brad Depine whose shirt sported dark crescents under his arms despite the air conditioning.

"Mr. Depine has been hand selected by the CEO to provide financial oversight and liquidity as required." If anything, Depine's saturnine expression deepened.

"This is Ms. Sophia Smith." Sophia was a slightly built blonde wearing a cream business suit. She appeared to be ridiculously young to be in a meeting about zombies. "Yes, she is a relation, a niece. As such, she holds my unequivocal trust. She is Dr. Curry's new assistant, augmenting Kendra."

Sophia looked tense, but controlled. A few people nodded to her. Next to her was another young woman, built considerably larger, though a family resemblance was evident. She wore utilities, a mostly empty equipment harness and a bored expression.

"Next to Sophia is my second niece, Ms. Faith Smith. Faith will be ... working on tasks as assigned."

The second Ms. Smith exhaled audibly and rolled her eyes.

"Durante will now run the Building Protection team, replacing the late Mr. Skorpio," Tom continued, picking up the pace. "Kaplan will run the Executive Protection team. We're suspending most Anti-Fraud operations, all book running for deals in process and delegating foreign travel itinerary reviews to individual travelers. With the spreading nation-state quarantines there are fewer of those anyway. These changes are intended to free up staff for an operations center that will support the collection of raw vaccine ingredients and the manufacture of vaccine. Rune will continue in charge of intel and will manage the ops center."

Down the table an arm in a pale designer shirt went up.

"No questions yet," Tom said. "Each of you is a proven, reliable teammate, known to me personally or vouched for by someone I trust. During this meeting, you will be brought all the way in on critical actions needed to assure personal safety, the safety of our families and the survival of the banking system which is funding the efforts to mass produce vaccine and find a cure. The actions we must take are..."

Tom paused and considered his next words carefully.

"...discomforting and extralegal. Discomfort is to be expected. If you are entirely opposed to this course, this is your last chance to leave. Requests for reassignment or resignation made subsequent to this meeting won't be honored until such time as our plan is ready to launch. This is your last opportunity to depart the platform without penalty. Staying may expose you to legal jeopardy and some personal risk."

He paused again and waited for several moments. No one moved. Rune, who had been read into the plan for a while, looked around the room as well, pausing briefly as he considered Jones.

"All right," Smith continued. "All NDAs remain in effect. I consider all you committed to our plan."

He slowly looked around the room, meeting the eyes of each team member in turn.

"Next, some announcements. The Bank didn't move fast enough at the start, so we didn't get our first picks for refuge locations. Some are going to be little farther away than I like. Consequently, I am setting up a study group to identify SAFEs."

He saw Paul and few others nod, but also noted a several blank looks.

"Not big metal boxes for money," Tom said, folding his arms across his chest. "Selected Area For Evasion. A place that isn't necessarily a long-term refuge, but which is situated away from the likely lanes of what I'll politely term *refugee drift*. If this all goes for a ball of chalk, the sudden breakdown in city and suburban infrastructure is going to generate a massive amount of refugees, which will promptly freeze every major highway."

"Travel during the first day after an incipient society-wide collapse will be very difficult," Kendra said, earning a squint from her boss. "Day two, forget about it." She steepled her fingers, the skin showing white at the knuckles. "The entire D.C.–New York–Boston axis is going to be impassable. Anyone who isn't already at one of the Sites is done."

A fraud analyst began to retort, but Tom cut him off. "She's not wrong," he said, favoring Kendra with an approving look. "I recognize there are those," he gave Depine a less favorable look, "who without background in this field find Kendra's analysis problematic. That's a lack of both training and experience...on the part of the skeptics. My physical security specialists don't tell you about anti-fraud or market making, so don't question their competence about security issues. Stay in your lane. I'll add that anyone stuck in the initial stampede is at high risk. So, Kendra's team will identify potential SAFEs—way stations if you will."

He glanced over at Rune and Jones. "Have a list ready for me to consider in three days. Next item."

Tom leaned forward, placing both hands on the table. He scanned the room again. Slowly. Deliberately.

"We *are* making an effective vaccine."

A hand shot up.

Tom shook his head, aggravated.

"Not yet," he repeated himself. "We now have an effective vaccine. In fact, we've got the first eighty doses. These doses are either being administered to personnel with the highest risk of exposure or to irreplaceable personnel in critical roles. Everyone in this room is eligible for the vaccine."

The same hand went up again.

"Where's the vaccine coming from?" the anti-fraud analyst asked. "How are we making it?"

"Dr. Curry will describe the process in a moment," Tom said, straightening. "I want to be clear on what you get in exchange for being part of this permanent team and maintaining absolute confidentiality. You're placed on the priority list for the vaccine, which is a multipart course of injections. You're guaranteed a seat for yourself and while you were selected in part because you have few or no nearby family, you will also be allotted up to three family member spaces at one of the bank's safe havens, depending on your role and physical risk."

Exciting buzzing interrupted Smith, who let it run for a moment before continuing.

"Next detail. We have sought and received permission to acquire and equip with much heavier weaponry than the limited number of pistols, Tasers and single use injectors now in our inventory. Kaplan will be scheduling in-house training. Wave to the crowd, Kapman."

Kaplan raised his hand and grinned. He had been lobbying for a while to buy some weapons with more authority than Tasers and pistols.

"The training is mandatory," Tom continued. "This means you too, Paul."

Good natured laughter sounded briefly. Rune's single-minded focus on work, his guitar and more work—in that order—were well known among his staff.

"For obvious reasons, it's now profoundly in your own self-interest to keep all such details secure," Tom continued, sounding more relaxed than he actually was. "For that reason, you aren't allowed to divulge or discuss any further details of this plan or our preparations outside the people currently in this room. Finally, in exchange for the personal and legal risks that this will entail, we'll place your family members on the secondary list for the vaccination schedule, making doses available after critical staff are all protected. Let me add: as NDAs go, ours has new teeth. If you break the NDA prior to completing the course of vaccinations, your protection is suspended. If you violate the NDA after vaccination is complete, your evacuation quota will be revoked and you will be indefinitely detained inside these premises."

Attentive silence met this statement.

"Dr. Curry, over to you."

Curry was getting into the swing of things. His grin was equal parts enthusiasm and evil genius as he tapped a key on his notebook PC, starting a short clip of an infected secured to a hospital gurney. It couldn't move, but the gurney shook from the zombie's struggles. The video froze on a close up the snapping jaws.

"Meet the source of our vaccine."

Below the conference room windows, Newark Penn Station provided a gemmed backdrop for the Cosa Nova evening meeting running into its third hour. Matricardi took a last drag and spoke as smoke filtered out from his nose, flavoring the air.

"Joey," the mob boss said, grinding out the cigarette. "Out of twelve bodies, we only got twenty doses. That's less than a third of the rate that Bank of the Americas is getting. Or at least, telling us they're getting."

Matricardi rolled a little vial around in his hand.

"What's the deal?"

"It's harder than the bank instructions made it sound," Traditore said, cautiously feeling out his boss. "Getting the spinal cords out without tearing 'em is a finicky job. The job itself, well it's pretty horrible so our guys tend to hurry through it. Basically, what we're doing is cutting up people. It takes a . . . certain kinda guy to be comfortable with that. We don't got as many people with the right mindset as you'd think. Also, the metering of the radiation used to damage the viral DNA while leaving the virus itself sufficiently intact to provoke an immune response is . . . well, it's finicky too. We've spoiled some batches because we don't have a well-trained radiologist. The bank's got a fuckin' microbiologist doing this. We got Tony Too-Smart runnin' our machine."

Tony, like the rest of the audience, wisely stayed silent.

The gangster looked out the window, listening. Tradittore couldn't clearly see Matricardi's face, and paused until his boss waved one hand in a circular "keep going" motion.

"Collecting the zombies ain't a picnic, either. We lost two guys who got themselves bit during the first week."

Matricardi looked back.

"What did you do with them?"

"You're holding it."

The Aeron Miller clicked a bit as the taller Sicilian leaned back in his chair, contemplating the vial as the lights struck golden highlights from the vial.

"Well, waste not, want not, I suppose," the mobster said.

He stretched an arm towards the buffet along the wall, and Khabayeva uncrossed her long legs and moved to open the humidor. She held up a Romeo Y Julieta and raised an eyebrow.

"No, no—something else. The Davidoff."

As she clipped and lit the cigar Matricardi turned back to the table. He set the ampoule of vaccine down on the rich wood of the table with a slight tick.

"You mentioned that the competition is getting stiffer?"

Tradittore's eyes followed the brunette's motions as she rolled the cigar in her long fingers, evenly starting the ember and shaking the long wooden match out before handing the lit cigar to Matricardi.

"We gotta couple trucks that we roll after dark, looking for obviously infected people, but usually we listen to the Essex County scanner." He looked back to his boss. "If we hear a 10-54, we try to beat the cops to the location. Sometimes we do, but even if the cops don't get there first, there's an even chance that Overture's guys, a team from the Triads or some other freelancers are laying claim."

Overture was the emerging power in New York. His Afro-Caribbean organization had consolidated power in Queens and Brooklyn and now vied for ascendancy with the Triads in Manhattan. The smart money seemed to be on Overture.

Matricardi blew smoke across the room and ruminated on the cigar.

"Nice." He glanced at the only woman in the room. "What do you think, Risky? You always tell me that you're more than a pretty face. So, fine, show me that I don't keep you around just because you're gorgeous."

"What we need are some specialized skills and to tighten up the organization." She recrossed her legs. "Reduce the wastage of, what did Joey call them?"

"Assets," Tradittore volunteered, his eyes narrowing almost imperceptibly.

"Assets." If the topic made Khabayeva queasy, it certainly didn't show. "We need to utilize them efficiently—no waste. Also, we need stop wasting collection opportunities by competing with cops and other organizations. The first one is simple. The second one is harder. Who can talk to cops, to other competitors and be believed by all? The bankers."

Tradittore leaned forward.

"Wait a second: Simple?" he asked with a smirk. "This I got to hear. You know a better way to cut off some poor stiff's head and pull his spinal cord out without snapping it or getting infected yourself?"

Matricardi eyed them both.

Khabayeva first met his glance and then looked back to the younger man.

"Is simple," she said, waving a hand dismissively. "Find butcher. A doctor. A coroner. A funeral home director. All of them would have a better understanding of how to extract the spinal cord. So, hire them, or bribe them, or...encourage them some other way."

"I like the funeral home director idea the best." She tapped the table with a long burgundy nail. "They have ways to dispose of the bodies—is one less thing."

Tradittore sat back slightly, deflated.

His boss looked first at his deputy and then at Oldryskya.

"That's not half bad," Matricardi said with a grunt. "Okay—Tradittore, set it up. I'll call Smith and see about the second thing."

He looked appraisingly at the woman again.

"Not half bad at all."

Without moving his eyes away from her he addressed the rest of the room.

"Meeting's over. Beat it."

Khabayeva stayed seated.

∽ ⊖ ⌒

"If this works, then the perimeter security issue gets much easier!" Durante exclaimed, examining his new toy.

The patch test kit resembled a single use diabetes monitor. Blood from a fine catheter passed through a membrane and then was introduced to a color sensitive paper patch. If the antibodies for H7 were present, it turned red. The failure rate was unhelpfully high—it would have never passed FDA testing—but it was better than nothing. Different models of varying degrees of accuracy were proliferating across the country.

"Will it get so much easier that you'll catch the next infected employee that wanders into the HVAC room," Smith asked, barely bothering to coat the steel in his words with a bare minimum of humor. "And thereby prevent my niece from having to beat it to death with a K-11?"

Faith Smith, having been thoroughly disarmed—who gives a Saiga to a thirteen-year-old, really!—and a building engineer named Schmidt who had been assigned as tour guide tasked to give her a familiarization tour of the skyscraper's infrastructure had found a zombie feeding on a recent kill. *Inside* his bank. She'd brained the afflicted former bank employee with a security baton that she'd been surreptitiously lent by a sympathetic guard. Then she had to deal with the emotional consequences of her first kill—not to mention, her uncle then had the pleasure of explaining the event to her parents.

Tom Smith wasn't going to let his new head of building security forget it.

Dr. Curry was demonstrating the kit and testing everyone present at the daily Plan Zeus team meeting. He moved to Tom Smith's side.

Wincing, the tall Australian held out a hand and looked in the other direction while Curry wielded the test.

He couldn't see Durante from this angle, but he could hear the grin.

"Boss, are you still scared of an itsy-bitsy needle?"

"Answer in the first part," Tom said, looking across the table. "It's a well-known fact that needles are the source of all that is evil in the world. So, yes. Answer in the second part. Find something else for Faith to do. Something safe. Filing. Hand folding pull-outs. Temp admin work. Something that keeps her in secure areas. Hell, spin it off to Rune."

At the end of the table, Rune winced. He had heard about the...challenges of reining in the younger Smith girl.

"Also, answer in the third part," Tom continued. "Gravy, *thank you* for volunteering to escort Brad on a little trip! You must remember to send us a postcard from picturesque Eastern Europe." Smith dabbed at his finger with a Betadine patch, his eyes glinting.

"And...this one is negative too." Curry was personally reading each kit and then dropping them into a bin proffered by Sophia Smith, before the pair moved onto the next person.

"Eastern Europe?" Durante looked over to their financier, who was looking unhappy but no real help, then returned his gaze to Tom. "How *far* east? Belgrade, Budapest...?"

Mostly blank looks answered his sally. However, Tom made a little "come on" gesture.

"Sofia...Kiev..." Durante continued, "Tbilisi..."

"Warmer..." Tom said, holding up his palm. "Your

job, once you have read the packet, is to figure out the details."

He slid a thick folder down the table.

"If we don't either dramatically increase asset collection, or per-asset realization, we aren't going to make our numbers for the planned courses of H7D3 vaccine," Tom said, turning serious. "I've no desire to buy from Overture or Matricardi—their Q and A isn't anything like ours. For that matter, Overture is starting to run his own coordination with some of the police precincts. If he gets tight with them, he can squeeze the banks. I'm going to try to head that off, but you and Brad are going to see if we can buy what we need."

Durante was still grinning. Big adventure! His erstwhile travel partner wasn't happy.

"Are we certain that the samples we collected from the London office came from this group?" Depine asked, reading an e-mail on his tablet.

"Not sure," Tom shrugged but stabbed a map of Eastern Europe with his finger. "We *know* that there is a large-scale production center of pharmaceutical grade vaccine at least as good as the best we are manufacturing. We are *confident* that it is originating in Eastern Europe, but not Russia or Belarus. Current intel points to a semiautonomous region of the country of Georgia . . . And we *think* that the actual producers didn't start out as a pharmaceutical operation . . ."

"The beer company?" Durante asked. "Didn't they mix it up with the Chechens a while back . . . ?"

"The same," Tom said. "Also mercenaries for hire according to our NatSec intel group. And now believed to be producing high-quality vaccine in saleable quantities.

Part of the background data on them is they have a long-term relationship with a former Russian/Soviet bioweapons expert. Presumably he's the one in charge of vaccine production. Fly to Tbilisi, make delicate inquiries, find the wholesalers, get us that vaccine."

"Why send me?" Depine didn't quite whine. "I'm not a biologist. Besides, air travel right now isn't safe!"

"Simple math," Smith replied, his tone hardening even further. "The board approved a global vaccination plan that will support up to thirty-thousand staff and dependents. We aren't confident that we're going to get to that number—so we need to buy more. If we buy from Overture or one of the others we run the risk of subpar quality as well as giving up leverage that we can't afford to sacrifice just yet. So, it's the two of you against potentially another few thousand courses of vaccine. I'll take that bet. You're a deal maker. Durante finds the wholesale source, *you* make the deal. Cause, admittedly, Gravy can't negotiate for shit."

Durante looked hurt. Depine opened his mouth but Tom cut him off.

"Lastly—you started off weeks ago by bitching about the costs when I wanted to initiate Zeus," Tom said, his eyes cold behind his smile. "So, while all your fat-ass buddies stay here nice and safe in New York, *you* get to go haring off into the wilds to be the bag man and negotiator. The G6 is over at FBO. Three pilots, all vaccinated, just like yourself. Mr. Bateman has authorized five hundred kilos of bullion and another twenty million in specie. We *need* that vaccine. Make the best deal you can make, Brad. You screwed up my well-laid plans for just such an emergency once. Do it again, you *won't* like the consequences."

CHAPTER 8

*"Whenever a doctor cannot do good, he
must be kept from doing harm."*
—Hippocrates, 362 BC

"The definitions of 'harm' and 'useful evil' can ... overlap."
—David Curry, M.D., Ph.D., Lead Virologist,
CDC Response Team, Year of the Fall 2

From: *Angels and Devils: The Practical Response to H7D3*
University of the South Press 2055

Kaplan's nose itched. He wasn't certain which of Smith's guests wore the offending scent—it seemed to be more sandalwood than floral, but that didn't really refine the possible suspects. The OEM director wore a uniform every bit as formal as the visiting cops' blues or his own boss's tailored suit. It certainly was less colorful than the Cosa Nova boss's white lapel carnation. The former operator carefully refrained from scratching his nose and concentrated on the principals while still keeping a careful eye cocked at their security.

The visitors had arrived in three parties. The NYPD contingent included several plainclothes cops, two of whom had rather obvious and unnecessary briefcases which they carefully sat down to the right of their respective chairs. A suspicious mind might note that they were the right size and shape for a shortened carbine or subgun. A second group consisted of only two gray-suited OEM functionaries, a bearded man and a hatchet-faced woman, each carrying a leather folio and multiple phones. The last group included a squad of what looked like private military contractors, albeit ones with an excess of spray tan and styling gel. Their equipment included double pistol rigs, hung low on the same thigh. That didn't count the knockout of a brunette who sat behind the head gangster.

The tone of the meeting wasn't . . . warm. Both Dominguez, now informally representing the entire Department, and Kohn, providing the same service for the remaining city government, were unhappy that they were sharing a room with a known criminal like Matricardi.

It had taken fifteen minutes to get past the obligatory pleasantries and onto the real business. Smith wanted everyone to turn their cards face up before he popped the question.

"You may need thirty-six thousand doses for the bank, but the department numbers twice that, plus dependents." Dominguez's voice was even but intense. "At the rate we are manufacturing, we might have full coverage for the officers in two more months. Probably three. But only if we don't have to constantly referee the banks, the criminals and independents who are, incidentally, going after the same raw materials that we are. And this asshole"—he jerked his chin towards the Sicilian—"is selling to whoever can meet the price, even as we protect him."

Matricardi smiled but refrained from comment.

Tom Smith didn't rise to the bait, but he still replied.

"I've got a couple of informal ways to determine how bad things are outside," Tom said, gesturing to the broad window overlooking the East River. "I measure how long it takes our trucks to fill up every day. Takes rather less nowadays."

Bank of the Americas, like other interested parties, had been collecting zombies for vaccines for weeks. Smith had labeled the units Biological Emergency Response Teams, or BERTs for short. The name stuck, and the various competing BERTs patrolled, ready to tase and bag zombies for use in vaccine manufacture. That the official PD policy appeared to be "live and let live" strongly suggested that they needed the teams collecting infected rather more than they needed to assert their own primacy.

"But I have been looking out this window since the Fourth of July," Tom continued. "I check to see how many smoke columns there are, which corresponds to the number of fires not being promptly contained by FDNY. I check the number of reported arrests and detentions, which apart from infected, are way, way down. I look at the amount of traffic on the FDR Parkway. It's getting a lot lighter. All those things correspond to how many LEO and emergency services we have left. And I can tell that the number is going down, fast. You don't have fifty thousand cops anymore. After your precinct consolidation, you might have half of that, optimistically."

The top cop was getting visibly agitated.

"Understand, Captain Dominguez, I intend no disrespect, but I can't bring you options if we don't share the same set of facts," Tom added placatingly. "And the fact is that the police department is fading."

"There are plenty of cops," Dominguez said, standing up abruptly. "Enough to lock the city down. If we get turned loose, we can clear out the five boroughs of the criminals that are profiting from this disease, instead of getting bled dry while they turn a buck."

He pointed at the New Jersey leader.

"If that happens, then your organization is next. I know that after Overture, you are the second largest illegal vaccine operation in the City."

"News to me, Captain," Matricardi said, spreading his hands disarmingly. "But I'm interested in finding more vaccine."

"We *are* the NYPD, and you think that you can dictate terms to *us*?" Dominguez looked angrily towards Smith. "If I think that you're holding back vaccine that we need, I'll arrest you here and now. I'm refraining from shooting this asshole," he added, flinging a hand at the Sicilian, "out of hand only because we have an arrangement with Bank of the Americas—but only with you!"

The tension in the room, which had been inching upwards, shot up several notches.

Tom looked around the room. Three different groups of security guards had gone from trying to out-bland each other to being fully alert, weight on the balls of their feet and hands close to their weapons.

The banker looked to the head of OEM.

"Ms. Kohn, before you allow this to escalate unhelpfully, perhaps you want to hear the entire proposal?"

Ding began to reply but Kohn forestalled him with a raised hand.

"Just before Independence Day weekend, we were running at half the pre-Plague numbers," she replied.

"Last Monday, the number of sworn officers reporting for duty was at thirty-nine percent of pre-Plague
levels and dropping."

The bright light filtering through the skyscraper's
tinted windows drew her face into sharp relief, severe
but determined. She regarded Smith steadily.

"So yes, your information is correct." Her glance
took in Smith and Dominguez. "Before we proceed
further, why don't we speak privately, we three?"

Tom Smith looked over at Matricardi.

"We four, you mean. I invited Mr. Matricardi for
a purpose. And I need the good doctor for a bit
longer, as well."

Ding gritted his teeth and shook his head.

Kohn smiled and replied smoothly.

"We accept."

"What do you mean, 'You can't do this'?" Rune
didn't often raise his voice, but when he did, he didn't
hold back. Despite that, he wasn't in danger of being
overheard. Jones had requested a private meeting
with her boss in the secure conference room. "Can't
do *what*, exactly?"

Kendra Jones was scared, but she stood her ground.

"I don't think I can be part of a plan, an operation,
that is violating the rights of the people sick with the
flu by murdering them for their spines."

Rune's deputy was clearly miserable, but she didn't
try to sugarcoat it.

"I don't think that this is moral, I know that it isn't
legal, and it feels like we are tearing down our own
civilization in order to find a quick solution," she went
on miserably. "There has got to be a different answer."

Rune let her have her personal space.

"I never took you as the conscientious objector type, Kendra," Paul said. "And understand that I mean that as a compliment. Unlike most of your cohort, or at least the ironic part, you have always had an edge... and you have busted your ass here. That's why you are my deputy as well as the handler for the scientist that is the best hope of saving our collective ass. What changed?"

"I, I knew what the bank and Dr. Curry were doing, even before the team meeting," Jones said, meeting his blue eyes without flinching, much. "Maybe it has to be done, maybe... But *I* can't do it. I know that the numbers are pretty bad for us—I can read a trend line like anyone else. Paul... We are probably going to *lose*. It's moderately bad already, and we haven't hit the take-off point on the curve. At this point there's no way to make enough vaccine to hold things together forever. I've seen the reports out of China. They're mass-producing like mad, ring-immunizing, everything, and they're still losing. If we're going to lose, anyway, why sacrifice our soul first?"

"And what do you plan to do?" Paul asked, trying to contain his impatience. "Walk away? Escape the city on your own while promising never to tell anyone what we did here? You think that CLD is all it'll cost you?"

Jones was pale, and held her hands together tightly. She nodded.

He shook his head and turned to stare at the dark wood paneling, visible between the regularly spaced blocks of anechoic foam that drank in their words, giving their conversation a flat quality.

"I like you, Jonesy," he said, shaking his head. "That's part of my problem. I don't just think that you a crackerjack deputy—I also think that you are a decent human being in a shitty industry in an even shittier spot. But no. You don't understand. Insiders that leave now know enough to put the plan at risk, to put everything at risk. You were in the meetings. You agreed to turn your hand and will to the bank's purpose. You took the money, the vaccine, the whole deal. No one gets to walk. Leaving, at this point, is not an option."

He turned back and looked directly into her eyes, focusing first on one and then the other. She hadn't moved from where she initially stood.

"The only way out is through. Nobody, and I mean nobody, wants to do what we're doing. Well, maybe the criminals, hell maybe even the NYPD, have found some psychos who like chopping people up. But I don't like it. Tom doesn't like it. Mr. Bateman, who knows damned well where the vaccine is coming from, doesn't like it. Nobody likes it. Everyone is horrified and disgusted. But. We're all in this together. Mutual assured destruction. You try to resign now and the best that you can hope for is a permanent inside job until the crisis is over, one way or the other. I don't think that I have to tell you what your other options are."

"What do you mean?" Kendra asked quietly.

"Recall what Smith's oldest niece is doing?" Rune asked with a humorless chuckle. "A fifteen-year-old Smith is taking human spinal cords and loading them in a fucking Cuisinart to make people paste. The thirteen-year-old? She beat a fucking zombie to death with a stick in our own basement. My boss—your boss—has sworn to uphold the security of this bank and the production plan above all other things, including the safety of his only family. His life, his fortune and his sacred honor. We're all putting that on the table so that, maybe, some of us survive. Maybe we can actually win, unlikely though it looks at present. So that maybe, even if we lose, we have a chance to rebuild and *not* go into a thousand-year night."

He reached out and clumsily if earnestly patted Jones on the shoulder. She barely avoided flinching again.

"So, knowing what the kids in the family are like, what do you think Thomas 'the fucking Train Engine' Smith will do to you if he thinks that his sacrifices, his honor, his family—hell, the entire plan—are about to be at risk as a result of your attempt to back out of this agreement?"

His deputy looked away and started to tremble.

Apart from the four principals eyeing each other across the gleaming table, only Curry remained in the conference room.

"You wanted the meeting private, Smith. Now it's private, including this ... person."

Dominguez wasn't happy about Matricardi remaining, but the cop's ire seemed to amuse the gangster.

"First some news," Smith said. "Dr. Curry turned up something interesting."

"'*Interesting*' interesting or 'bad' interesting?" interjected Matricardi. Clearly he wasn't prebriefed on whatever the development might be.

Curry stood at his place, but didn't approach the head of the table. Instead, he watched the outsiders like a cat aware that there were large dogs just outside his yard.

"Although the citywide attempts at ring vaccination have bought us more time than we had hoped, the rate of infection is up," the scientist said, referring to the strategy of firewalling outbreaks with circles of vaccinated persons. "That's the 'bad interesting' bit. The proportion of infections due to bites, or blood contamination of some sort is now greater than that of the airborne virus. That is the 'even worse' interesting bit, if you will."

Kohn looked at Curry for more amplification and then turned to Smith, who took up the narrative.

"I can see you thinking 'why does this matter?'" Tom said. "First, it means that the number of already infected people is sufficient to spread the disease by contact faster than even the initial airborne attack, which was already a high speed vector. Second, the propagation models we are using, from the CDC's to the ones we built in house, are all using the previously observed infection rate. Third, and this is the kicker, the change to the disease propagation rate blows our plan to use vaccination to contain the disease out of the water. This means that we'll *not* hold the entire city. The bite propagation rate has thrown that out as a possibility."

Dead silence persisted for several moments as everyone digested that happy news.

Matricardi wasn't shy.

"And?"

"The only way we'll gain enough time to inoculate the largest number of people and get them to safe areas is to work together, organize the city, coordinate the efforts of the various city actors and accelerate vaccine production." The banker slowed his rapid fire delivery.

"We hold the line for as long as we can. Maybe the CDC and the government will pull a miracle out of their hat. Maybe the Plague will burn itself out."

Curry snorted.

"Is there seriously a chance that could happen?" Kohn looked intrigued. "I have been told it may just go away, that the virus is breaking down."

Tom slurped some more coffee and waved at Curry, who stood back up.

"In genetic engineering terms, this virus is made of spit and bailing wire," Curry said. "The rate of transcription errors for the secondary expressor, which is the actual modified rabies virus, is creating some variants that are not viable in any host. However, others are, and those are enough to keep the transmission going long enough to infect the planet, unless the devolution of the dominant H7D3 strain accelerates unexpectedly."

"Thank you, Dr. Curry," Tom said, nodding at the scientist. "I think probably Sophia needs your guidance at this point."

"Out of the room for the rest of it?" Curry asked curiously.

"Out of the room for the rest of it," Tom said, nodding.

"So, the virus is dying, but probably not fast enough to save us," Kohn said, after the microbiologist had left the room. "Why would we cooperate to hold the line only in order to afford your bank enough time to escape? I find that unacceptable."

"Because the bank is constructing and outfitting long-term refuges for critical personnel." It was Tom's turn to play his final ace. "In exchange for working with me, I'm going to make room for all three of you."

"And our families?" Dominguez asked.

"And a select number of critical staff as well," Tom said with a nod. "I'm letting you buy into our plan. Break security? You get left behind. Fail to deliver on cooperation? Same thing."

"Where are these safe areas?" Kohn said thoughtfully. "How large are they?"

"Madame Director, that's 'need to know.'" Tom leaned back. "And you don't yet need to know. However, consider my actual job here at the Bank. It's to ensure that the Bank continues. Period. Dot. And I was given quite a nice budget to ensure just that prior to the Plague and more funding since. Before I read you in, and before you think about forcing the issue, allow me to share that the one *certain* way to cut yourselves off from this parachute is to try to strong arm us. The first question that matters is, 'what do we need from each other?'"

The three groups of security specialists were in the large foyer outside the bank's executive conference room. Groups of chairs, a light buffet and windows provided natural places for them to gather separately. Kaplan noticed that the Cosa Nova woman was by herself, looking out a window.

Her conservatively cut, dark business suit didn't hide her knockout figure. It was complemented by tall heels, whose soles flashed red when she walked back from the coffee urn to her window perch. They might as well have been a spinner lure in front of a lunging bass.

Roooowf.

Kaplan decided that as long as no one was making her acquaintance, there was no reason that he shouldn't be an attentive host. He stopped by the OEM staffers and cops first, inquiring if they needed anything. The Jersey boys were next, and despite some flexing, which might have been an involuntary reflex upon the approach of any other male, they too needed nothing.

As Kaplan strode confidently to the woman, he noted that her right hand never strayed more than a finger's width from her cream clutch, which seemed to have rich leather and deep, hand-sewn seams.

"Miss Khabayeva, my name is Jim Kaplan." Kap was all professionalism and charm. "I run security for the building. Is there anything that I can get you?"

She held out her hand.

"Oldryskya Khabayeva, 'Risky' to my friends."

Kaplan enjoyed the benefits of a great poker face, but this woman was giving nothing away. As he shook her hand, he noted the perfect manicure, a pleasant floral scent and startling violet eyes. Had to be contacts. He took her extended hand and enjoyed her firm hand shake. No limp-wristed, damp-palmed ingenue here.

"My friends call me Kapman. Nice to meet you."

She glanced at him, obviously considering something.

"Our security people told us that you were recently promoted. Congratulations."

Kaplan figured that they had information that was probably almost as good as what the bank had on them.

"It wasn't how I would have chosen to get ahead," Kaplan said. "But a zombie apocalypse is sort of like a war, am I right?"

"Dark humor, yes, I understand that quite well." She tilted her chin a bit. "I grew up in the wreckage of the former Soviet Union, so a touch of nihilism is quite familiar. Your Mr. Smith seemed to have the same sort of humor, when we last met. Have you worked with him long?"

"Tom?" This was not going the way Kaplan envisioned. "Yeah, we've known each other, off and on for a pretty long time. Only just started to work together again recently." He pointed towards the window and some of the smoke columns in view. "Pretty much since that started happening."

She followed the direction of his gesture.

"Yes, the burning is more now. In New Jersey too. One wonders if the fire can be put out."

She looked back to Kaplan. He thought that she might be studying his face before she turned to look out the window again.

"Do you think it can be put out? Do you believe in this plan of Mr. Smith's?"

She was definitely not into him, Kaplan decided. He could guess from her questions who had caught her fancy. Fucking SAS pretty boys.

"Probably," Kaplan said, shrugging. "Tom's a planner. Long-term plans, short-term plans, mid-term plans, contingency plans woven in and out of each of them. He wants to keep the bank going, somehow, because we are going to need some kind of economy in order to recover from all this. The banks have the money and the incentive to make that happen. Plus, he took their salt. You know the term?"

She glanced back sharply.

"Yes. Where I grew up isn't so far from...places where that matters still. Very much."

"So, what you want is for me to convince the chief of police and the mayor that we need to not only tolerate the gangs that are collecting infecteds and making vaccine, but actually cede effective police control of much of the City to them and endorse their activities?" Kohn's fingers tapped the polished wooden table. "What makes you think that I can do that, Mr. Smith, even if I wanted to?"

Kohn was conversational. Dominguez looked like he might do himself an injury throttling his barely controlled rage. Matricardi's earlier smirks hadn't helped.

Tom understood negotiations and appreciated where his opposite numbers were, emotionally. Frankly, the cool response from Kohn concerned him more than the twitching in Dominguez's right hand.

"Ms. Kohn, I want rather more than that. I need you to help me organize a citywide agreement. The City and the police"—Smith carefully didn't add "what remains of them," but gestured to the captain instead—"the banks which have resources sufficient to contribute," he tapped his own breast, "and the entrepreneurs who have already shown a degree of initiative," he inclined his head towards the chair where Matricardi slumped cheerfully, "must work together to reduce the wasted competitive and policing effort in order to eliminate more infecteds, faster, and accelerate vaccine production. Competition is normally a good thing. Unrestrained violent competition, war if you will, means everyone loses."

He pushed a carafe of sparkling water towards the cop. It slid easily in its puddle of condensation. Looking back to Kohn, he answered.

"At least when it's merely the four of us, can we use less formal address? Call me Tom. Why do I know that you can deliver? For a couple reasons. For example, I think that the mayor is out of the picture in his less than totally secret private estate on the east coast of Antigua, where he has been these last several weeks."

Both Kohn and Dominguez froze at that, but Dominguez flicked his eyes rapidly at both Smith and the gangster. His hand twitched a bit more.

"The deputy mayor is, pardon me, your bitch," Tom continued. "And I know that he has yielded operational control for the NYPD-led vaccine materials collection and infected control up to the OEM. I know that you and Rafe here go back a fair piece and I know that you are already closely coordinating with the police regardless of the mayor's intentions. I know that you are covering for the dozen or so people who really run the City and have promised them your protection in exchange for ongoing and future considerations. I also know that Matricardi's competition is already trying to cut a separate, if smaller deal, with some of Ding's colleagues, though without his knowledge."

This time Matricardi reacted, adjusting his posture so that he was sitting, if not straight, then at least more attentively. Dominguez hadn't yet unfrozen from the revelation that Smith knew about Antigua.

"Hey, we've gotta protect our interests," Matricardi said. "And it ain't like we're the only one. Seventeen is so far up Overture's ass the precinct chief's practically family. We've had people killed by cops working for them, direct. An' worse than killed!"

"Which is an example of the issues," Tom said. "We're trying to save our civilization, our respective organizations, our families and ourselves. We're not going to succeed if we simultaneously have to fight what amounts to a civil war.

"Mr. Matricardi's organization and the banks can

deal directly with the City through you and no one will itch, as long as the captain of the most prestigious precinct seems to be in agreement. You get to retain the trust of the power brokers who, incidentally, are all already largely absent—so I have to wonder... How will they compensate you, caught in a city overrun with infected?"

He sat back.

"Well, *Tom*, let us suppose that you are right?" she said, smiling thinly and effectively ceding the points that Smith had made. "How do we know that you can reciprocate?"

"I give you the location of one of our refuges as a gesture of good will," Tom said. "We exchange trusted subordinates to participate in our respective organizations. I guarantee your evacuation not later than the flight before my own extraction and that of my family. You keep the number of 'insider' personnel to our agreed-upon limit. You go over, it's on you."

He looked over at Matricardi, who still hadn't spoken.

"Cosa Nova gets the same payout," Tom said. "In addition, they gain the benefit of our summed intelligence and use it to serve as a counterweight to Overture and the remaining Triads in lower Manhattan. Cosa Nova acts in our combined best interest and they contribute to the vaccine stockpile while endorsing the integrated approach to sharing infected territory. They also agree to a price structure that permits the city and the banks to buy what they need. In exchange, you don't raid them. If you raid anyone, you raid those who are not party to the agreement."

Smith added one final point. The entire point.

"The purpose of this agreement is to build a citywide cartel and give the whole system the longest possible interval to turn the situation around. If that fails, our group of four will have something and somewhere from which we can rebuild. I like to think that despite our differences, we can all agree on that."

"I like it," Matricardi said. "Oh, there are details, but in general I like it." He looked to Dominguez, and laid a hand on his own lapel. The carnation caught the pale light from the window. "Captain, with the deepest respect, I pledge to cooperate with you and your colleagues."

Dominguez met Matricardi's look, his eyes narrowed.

"If we can actually stop the Plague, or worst case— survive this for real, and get the family out, then I'm in." Dominguez looked back over to Smith. "Secrecy is going to be hard though. How many people actually know about the whole plan?"

"This part of it?" Tom relaxed a fraction. "We four. The refuge locations, disease forecasts and the long-term chances? Maybe thirty in North America. As we get closer to pulling the handle, to actually evacuating, the number will go up."

"I'm in." Dominguez nodded. "Provisionally."

"I agree as well," Kohn said decisively. "The Devil will be in the details. We will have to discuss quid pro quos of course, and select the liaison personnel..."

At the head of the table Tom looked to the Cosa Nova chief.

"Will you make it unanimous?"

"I think we got a deal." Matricardi stood and stretched. "I know just who to lend out for the bank team. Say, anyone else hungry? I could murder a lasagna."

CHAPTER 9

"I'm like any other man. All I do is supply a demand."

—Al Capone, 1923

"No, Mr. Mayor," Joanna said, smiling calmly at the crystal clear image of her titular boss. "There is no danger that Bank of the Americas can conceal their preparations indefinitely. They have several long-term fallback points in development. The agreement requires them, in the event of catastrophic emergency, to share them with us."

She carefully omitted details on what, exactly, constituted "us."

"How the hell can you ensure that they don't betray the agreement that *you* agreed to without my permission, Kohn!" Hizzoner didn't quite snarl. "You said that you'd consult with me on anything that was serious, and this is damned well serious! You can't trust those fucking bastards—doing so is fucking stupid."

Joanna was affected by his famous temper just as much as she was by the sharp, persistent scent of chemical disinfectant, which was used daily to wipe down every surface in the OEM offices.

That is to say, not at all.

"Sir, conditions are increasingly perilous," she said.

"We are still losing ground to H7D3, despite all of our efforts." She gestured to Gauge, who spoke up.

"Mr. Mayor, on your orders we immediately instituted the vaccination program and it's ongoing. We continue to suppress the worst reporting about the disease, and the state legislature backed the suspension, sorry, the *realignment* of some civil rights. We're continuing the program of compartmentalizing blocks with severe rates of infection and lastly, we are getting more National Guard presence."

"None of that excuses your freelancing, Joanna!" the major retorted, ignoring her underling.

"Sir, I am supporting your agenda, as agreed, but there is not time any longer to run every late breaking decision through you, unless you can return to the City."

"Out of the question!" the mayor snapped, though more calmly this time. "My family's here, and we have on-island redundant communications links to every relevant capital and government department. I can run the City fine from here, and I can sure enough bury you if you disobey me again, Joanna, no matter where I am."

"Of course sir," she answered. "But Mr. Mayor, on a different topic, we sent the first course of human sourced attenuated vaccine via your courier team last week, as authorized per your signed finding. Did you complete the round of primer injections for all the adults? Precise timing is required for the application of the booster injections."

There was a brief pause as the mayor adjusted to her not so subtle reminder about the source of the vaccine. And who authorized it.

"Yes, yes, of course," he replied. "Look, I have to go. Keep me informed and don't sign anymore agreements with any fucking gangsters unless you consult with me, understood?"

"Yes, sir," Joanna replied, almost demurely.

The screen went dead in the secure OEM conference room and Schweizer moved to unplug the system, doubly ensuring that they had complete privacy.

"That could have gone better," offered Gauge, stacking the unneeded briefing folders on the table.

"'If the population knew with what idiocy they were ruled, they would revolt,'" stated Joanna.

"Ma'am?"

"Tell me again, what did you study for your master's degree, Sarissa?" the director of the OEM inquired. "Any history, or the classics?"

"No, Ms. Kohn," replied Gauge. "Women's Studies at Berkeley, and an MBA from Brown."

Joanna flicked her eyes over to her second associate.

"Poli-sci at George Washington," Schweizer said, correctly interpreting her glance as a question.

"Charlemagne, Sarissa," Joanna explained. "The quote is from Charlemagne, the first emperor in the west after the fall of the Romans. He owed his position to his father, Charles Martel, better known as Charles the Great."

"Battle of Tours," offered Schweizer, with a snide look at his competitor. "Charles the Hammer, first of the Frankish kings, filled the power vacuum during the Muslim invasion of Europe."

"Better, Ken, but not quite accurate," Joanna said reprovingly. She liked her people to practice their competitive skills on each other, but it wouldn't do to let one or the other too far ahead. "Charles Martel wasn't the king, his title was Mayor of the Palace for the last of the Merovingians, the line of kings that ruled a dwindling European kingdom. The mayor of the palace was the true power behind the throne of the Merovingians, and set policy and led the army, which Charles used to reclaim central Europe from the Turks. Then he consolidated the petty dukes, thereby reestablishing Francia and starting his own royal line."

"Um, yes ma'am?" Gauge wasn't certain where her boss was going with all this.

"My point, Sarissa," Joanna said patiently. "Is that Martel's grandson was Charlemagne—Charles the Great—and he climbed great heights, eventually rising to be the Holy Roman Emperor. He shaped the future of Western Civilization for ten generations. Like any competent ruler, he appreciated that bad rulers didn't last long, especially when those ruled became aware of their leaders' incompetence."

Joanna saw Schweizer's eyes glittering appreciatively. She went on.

"Crises come and go, and the City persists. Our mayor has chosen to absent himself during this crisis. A great crisis which we are managing, ably and quite visibly. When the dust clears, who will be leading the entire city? Who will be new king, Sarissa?"

Gauge and Schweizer shared a bright look, as each calculated their own trajectory, while Joanna continued.

"So, I would say that our meeting went quite well."

"Right, right." Tom was clearly impatient. "Yes, Brad. Got it. If you're confident that this is the guy, then you have the authority to make the deal."

Depine was getting twitchy as the meet with the independent vaccine manufacturers drew near. Rune could only hear Smith's side of the conversation, which continued.

"The amounts involved will be high, but not impossible." Tom went on with his half of the call. "You've got the testing kits to verify quality and you also have the liquid assets for the first shipment. Get. It. Done."

A pause.

"Right. Smith clear." The head for Security and Emergency Response snorted and didn't quite slam the receiver into the cradle.

"What an asshole," Tom said, sighing. "The thought of having to deal with him for possibly years in a fallback shelter just does not please."

He glanced up and frowned. "You look way too happy. Whatcha got?"

"Just some routine updates—so you first, Boss," Rune replied, trying manfully to erase his smile. "Do we need to backstop Depine and Durante? Judging from what I heard . . ."

"No, we're good, I think," Smith said. "Seems that this is Depine's version of the usual pre-mission jitters. Durante's last e-mail states that other than sweating through his suits faster than usual, Depine seems ready to go for the face-to-face with the vaccine outfit later today. The samples that they have tested all check out. Your turn."

"Cosa Nova's representative just got badged up and is heading to orientation," Rune said, willing his cheek muscles into immobility. "Since you made the deal with her boss, she'll be at the first team status meeting."

This was going to be good.

"Okay, fine, ho . . . wait," Tom said, squinting suspiciously. "She?"

"Oh, didn't I say?" Paul studiously looked at his Moleskine for the notes as though he hadn't already memorized the name. "Matricardi's liaison is that hot brunette from the restaurant. Same one as went to the last chat before you bosses kicked everyone out of the room. A Ms. Oldryskya Khabayeva."

"Of course." Smith sighed.

Matricardi didn't miss much.

"All right, as soon as we get the other two in today, set up a welcome aboard chit chat with the department heads and myself," the tall Aussie went on. "Oh, and if you haven't already . . ."

Rune finished for him, " . . . get a complete 'go-to' for each primary. Got them here, Boss."

He laid the relevant intelligence summaries for each liaison on the desk.

"I'm also doing a deeper dive on the principals," he added. "When I develop anything useful I'll let you know."

"Hey Tom," Kaplan whispered as the cargo van turned a corner. "I heard that Matricardi is lending you a real hottie for a liaison. That true?"

There were many vaccine producing entrepreneurs outside the sanctioned list of proposed members for the City-wide H7D3 cartel. This was the result, in part, of the easy availability of incomplete information: the basics of making an attenuated vaccine were but a few Internet clicks and a complete disregard for the law away. Most of the street-level operations were little more than a small crew running a single truck, processing in a cobbled together lab using an old X-ray machine and repurposed sweat shop labor for packaging and "enhancements." If the X-ray machine was on the blink—oh well. A little food dye and a few micrograms of methamphetamine provided enough authenticity to assure low information or desperate buyers that their "medicine" was genuine.

While a few of the most careful players also made or bought some higher quality vaccine for themselves, these teams were niche players without top cover. The larger criminal elements had no objection to clearing the playing field of riff raff, especially if there was some profit on the table for them.

The first tentative cartel operation between the City, organized crime, and what Matricardi liked to call "really organized crime"—the banks—was to destroy the independent chop shops in Manhattan.

The normal circadian rhythm of a healthy person reaches its ebb, measured in alertness and capacity for work, between two and three a.m. Since time immemorial, humans planning to wreak mayhem upon other humans have taken advantage of this rhythm to initiate hostilities at that time, striking while their targets were unfocused or asleep. Modern western militaries and nearly all special operations types had extensive experience in planning and executing success-ful surprise attacks in the wee hours of the morning. Conversely, they tended to buttress their own protection in the form of additional sentries and cameras during that time of day. You could say that these units had written the "book" on surprise attacks.

The franchise of Mara Salvatrucha 13 or MS13 as

it was popularly known, that was running zombie collection and vaccine production near Canal Street had
modern weaponry, surprisingly adequate lab facilities
and two collection vehicles.

Unfortunately for them, they didn't have the "book."
Or maybe they simply neglected to read it.

Smith was standing crouched in the darkened cargo
space of an ad hoc BERT truck. Adapted from a Hyun-
dai panel van and seized from its operators a short
time previously, the vehicle had clearly been used to
transport zombies for processing. The sweet and sour
smell from the rotting blood and accumulated filth
was enough to make his eyes water. Holding on to
the internal ribs of the shell, the rest of a combined
assault team composed of Cosa Nova shooters, Kaplan
and himself swayed with the motion of the truck as
it passed over a speed bump before turning into the
alley leading to the clandestine production facility.

Launching operations during the early morning
hours was a habit for the "spec-ops" crowd. Another
habit of operators was to take advantage of stressful
situations to have a little fun at their buddies' expense.

Parachute rigged just before the drop? Check.
"That rig looks a little screwy to me, wouldn't jump
it if I were you."

Four-hour pressure-chamber ride? Check. "Man,
have I *got* to take a dump. You mind? Pass the bucket."

Getting ready to spring an ambush? Check.

Kaplan had chosen a common wrinkle. Needle the
boss over his potential love life, or lack thereof.

"Loved those red-soled high heels at the meeting,"
he added to his first statement. "What's your play?"

"Meh," Smith replied, a little too tonelessly. "It's

all the same to me." Of course a real veteran knew that the closer to the mark that any joke might be, the more critical it was to give nothing up.

"Suuuuure. So, you're okay if I take a shot..."

Smith's eyes glinted dangerously.

"Shut it," Tradittore grated, his hand covering the side of his head with an earpiece as he tried to monitor the communications for the operations. Tom couldn't make out the popping of the enamel as Tradittore ground his molars, but he could imagine it just the same. Between the intel summary and Tradittore's clear interest in Matricardi's "assistant," it was likely that the Cosa Nova lieutenant's agitation was only partially from the stress of the op. Which was considerable.

The former government political analyst and fixer turned mob wise guy had grown in influence within the Cosa Nova since the crisis had progressed. It was his idea to try to close out the niche players. The smaller groups were very difficult to infiltrate, but the NYPD, Rune's team and Matricardi's group had independently corroborated information that they were feeding the black market for vaccine outside the City, benefiting from a considerable markup exceeding what the "Gang" had negotiated with each other. They'd also violated boundaries and aggressively operated in Matricardi's territory. Worse, the information from the consolidated police precincts was that they had swept up civilians who appeared to have stage one symptoms, and then skipped the confirmation blood tests before adding them to the pool of "raw materials."

A day ago Tradittore had proposed to his boss that they simply terminate all the noncartel operations inside the five boroughs. Once Matricardi had approved the notion, he briefed the smaller inner circle of BotA collaborators. From there, the results would be presented to the still dithering much larger cartel, and perhaps drive a decision that it was time to move. The first four players would present the end of the independents as a step towards enhancing safety and policing in the city.

The surprise twist was that Matricardi had directed his deputy to run the operation himself.

In person.

The mob winnowed its ranks of the less capable somewhat differently than a bank. The best sharks tended to rise to the top, regardless. Matricardi appreciated the metaphor.

In addition to the joint Jersey and BotA team assaulting the Canal Street site, there were two other operations starting simultaneously, mostly run from the Hercules and Ajax units fielded by the Emergency Services Unit of the NYPD, now openly controlled by OEM and led by Dominguez. Previously used to maintain a rapidly deployable and up-gunned presence near high-value targets in Manhattan, these armored trucks and more heavily armed officers had been used to collect the police department's share of zombies. They might also eventually enforce the terms of agreement between all players.

Tom had decided to tag along. He had a feeling that they might find a considerable stock of vaccine on site and he wanted to ensure that product of questionable quality was put to the torch. He didn't really expect that Matricardi would so obviously screw him by under reporting and reusing the material, but he did elect to help Matricardi by keeping "honest men honest."

For values of the word honest.

If it annoyed the Cosa Nova lieutenant, that was pure bonus.

Tradittore had been more than a little apprehensive—he was no operator—and timing was going to be tricky. Over the radio he heard the cops prepare to launch their assaults.

Outside, Spanish could be heard over the truck's diesel engine, which in turn was almost drowned out by the shriek of a rusty garage door being rolled up. The truck lurched forward.

Tradittore raised his hand as the truck began to brake to stop.

"Go!"

The modified roll up door on the truck fell away, revealing three surprised gang members standing in a courtyard lit by a fire in a fifty-five-gallon drum as well as the interior flood light that lit the open garage beyond. Despite being armed, they didn't get off a single shot as the first two Cosa Nova shooters serviced their targets with easy central nervous system hits.

Tom and Kaplan followed the Sicilians out of the truck, jumping down last. Their AR carbines were legally short-barreled rifles, or SBRs, courtesy of Rune's shopping trip earlier. The decreased overall length and pistol caliber weapons permitted the handier use of the suppressors, which kept the sounds of the first shots to a loud clapping sound, similar to a chair falling over on a hard surface.

The use of similar weapons by the first shooters out had kept the reports down, and no obvious response to their presence had started yet.

The Cosa Nova crew split into three teams as

Tradittore directed them toward the priority targets, including the suspected upstairs lab and the bunk area. As the Jersey shooters went upstairs, Tom and Kaplan soft footed up to an exterior door. Tom twisted the door handle and found it unlocked. The second man placed his right hand on Tom's shoulder and squeezed, indicating his readiness. Tom swiftly opened the door and followed it all the way around, ensuring that no one was standing behind it. As he cleared from the wall towards the center of the room, he saw a man in a loose business suit look up from his desk. Demonstrating excellent reflexes, the seated man darted a hand at a pistol on the desktop.

Kaplan had already entered behind him. His suppressed weapon coughed simultaneously with Tom's, their combined efforts dropping the suddenly limp body across the desk even as the dead man's hand covered the gun.

A fusillade of shots rang out upstairs, then tailed off. Tom cocked an ear for a moment, but there were no other sounds so he scanned the room more completely.

A large stainless-steel refrigerator was set into the next room. Opened, it revealed several Styrofoam racks of the now familiar vaccine ampoules. Manufacturing dates were scribbled on the stickers decorating each rack.

"How much is that worth?" Kaplan whispered.

"Don't matter," Tom replied. "We're gonna burn it. Hold open your ruck."

Kaplan knew that he was looking at hundreds of thousands of dollars but letting his carbine dangle from its friction strap he shrugged out of his pack and held it open as Smith dumped the vials in, two racks at a time. The chore was completed in less than a minute and they started up the stairs.

Behind a door, they could hear Tradittore's distinctive voice. Knocking on the door very loudly, Tom yelled: "It's Smith, I'm opening the door."

He waited a moment, and slowly opened the door, giving the Sicilians time to see him. All were aiming towards him, but dropped their muzzles as soon as they saw Smith. Tradittore lowered his last.

"Took your sweet time."

Tom glanced around the room. In the corner of the lab area, one of the Cosa Nova shooters had returned to bandaging a second. Two more Mara Salvatruchas lay on the floor, unmoving. The shorty version of a Kalashnikov protruded from under one body. Broken glassware and debris from medical devices crunched underfoot.

"What's the hold up?" Tom asked.

Tradittore gestured at a wide but shut door at the other end of the room. The surface was bullet scarred but intact.

"Third door." He smacked it with a palm. "The hinges are internal and there are least two more inside. I think it's a safe room. Our rounds bounced."

"What's your plan?" Tom asked.

"We blow it, then shoot what's left."

"Works for me," the banker replied. "We'll go back down."

Before he could step back, the locked door began to open, prompting the assaulting team to hastily raise their weapons.

The door finished swinging open. A pair of very

young women, clearly not yet eighteen, were revealed. Behind them was a sleeping area.

"*Manos arriba!*" Tradittore jerked his carbine up, and the clearly scared girls raised their hands up, revealing that their midriff-length shirts were not cut with modesty in mind.

One of the Jersey boys whistled.

Kaplan and Smith didn't react as Tradittore sent the two remaining shooters into the room to clear it. Finding nothing, their shouts of "Clear left, clear right" lowered some of the tension in the room.

One of the women stepped a little closer to Tradittore, sizing him up.

"You aren't going to hurt us, yes?" She had survived with one ruthless gang and seemed to understand which currency might buy her security for a time with a second. She lowered her hands, one resting on her hip and another tugging her shirt downwards, ostensibly for modesty's sake but serving to tighten the thin fabric across her chest. "We can be friends."

"Sure, we can be friends," Tradittore said with an easy smile. "You two just stand there for now."

He gestured the two teenagers towards the wall, where they obediently shuffled while carefully not looking at the two bodies leaking on the floor.

Letting his weapon aim back towards the floor, Tradittore turned to address his men and organize the withdrawal.

"Sacks, get Little Mike down the stairs if he can walk. Let the other two know that you are coming so you don't eat a bullet. Sammie, you and I'll search these two, then the lab. You banker boys can check the bunkroom. Priority to vaccine, documents, then cash."

Tradittore sounded confident. He clearly thought that the op was already over.

The Bank of the Americas pair looked at each other and watched as the injured man stumbled downstairs. Kapman's eyes scanned the pair of women who stood, mostly still, against the wall. The hips of one girl tilted from side to side as she shifted her weight from one foot to the other and back again. Tom frowned a bit as he noticed his partner's eyes lingering.

It was neither the time nor place for eyeball liberty.

They crossed towards the bunkroom as the Cosa Nova pair approached the women, grinning in anticipation of the "search." Tom entered and began to yank open drawers. Kapman paused just the other side of the door, keeping an angle on the activity in the lab.

The women smiled back at the Sicilians, sharing a knowing look between themselves. The one closer to Tradittore ran a hand up her leg, raising the hem provocatively.

Tradittore chuckled throatily as stepped closer, blocking most of the view from the bunkroom. He ran his hands around the woman's waist, and addressed his partner.

"Sammie, what do you think? Any contraband?"

Sammie had leaned in to sniff the hair of his "target" but his reply was interrupted by a needle-sharp ice-pick that the teen rammed into his right eye. He froze and made a *glurk* sound just as Tradittore's searchee produced a black compact pistol from under her skirt and pressed it into her target's side, pulling the trigger as fast as she could.

Kapman took a single sideways step back into the room and serviced both targets, dropping each woman with a pair of rapid shots. Tradittore stumbled back, cursing, and emptied his magazine into the corpse at his feet as Sammie finished falling to the floor. His fresh corpse drummed its heels against the industrial tile floor.

From start to finish the action had lasted under three seconds.

Kapman added one more headshot to each body as Tom exited the room and scanned the scene. He looked at Tradittore who was pressing his hand to his ribs, but was still on his feet.

"How bad?" he asked the Cosa Nova.

"I don't know," Joey wheezed. "Motherfucker hurts. That fucking bitch—"

"Shut it. Let me see."

Tom brushed the injured man's hands away and opened the velcro on the plate carrier as Tradittore kept up a steady torrent of profanity. The shirt under the armor was unpunctured and unbloodied. Tom looked under the cloth and observed a large bruise already blooming.

"You got lucky. The armor kept it out."

He looked down at the brass on the floor and picked up a case ejected from the dead teen's pistol.

"A twenty-five," Tom said. "That wouldn't even penetrate the soft-armor. Like I said, lucky."

"Lucky," wheezed the mobster, drawing the word out.

"How did you know?" Tom asked Kaplan.

"The girls weren't scared enough," Kapman said, his right hand still on his AR grip. "They had a plan. The one with the gun kept rubbing her thighs together, like she was horny. I don't care how seductive you are, you watch your man get shot, you don't feel sexy.

She was moving her legs together to check that the pistol she grabbed while she was behind the door wasn't about to fall out of her underwear."

"I thought for a second you were distracted by the jailbait," Tom said. "Shoulda known better, Kapman."

"It's all good, Boss." Kaplan turned to hold security, facing the two doors leading out of the room. "I like a piece as much as the next guy, but no matter how good they look, somewhere, some dude learned the hard way that she was too far to the right on the crazy-hot matrix. I just read the signs."

The security specialist jerked his head at the dead Cosa Nova shooter, whose face was still decorated with a knurled red ice-pick grip.

"We taking that with us?"

Tom looked over at Tradittore who had his kit back together and was fumbling with a cell phone.

"Not our problem," Tom said, jerking the stair door back open. "Let's go downstairs to take care of that job."

In the courtyard, Tom relieved his teammate of the pack full of vaccine and began shaking it into the burning trash barrel. The chore took a minute.

"What the fuck are you doing!"

Looking up he saw Tradittore exit the door and start to raise his weapon.

"Little late for that, Tradittore." Tom tilted his head sideways even as he continued to dump the last ampoules into the barrel, the merry tinkle of glass a counterpoint to the grimness of the scene. To one side Kapman had a perfect sight picture centered on the Sicilian's face. "He saved your ass back there," Tom added lightly. "Be a real shame if he had to ruin his hard work, don't you think?"

Tradittore's man returned and immediately shouldered his weapon, training it first on Kapman, then Tom.

"Fuck it and fuck you, pretty boy," Tradittore said, disgusted. He let his rifle hang once more. "Do you know how much money you're burning?"

Tom looked back after the last good shake consigned a final ampoule to the flames.

"You can't spend it if you're dead," Tom said, meeting Tradittore's eyes. "This is dirty vaccine of shit quality. All it's good for is taking money from desperate people in exchange for making a considerable number of them into zombies. It burns."

The red flames continued to reflect in Tradittore's eyes after Tom turned away.

"Ken Schweizer, OEM." Schweizer introduced himself to the neatly dressed black-haired man across the table.

"Ramon Gutierrez," came the answer from behind a pair of five-hundred-dollar sunglasses. "I represent the business interests of Mr. Overture."

Gutierrez's suit looked loose and comfortable. He had eschewed a traditional suit and tie in favor of a open-necked guayabera, the traditional lightweight linen shirt of Central America and the Carib. It was as much a symbol of his role as the subdued NYC OEM logo on Schweizer's binder.

"Thank you for making time for me despite your busy schedule," Schweizer said, glancing around. Although Schweizer was alone, his counterpart had brought along additional trappings to highlight his place in Big Mac Overture's enterprise in the form of two looming, dreadlocked bodyguards.

Gutierrez tipped the neck of his beer towards Schweizer, acknowledging his statement, before taking a healthy pull.

The hustle and bustle of the Crown Heights bodega provided enough background noise to afford them some privacy, so Schweizer proceeded.

"We have an interest in maintaining a good relationship with all of the important city departments, Ken," he said. "NYPD, FDNY, sanitation—so I'm glad to hear that you want to talk. OEM has an important job, but it usually takes a while for you to get around to the little people in Queens, man."

Queens, and to some extent Brooklyn, had become a home to successive waves of immigration from the Gulf of Mexico and places south. Trinidad, Cuba, Haiti, Jamaica, Barbados, Puerto Rico—all had contributed to the melting pot in New York City. The intelligence that OEM had from the police and the FBI revealed that Overture had made his bones by consolidating power in his borough, much as Matricardi had done in Jersey.

Like Matricardi, he also appeared to have leaned into the H7D3 crisis instead of running away from it.

"I assume that you are aware that the City is contemplating a partnership with certain business elements to regularize the production of vaccine," Schweizer said. "An important component of that is cooperation."

"Well, the term 'City' is a pretty big stretch, wouldn't you say, Ken?" Gutierrez said, smiling. "I mean, if you'd said you were working within Manhattan, or North Jersey, or even Staten Island, I'd probably agree. But Brooklyn and Queens already belong to my boss. And he's moving in the other boroughs too. We know that you are rolling up MS13 and the Triads. Like my boss always says, gives us something in common."

Schweizer sipped his water before replying.

"We have a working relationship with banks and other . . . irregular business interests. As well as the NYPD," he said. "I see some value in maintaining a channel between us, to avoid potential conflicts of interest and to share breaking information."

"Everything is negotiable," Overture's man said, drinking more beer. "So let me show you 'round. Give you a sense of what we have to offer." He stood up.

"C'mon, it's just around the corner."

Schweizer paid attention to the way that Gutier-rez's eyes glinted.

That couldn't be good.

"You take the good with the bad," Tom Smith thought aloud, feet propped up on his desk during a rare moment of reflection. Summer had nearly gone. The fireworks, the parties and the drunks all proceeded as normal, or near enough.

How New Yorkers managed to just . . . keep going was a matter of wonder for the tall Australian import.

The previously concluded city wide meeting had taken most of two days to negotiate, but finally the City, the police, OEM, many of the banks and insurance firms and most critically, the . . . entrepreneurial groups had finally met. Encouraged by the success of the first efforts to consolidate the market, some actual progress had been made towards establishing the rules of the road for how the various groups would cooperate, or more properly, compete civilly.

The cartel was in business.

It appeared to Smith that the salubrious effect upon the leadership of the "Gangs of New York" of watching a zombie turn from inside a sealed room while most of their security was disarmed was a dramatic acceleration of their decision-making. The agitation of watching security literally bludgeon to death what had only moments previously been an attractive secretary probably added to their sense of urgency.

Hey, whatever it took.

Not only the bank but the entire cartel was slowly gaining on the critical vaccination curve, although BotA was still under-producing if they wanted to meet the magic thirty thousand courses of vaccine mark, covering the currently projected number of staff and dependents.

But they were gaining. The new equipment, the shared intelligence, the updated firearms, it was all working. The city truce was holding. The rate of infection had stabilized even.

Rune walked in and did a double take. His boss, who had been brooding for weeks, was actually smiling. Paul thought that Smith looked happier than Dita von Teese's pasties.

"How are you doing this fine morning, Paul?" Tom called out.

"Um, decent?" Rune tried to echo his boss's apparent upbeat mood. "I did some digging on our cartel partners. I have a hit on OEM that you should see. Summary on page one."

He slid a red folder across Tom's desk, retaining a copy.

"I did a routine credential check on everyone," Paul said. "Kohn's had an odd break in transcripts. I went a little further and from middle school through high school, she was in what amounted to a low- to medium-security residential program for juveniles."

"What fo—" Tom's eyebrows crawled up his forehead as he flipped ahead. "Well, *that* would do it."

"She was tried as a juvenile," Rune said. "Paragraph three. But, between the murder method and her counselor's reports, she's not what you call fully wrapped. You don't just spring back from 'extreme homicidal psychosis.'"

"Hmm . . . okay," Tom said, leafing through the report. "I'll have to parse the psychiatric diagnosis for longer than I have now. How did you get this? These records are supposed to be sealed."

"Head of Global Intelligence for a top five investment bank versus podunk flyover state secure digital records system," Paul said, miming typing on a computer. "Hardly fair. But the point is, what do we do now?"

"Do?" Smith asked, puzzled. "Why would we *do* anything? She's clinically psychotic and appears to have limits different than the average civilian. In our current situation, that's a *feature*, not a bug. She is entirely efficient in her job and we need her in that role."

"But she used a c—" Paul said.

"Stop," Tom said, closing the folder. "This world's falling apart faster than *any* government can get ahead of the virus. The only way for *any* functional core of civilization to survive is to create vaccine from, I hate repeating this, *human spinal cords*. To do that, we need a city official who is willing to countenance and abet the murder of thousands of infected. Kohn is that person. Now we know why. Good job. That she wasn't entirely wrapped was sort of obvious but with this we can plan more specifically. For now, tell me about the four main sites we got for Zeus."

Rune had to recalibrate his headspace for a moment, then proceeded.

"It wasn't cheap," Rune said. "But Site Maple in Maine is nearly fully provisioned and we have a complete skeleton staff in place. Site Grape near Champlain is at sixty percent, more or less. Site Bugle is forty-plus. The bad news is that the Blue Ridge site is a problem. We have the title, a cover story and some contractors lined up but we're way behind on most everything else."

Smith declined to let a spot of bad news derail his outlook.

"That's better than I hoped," he answered, his tone reasonable. "We got a late start so we're behind the ball. Okay, give me options, Paul."

Rune was ahead of this question. Smith never accepted a situation report but that he asked for candidate options.

"The easiest thing to do is to pour everything into the first two and walk from the others. But at a guess, Bateman won't go for that."

"Got it in one," Tom said. "You know the argument. What about . . ."

As Smith's desk-phone rang he glanced at the number, then held up one finger towards Rune and punched a button on his handset.

"Durante's satphone," he said, putting it on speakerphone. "This is Smith and Rune, you're on speaker, Gravy."

"Hey Tom, hey Paul." The connection was pretty

clear. "The good news is that the vaccine checks out and we can buy some, maybe a lot. The bad news— okay, the not so bad...okay, the 'would be hilarious under other circumstances' news—is that Depine is dead. Apparent massive heart attack."

"No shit?" Smith was surprised. "When?"

"Like half an hour ago," Durante said, his voice artificially light. "He didn't make it through the introductions. Grabbed his chest and went into Cheyne-Stokes right in front of God and everybody. Two minutes later, doornail. These guys have a doctor and he's already been pronounced. I'm negotiating for us now, right?"

"Got it, you're not alone," Smith replied. "Yeah, you're empowered to act for the bank. Get the authorization letter out of Depine's brief case, get familiar with the top line numbers. We need a minimum of another two thousand complete courses to make the trip worthwhile. Get more if they can spare it, especially the booster. Twice the base figure wouldn't be too much. Three times might solve most of our problems."

"Okay, I'm on it," Durante said, his tone becoming cagey. "By the way, this guy seems to be from one of the outfits we used to run with. Remember Mr. Invisible who craves fish?"

There was a pause, then Smith's eyes widened.

"Damnit," Tom muttered, rolling his shoulder to relieve some stress. "If that's who I think you mean, do not, repeat do *not* negotiate with the brew-mistress if you can help it. She'll look like a creaky old lady that's got the face of an angel. Do *not* trust that face. But we need that vaccine, copy?"

"Um, okay?" Durante said, puzzled. "Whatever it takes, roger."

"Make the deal and get back, we need you, yesterday. Smith clear."

"What was that about a mistress, Tom?" Rune asked when the connection was closed.

"*Brew*-mistress." Smith leaned back in his chair and looked at the ceiling. "If Durante meant who I think he was referring to, well, remember your guesses on the rumor about a nuke in the Bahamas, or that nuke bluff that the tangos used in Paris maybe seven or so years back?"

The intel analyst nodded.

"Natch."

"There's a decent chance that they're more than just rumors," Tom said with a frown. "But...suffice to say that his outfit has some very experienced older ladies who run the brewing business, and they are purely hell on wheels when it comes to bargaining. Durante is gonna get his clock cleaned."

"Ask Bateman which he would rather have: another thousand kilograms of gold or another couple thousand courses of vaccine, right?"

"Rune, Rune, Rune," Tom said, shaking his head. "Rich Bateman is first and foremost a banker. I don't want to have to bring a comfortable chair and a packed lunch while I wait for that answer."

Dominguez found his wife's body before the kids saw her.

Small mercies.

He had rushed to her body, but the veteran cop had seen overdose deaths before. He didn't need the empty bottles of Tramadol and oxy to diagram the story. Any cop will tell you that a body smells a certain way, even before decomposition is obvious. The careless arrangement of her limbs, the cyan tint to the skin around her lips and on her hands all screamed OD.

He still checked her pulse and breathing because that's what you do, and because he loved her. But his heart broke the moment he saw her from the bedroom door.

He'd promised her that there was a way out, that he was working on a way to save their family.

She had wanted to flee the city and go somewhere else, anywhere else, really. The problem was that there wasn't anywhere much safer than the guarded neighborhoods where many senior city officials and cops were sheltering. He couldn't tell her the details of the plan, not yet. One thing that his wife wasn't was secretive. She would've wanted to find a place for her parents, the cousins, los abuelos . . . everyone.

Impossible.

The rhythm of her life had changed. No more shopping—it wasn't safe. No more shows—too many people. Fire the maid—she visited too many houses. And yet, life went on with a disturbing degree of normalcy. Ding went to work, the bills came in, the TV shows ran, though perhaps with a touch more reruns.

And yet, behind every decision outside the house, death lay waiting. Perhaps she elected to find death on her own terms. Maybe she couldn't bear the thought of watching her children turn. Ding would never know.

For a short while he sat on the edge of the bed, not so close as to get the pooled vomit on his uniform, but close enough to touch her hair one more time. Spread in a semi circle, and somehow free of the ejecta, a partial lay of the tarot deck that she'd been using for weeks was arranged beyond arm's reach of her body.

She had tried to teach him the suits and the Arcana, but mostly he listened because it seemed to ease her mind for a time. She read a message in the cards, and had something tangible to explain the craziness and ever-present dissonance of life during a lethal but slow moving and inescapable pandemic.

Dominguez looked at the cards.

Ten of Cups. The cycle completed.

The Lovers. Through love we see heaven.

The Judgement.

Dominguez swept the deck away and stood. He didn't need the cards to tell him who was responsible. Swaying a little, he covered her with a bath sheet and carefully avoided looking at the tall dressing room mirror that he had to pass before he could exit and close the bedroom door.

There were basic arrangements to make and he had to get the kids out of the house before he could tell them.

The secure conference room was once again in use. Smith looked at his three new liaison officers. The cop, Detective "Call me Tango" Tangarelli, was in full LEO banking mufti, complete to the nineties-era Brooks Brothers' suit and Bates all-leather "tactical" dress shoes. The city council liaison was Kohn's man, an OEM analyst named Ken Schweizer. In a room noteworthy for its blend of opulence and functionality, his classically severe, dark gray two button suit and muted tie were distinctive by their very understatement, reflecting the nature of his true boss.

The third liaison was Oldryskya. She at least looked as though she was ready to work. Her men's cut business suit jacket was open enough to show an empty shoulder rig underneath. Her boots were the same brand that Smith had been purchasing for his team: Striker low rise. She noted his scan of her appearance and calmly returned his gaze.

"My name is Tom Smith," Tom said, all business. "I'm running the business continuity, disaster readiness and security team for Bank of the Americas. Your primary purpose, beside liaison, is to ensure that my pledges to your bosses are redeemed.

"You'll have complete access to critical parts of the plan, more than nearly anyone else in the bank. Only the people in this room right now have the same level of understanding. Each person is a trusted part of my inner team within the Security and Emergency Response department. If you discuss what we share inside this room with anyone not inside this room right now, you violate the agreement that your parent organization has signed with us. The only person that you may tell is your direct boss. If they leak the information that you learn, it's on them, and the deal is off.

"However, we maximize the tooth to tail ratio around here," Tom continued, tapping his own security badge, which hung on a bright blue lanyard from his neck. "We're in the middle of a crisis that has required tightening personnel access. As shorthanded as we are, I can't afford any unproductive staff. So, you're going to be directly supporting my team.

"Step one, if you intend to carry a firearm or other weapon during your tenure here, you have to be cleared by our building protection team lead." He looked down the table to Kaplan. "Kap, raise your hand. That is the person to talk to after the meeting. Once he clears you we'll add another credential to your badge so you can carry concealed in any BotA controlled building."

Tangarelli started to raise his hand and Smith noticed.

"*Everyone*, including me, has passed that training screen," Tom said definitely. "No exceptions for anyone, not even law enforcement."

Kaplan had lowered his hand earlier, and now he displayed a toothy grin. Twitting cops was a hobby.

"Step two will be to get you sorted onto teams that can use your skills. Department heads, make it your business to talk to all three and figure out where they can best assist."

"Any questions on one and two?"

Schweizer put his hand up.

Smith looked at him and continued.

"There being no questions for now, we'll proceed to the regular agenda."

Oldryskya smiled.

The trading recovery site dated back to the weeks after 9/11. When the towers were brought down, many other buildings were destroyed or damaged beyond immediate use, affecting not just Morgan Stanley and Deutsche Bank, but several other banks. BotA had previously optioned space across the river in Jersey City and had since developed it.

Traders dislocated by any future disruptions to Manhattan proper were only a short ferry ride away from a second, complete office where they could keep their bank "in" the market. There were additional facilities farther away, both in northern New Jersey as well as in the other direction, in upstate New York.

The days of paper slips recording transactions in the bidding pits of commodity floors and trading houses were long gone. Everything was electronic now, and all trades were transmitted between several points before they were sent to reconciliation houses for the end of the trading day. There were several little details, not well understood outside the financial services community, that profoundly affected world markets.

First, banks had begun offshoring their data and reconciliation operations a decade earlier. A volume in the millions of trades per day meant that modest savings in transaction cost per trade added up in a hurry. There was a relatively bountiful supply of technically savvy, college educated hires in cities such as Mumbai, Delhi and Chennai. What's more, they could be had for far lower salaries than the analysts and accountants in New York, London and Paris. Banking executives were happy to gobble up profit margin. The discarded staff? Pity, that.

Second, and perhaps as important, was that although the Internet passed signals over fiber effectively at the speed of light, the physical distance that a server lay from a primary Internet trunk line created tiny delays, measured in milliseconds. However, this small drop in efficiency had become relevant in the world of high speed trading where tens of thousands of transactions might be executed every minute. Reducing even infinitesimal amounts of latency yielded significant advantages, so physical proximity to a primary Internet trunk line became very important in trading, especially in currency markets.

As a result of these structural changes to bank operations, any changes to working schedules in Asia or even small changes in the speed of high-bandwidth Internet trunk lines used by banks meant big impacts for the sector as a whole.

Virus ravaging Asia and driving people out of work, or into the morgue? Not good.

Reduced high-tech workforce maintaining critical telecoms infrastructure? Even worse.

Bateman and Smith stood side by side at a super trader position at the bank's Jersey City recovery site. The specially telemetered work station showed the fluctuating amount of bandwidth and associated delay that affected this particular desk. A twin display showed the same values being recorded in an identical workstation in the home office across the river.

"You can see that the delay between our buy order and the execution from this location is about eighty milliseconds slower than the same trade from our main floor back on the island." Smith didn't have to connect the lines for Bateman.

"Well, shit," the CEO said, running the numbers in his head. "What percentage of the main floor with the cleaner connection is manned? And what if we move folks back in?"

"Twenty-five percent at each of our four locations, including Manhattan." Smith's tone wasn't encouraging. "Piscataway's latency is another ten percent worse than this, and Westchester is double that. If we bring people back to the main floor, we risk transmitting the virus. We have had only one employee turn since Skorpio, but still . . ."

Smith was not anxious to increase employee density.

The CEO stared hard at the monitor as the needles on the virtual dashboard wavered slightly to the right, and then returned to their original position.

"How is this hitting Goldbloom, MetBank and Cities?" Bateman asked. "If we're all affected equally then maybe it doesn't matter."

"The bottleneck is actually reconciliation," Tom said. Then the security executive dropped the other shoe, switching to a view of the latency issues across the world. "I'm putting boot to arse and we're re-onshoring about eight percent of the book every night, and that proportion is rising. Staff are working much longer hours—pretty soon we won't have time to finish the previous day's trades before the market opens the next day. Asia is taking a hammering—the cities there are in turmoil, much worse than we have here. The entire forecast curve failed to allow for the faster spread of the disease in Asia. So, yeah, everyone is affected more or less equally. That isn't the problem."

"You made me a believer, Tom," Bateman said angrily. "We need to press as long as we can to save as much as we can. So, what *is* the problem?"

Bateman squinted at the wide, tiered flatscreens dominating the trader's desk, as though there was an answer to be found in the multicolored text that scrolled from top to bottom, like it could never end.

"This is the critical employee graph for outside the main bank," Tom said, bringing up a series of line graphs marked in red and blue. "The blue is no-shows. The red is turns. Both are increasing exponentially. New Jersey has had thirty-seven turns compared to our one. No-shows may be turns or may be...just gone off to wherever they think is safe. We don't even have the people to try to find out what happened to our people. Chennai is shut down. Mumbai is at fifteen percent staffing and missing enough critical staff it may have to be shut down. Delhi's much the same and as you already know Hong Kong is suspended. Internet bypass activity is also increasing at unsustainable rates. Major rings are out of contact already and are having to be bypassed. Singapore had nine rings and it's dropped to four. Shanghai just had a power outage that hasn't been rectified. Its ring is running on back-up generators and they'll only last a few more days."

"We're doing okay here in New York, for values of the word okay. It's everywhere else that doesn't have our resources that's going. If the world can't complete vaccine firebreaks around critical worker population, it's over, Boss."

Bateman slowly turned to look him in the face. He didn't have to ask.

Smith answered anyway.

"We are down to weeks."

CHAPTER 10

"PRIORITY MESSAGE. At the direction of the Secretary of Energy and with the agreement of the Nuclear Regulatory Commission, all generating units in Region Two will implement Condition Charlie Modification Three. Site operators are required to make final preparations to implement indefinite site isolation. All operators will reply by endorsement with confirmation of current inventories of critical spares, backup generating capacity and security equipment (see app. A). Report compliance not later than 9 AM, 20 July, Eastern Standard time."

—Excerpt, NRC broadcast to operators, July 20, 2012

From: *Collected Radio Transmissions of the Fall*
University of the South Press 2053

The macadam assembly area was teeming, but the activity couldn't even be charitably characterized as controlled chaos. Chaos would have been an improvement. A neat row of six towed 105mm howitzers lined one side of the fenced compound, each sheltering from the early morning dew under taut olive drab covers. In ones and twos, the Army National Guard reservists of Battery A were slowly accreting into sections, building piles of rucksacks and personal equipment, while others were pulling last second maintenance on the unit's prime movers.

An angry sergeant in dirty advanced combat uniform, or ACUs, was bent over the power pack of an LMTV. The light tactical truck had replaced many of their ubiquitous HMMWVs or Hummers only a year previously, and was strong enough to both tow the battery's cannons and carry a load of soldiers and their personal equipment. The cab was tilted forward to allow access to the engine compartment. Neon green antifreeze stained the frustrated NCO's uniform, and he vented his frustration at the maintenance sergeant replacing the cracked coolant hose.

"If you Nasty Guard no load nondeploying assholes actually did the routine maintenance," the sergeant said, berating the mechanic, "We, and by we, I mean ME, could be prepping our gear and making sense of this cluster instead of babysi—"

"Sergeant Copley!" yelled a figure, jogging towards the deadlined truck. "First sergeant wants to know how long?"

"Have this truck up by the time I get back, hear?" Copley bit off, looking at the sweating motor pool noncom. They might be peers in rank, but Copley's multiple tours to Iraq made him a respected figure. No one was anxious to cross the section chief. It didn't hurt that he was both large and known for being regulation, earning him the sobriquet "Worf." Despite the August humidity, the wrench turner redoubled his efforts.

"It's okay, Randall, I'll come back with you and tell him myself," Copley said as he hopped off the LMTV's running board and started trotting towards the one story brick building that served as the armory for Battery A, 1st Battalion, 258th Field Artillery (Towed). "Any new word?"

"Just that we're activating in order to augment JTF Empire Shield," answered Specialist Cameron "I'm the Gunner" Randall. He was another veteran of Operation Iraqi Freedom who was supposed to leaven the National Guard arty unit after leaving the RA, or regular army two years earlier. The call up that had brought them to assemble had been rumored for weeks, but in typical Army fashion, they were notified at the last minute. Copley had received a text from 1LT Pozzo, the battery executive officer, after dinner the night before. Then he had spent two hours digging through his boxes of kit in order to make up for the known deficiencies in the TOE for his section.

"Hey, Sergeant." Randall leaned in close to avoid being overheard. "What are you doing with your family?"

"Reenie is taking the kids west to her folks' place in Pennsylvania," replied Copley. "You?"

"Hell, I'm divorced," the specialist said. "My ex lives in Minnesota and I visit my kid in the summer."

They reached the door and quickly stepped into the National Guard battery commander's office, where the CO, XO and first sergeant were consulting a notebook PC, a sheaf of paper and a steaming mug of coffee, respectively.

"Sergeant Copley, good to see you," Captain McCabe said, as Copley exchanged nods with Misiewicz, the battery's senior noncom. "How many no-shows you got in your section?"

Battery A only had six howitzers, often called "tubes," organized in three sections of two weapons each. Each section was notionally led by a staff sergeant, though in Copley's case, his combat experience substituted for the extra rocker. Each section should have mustered fourteen soldiers. Copley was assigned twelve.

"Eight on hand, sir," he replied, answering the CO's question. "One more said that he's still en route."

"That's more than the other sections," stated the captain. "Take your section, one LMTV, one unit of fire, complete personal equipment including small arms and proceed to Fort Hamilton with the XO and the Fire Direction team. We've got orders to reinforce Joint Task Force Empire Shield."

JTF Empire Shield had been running constantly since 9/11. It had since evolved into a standing force composed of rotating units of the National Guard, drawn primarily from state units. The deterrence and defense mission had traditionally been focused on logistics hubs such as Penn Station and La Guardia airport. It seemed that the mission was expanding, extending coverage to more locations in metro New York.

"We'll send the other two sections and stragglers," the captain continued. "But they want bodies ASAP."

"Do you have any more information on the callup, sir?" asked Copley, with a glance at the first sergeant, who was still absorbed with his coffee. In a strack regular army unit, like the one Copley had served in during his last deployment, the First was the enlisted font of all knowledge and had his finger on the pulse of not just the command, but was tied into the senior noncom network all the way to division. The First for Battery A was . . . not cut from that cloth. "I mean, this zombie thing has been going on for weeks, and it seemed to be leveling off—what changed?"

McCabe ran his hand through his salt and pepper hair. The Guard promoted much more slowly than the regular army and at forty-eight he was both older than some regular army full colonels and younger than other captains in the 258th.

"Hell, I don't know what has regiment in a twist, Copley," the captain answered. His eyes were red and his ACUs rumpled. "They've been steadily calling up the infantry guys these last two weeks. The last of the Sixty-Ninth just deployed into Staten Island last week. I don't know what they expect a few more thousand Guard to accomplish in a city of twenty-five million, either. Just take the truck, follow the XO here, and report to the JTF."

"Sir, are we dragging the tubes with us?" interjected Randall.

"Negative, this is going to be an INCONUS presence mission," the captain said, using the abbreviation for being INside the CONtinental U.S. "I don't think that the brigadier is going to call for indirect fires into Manhattan just to knock over the occasional zombie."

Oldryskya Khabayeva had adopted the same business dress as the rest of Smith's team. Three-piece suits and six-inch heels were both out. Sports jackets, and low-profile tactical trousers with comfortable, lightweight all-leather boots were in. Following the welcome aboard meeting, Khabayeva, Schweizer and Tangarelli briefly grouped together, as any three strangers dropped into a new and stressful environment might. The OEM rep quickly oriented on the refuge design and preparation team while the cop supported the executive and building protection forces. Risky offered to assist in the laboratory with the older Smith girl, but was rebuffed by the doctor there.

Curry didn't want anything to do with her and politely but firmly declined her assistance. His flat appraisal of her telegraphed his answer before he said a word: *thanks, but no thanks, miss. I already have enough hands.*

However, the BERTs needed help. She learned Durante had relieved Kaplan on that detail as soon as he had returned from Europe after some vague mission for Smith. She hadn't exactly flirted with him, but she wasn't above taking advantage of the subtle striking power of her perfume when she approached him in the bank's underground garage. Durante saw her coming. Even the unflattering overhead florescent lighting couldn't dampen her looks.

"Do you shoot?" he bluntly asked her in reply to her offer of assistance.

"Since I was little," she answered. "My stepfather taught all of his daughters. Light arms, mostly Kalashnikov, but also other marques. Now I have access to American guns."

"Nice accent," Durante said. The taller man gave her a second glance and returned to checking and racking reloaded Tasers in a large, open topped equipment case. Each unit was shoved into a foam slot and retained with an elastic band. "Where you from?"

"I was adopted, I think somewhere in the Ukraine, but I grew up in Tashkent, and yes, the one in what you Americans call the 'Stans."

She had answered the question several times now. Her nearly impeccable English retained the faintest whisper of a Eurasian accent.

"Nice country in spots but that's a tough place to be from, squeezed by the Kazhaks to the north, and surrounded by a tangle of borders shaped like a dog's hind leg." He finished and stood facing her, giving her a harder look. She was in fact pretty damn gorgeous, but she had some muscle mass and it looked toned, so that she wasn't merely supermodel skinny. "What do you do to stay fit—CrossFit?"

"Have I tried to tell you all about it yet?" the dark-haired woman said with a slight smile. "I don't think so. It is simple, I run and swim and do a little climbing. Off season I use gym to keep my upper body stronger than average, though I'm discouraged from getting too hard. Mr. Matricardi does not consider muscular to be . . . pretty."

"All right." She could see Durante thinking about it. When he frowned slightly, the scar on his forehead turned white, disappearing into his hairline. "We got a short safety brief in a few minutes and then we roll later this morning. Why don't you sit in, and then plan on being an observer only on the next run?"

With loud snaps he seated the catches around the edges of the case.

"Only an observer?" Oldryskya eyed the vests that held armor and pouches. "Mr. Smith said 'no tourists,' no?"

"Look," Durante replied, looking up at Risky intently. "Even when everything is perfectly arranged, things can go wrong. Zombies or thinking people, the enemy always gets a vote. So if you want to get stuck in, first you watch. And I'll watch you."

He relented.

"Afterward, if you still want, we can get permission

to make this a little more routine and you can help with the actual op," Durante said, before adding firmly, "This time, you stay in the truck cab, see?"

"The cab I can handle," Oldryskya said. "It's the trunks that I don't like. Can I borrow a plate carrier? I have pistol."

"We got some gear that should fit," Durante replied, slightly puzzled at her last comment. He shook it off. "One thing, though. What we do with trucks isn't pretty and the teams have to work together closely. There is, to be clear, actual, no-shit, danger in this task."

Oldryskya let her eyes grow a little wider and replied.

"Danger," she said, her eyes wide and smiling slightly. "Oh, my. Not that."

"I need them gone, right now!" Dominguez was in uniform, the two silver bars of his captaincy gleaming again the dark blue uniform. He gestured sharply at Joanna's staff, some of whom shrank back from his sudden, visible anger.

"Good afternoon, Captain," she answered, remaining comfortably seated behind her desk. "Ken, please take the team to Conference Room Two and continue. I will join as soon as is practical."

Dominguez stood to one side of the door through which he had just stormed, disregarding the administrative assistant who remained outside, white faced. The group, including Gauge and Schweizer, filed out, the latter flicking his eyes back and forth between his boss and the policeman.

As the door clicked shut, Dominguez met Joanna's eyes.

"Enough," he said, making a visible effort to master his temper. "There's been enough and I want to take Matricardi in. His arrogance and his blatant commercialization of a huge part of our vaccine supply is encouraging all the other gangs, and the banks. It's fucking with my officers, it's illegal as hell and it's slowing the vaccination of our core service team."

"The agreement is clear," Joanna replied. "Not just the cartel agreement, but our agreement, yours and mine. That agreement explicitly covers strategy, *my* strategy—and my strategy includes Cosa Nova."

"I don't care!" Dominguez retorted, his voice rising again. "He's dirty. My guys are tired of associating with criminals! We don't need them and even if we did, what price do we pay if we ally with scum like Matricardi, who are making money on fear and misery, enabled, *enabled*, by us?"

Joanna's eyes narrowed. A challenge now, as the situation hung in the balance, would not be tolerated. She understood human nature quite well, even if she didn't always share it. Dominguez's objection wasn't to the task itself, of cutting up infected. No, it was simpler than that. His personality couldn't reconcile that he had to not only endure the presence of persons he had always labeled as bad, he had to actively assist them. The City was in fact upside down, and Dominguez's mind wasn't plastic enough to handle the dissonance of the new framework.

It was a serious handicap.

She would have to appeal to the old framework of values, then.

"You will carry out my strategy, as agreed," she said coldly. "You will work with whomever you must, directing the remaining members of the department and producing vaccine."

"Butchering the citizens of New York you mean," spat Dominguez. "Creating a market for the likes of Matricardi! Using up my cops, even our families, in order to gain more power."

"Making a life-saving medicine which is our only hope of surmounting this emergency is what I mean, Captain Dominguez."

Joanna had seen tensions build in Dominguez since the loss of his wife, but hadn't forecast a rupture so early. She had to keep the careerist under control.

"Don't you think that I don't see your plan, Kohn—I know about your aspirations. It was good enough when—"

"No Rafael, you do not know my plans," Joanna said, finally standing. She briskly tapped her knuckles on the desk blotter. "If you must arrest someone, then address your need by solving the problem of members of your department working with Overture. Address the problem of Overture controlling more and more of Queens and the Bronx. But. Leave Matricardi alone."

"I'll expose the whole thing if I have to, *Director* Kohn!" Dominguez began to turn. "We can go down together then. At least before this city is overrun with zombies, I'll have the pleasure of seeing your arrest."

He turned to leave but was frozen by Joanna's silvery, tinkling laugh. She held the back of one hand to her lips, her eyes alight.

"You may arrange your own demise, Captain Dominguez, but mine?" she said, lowering her hand to a locked desk drawer. She rapidly punched in a combination as she continued talking. "I have a signed letter from the mayor, personally authorizing me to take any steps necessary, any steps at all, to combat H7D3. This includes deputizing you to lead the police response."

"So?" Dominguez replied, but he lowered his hand from the doorknob. "Who cares about a signature now?"

"Do you have a letter like this Rafael?" Joanna asked, as she held up a sheet of paper. "A letter granting you broad powers? The authority to *process* vaccine? I rather think not. Of course, as long as we are partners in this effort to save the City, all of your actions and the actions of the department, are fully covered under law, under my authority. Of course..."

She sat down again, leaving both hands on the desktop.

"Imagine my terrible shock if I learned that our respectable captain of Precinct *One*, the acting assistant chief, the savior of Manhattan," here Joanna raised one open hand to cover her mouth again, this time in stylized horror, "was running a human-parts chop shop while being in league with the most vile elements of the criminal underground. I just do not know what I would do, do you?"

"You fuc—" Dominguez began.

"And there is the question of who will care for your children," Joanna said, continuing with timing too impeccable to be an accident. "Without you, it will be difficult to assure their security in the event that the city falls and we need to use our final contingency with the bank."

"You wouldn't, you, you couldn't!" Dominguez sputtered, but much more quietly than before.

"Better to say that I do not want to, Captain," Joanna replied, reassuring him. "But I can, and I shall if I must. There is too much at stake for you to suffer a crisis of conscience, or allow your intemperate rage to conceal the true objective, however it is attained. And if the City should fall, we must be ready to carry on, wherever the tide of this disease pushes us."

Dominguez held her gaze for a long moment.

"We can continue to work together," the composed OEM head said. "Or not. Now, you must, as the saying goes, 'get your game face on,' Captain. We have a meeting with our partners shortly."

So fractionally that she wouldn't have noticed had she not been utterly focused on her target, Dominguez's uniform jacket tightened across his shoulders.

Kohn wasn't sure whether it was resignation or . . . something else.

The foursome that formed the nucleus of the cartel had settled into routine weekly meetings. This one wasn't going smoothly. Tom knew that Dominguez had never been particularly "happy," but now he was permanently simmering with barely controlled anger. Usually, he couldn't be bothered with Matricardi's concerns, even if Smith was. Dominguez could count on Kohn to take his side.

However, this time Tom had the unexpected support of Kohn, and Matricardi had the floor. As usual, he sported a white carnation in his lapel.

"One of my teams got shot at last night," he said angrily. "Wasn't the first time. Shooters belonged to Overture. When the cops showed up, they sided with the other guys and threatened to arrest us—and our truck is the one with the bullet hole in it!" He chewed on an unlit cigar. "We got a deal, right here, amirite?"

Smith and Kohn nodded. The cop looked across the room at nothing in particular, flipping a deck of garish cards in one hand.

"Well?" the Sicilian insisted.

"The department is under severe stress," Kohn replied obliquely. "No-shows are continuing. We are actually collecting fewer infected even though the service call rate is up. As we feared might occur weeks ago, some parts of the city have made informal deals with the contractors in their immediate vicinity. The captain and I can not control it."

Though her words were conciliatory, the tone was anything but.

"What we are experiencing is happening in all major metro areas," Kohn reported. "Entire areas of L.A. are simply cordoned off. As far as I can tell, most of the federal government has continued working in the District, but a curfew is in effect and all local law enforcement has been federalized. Chicago has an extraordinarily high homicide rate that only slightly exceeds their worst pre-Plague years, but indicators strongly suggest deliberate under reporting. The military is mostly isolating itself on bases. I do not believe that we can contain the disease. We are approaching end game."

There was silence for a short time and then she continued.

"Locally, the 'acting chief for the eastern boroughs' is reputed to have informal ties to the, uh, contractors," Kohn said. For some reason, she couldn't quite say "criminals." "His concerns mirror my own, but he appears to be anxious to believe that we can prevent total collapse. Overture has offered him a story that he can believe in."

"I was able to purchase a large lot of medical grade vaccine," Tom said, trying to calm things down. "It might be enough to let us accelerate the schedule if it all tests out."

"Doesn't matter." Dominguez's voice startled them. "Doesn't make a difference. We need to talk about moving up the evacuation. The force is starting to fold." He didn't really look at anyone as he spoke. The card deck in his hand scritched on his armrest.

"Out of the question," Tom countered. "We don't *know* that collapse is inevitable. We just got a shot in the arm in the form of a new batch of National Guard. They are going to cover the high-value targets in Manhattan, Brooklyn and Jersey City, as well as transportation infrastructure. That should let you shift officers to reinforce areas on the periphery as well as give some teams a rest."

"A couple thousand more guardsmen spread across a city the size of New York?" Dominguez said, unimpressed. "That's like trying to stiffen a bucket of spit with a handful of lead shot. We should be looking at evacuation options and not trying to help you make some extra profit."

"This isn't about profit," Tom insisted. "This is about giving the system as long as possible to find a solution to the virus. If, IF, we evacuate, the timing is my call—as we all agreed. And I can't make that call until the bank pulls the handle. I'm still here. My family is still here. You get your seats out when I get the direction from my boss. If you can find a better arrangement elsewhere, I suggest that you take it."

The cop stood, neither angrily nor especially forcefully. He simply stood up.

"I'll push on the precincts next to Overture," Dominguez said, his voice flat. "Slow down their deal, maybe. Might need some of that vaccine you bought, Smith, to sweeten the pot. There still isn't enough to go around. But we're out of time. You'll see."

He left the room without fanfare. Tom and Matricardi looked the question at Kohn.

"His wife overdosed," she said. "Fatal. All he has are the kids."

"Ah, shit," Matricardi said with a sigh. "Makes sense now. How can we help? This is still the best deal—for all our sakes we gotta make this work."

Kohn looked at the door that her colleague closed.

"I know that it seems grim Mr. Matricardi, but I agree with Mr. Smith. We just need to hold fast."

Tom looked at her, sensing something that wasn't quite right.

"Put together a backpack with fifty complete courses of vaccine." Smith was working through his afternoon to-do list and Rune was scribbling.

"Who they going to, Boss?"

"Dominguez," Tom said. "He needs them fo—" Smith's personal cell went off and he glanced at the number, holding up one finger towards Rune.

"Smith . . . Uh-huh . . . Well, that's good, at least . . . Wait, what . . . ? How many zombies . . . ? How the hell do you AD an auto-injector in your thumb . . . ? A *crowbar*? For fuck's sake, Gravy, she's a fucking thirteen-year-old girl. In what fucking world can two Tier One operators backed by the effectively *unlimited* resources of an international investment bank *not* keep one thirteen-year-old from picking fights with zombies ... in my *own building* ...? Sure, sure, that's what the traveling salesman said to the mother superior. See you in two. Out here."

Rune decided that silence was the better part of valor, so he *only* looked the question at the visibly agitated Smith, who was strapping on a pistol belt loaded with four mags. He started talking even as he opened a desk drawer and withdrew his SIG.

"Faith decided that filing was boring and went for a walkabout in the basement," Smith said angrily. "Bagged nine infected and managed to tranq herself with an auto-injector. She should be okay, but her mother is going to murder me if she finds out."

The intel's specialist's eyes bugged out a bit, but his boss was too preoccupied to notice. Mostly Paul was just glad that his name was neither "Durante" or "Kaplan" at this point. Kaplan ran physical security *and* executive protection for all the American BotA locations now, and since his return Durante ran all special projects including the BERTs and what everyone called the "keep Faith out of trouble" watch. Just so long as Smith didn't immediately recall that it was Rune who gave Faith the filing assignment ...

"No idea where she gets this wild streak." Smith slapped a magazine home and let the slide go home. "I swear to the white Christ ..."

He started walking out of his office but was already trotting before he made it past the admin's desk, and continued accelerating towards the elevator lobby. " ... fucking Durante ... so much to ask?"

Smith's speed was a good thing in Rune's opinion,

because it kept his boss from seeing the borderline insubordinate smirk on the smaller man's face.

Yeah, no idea where she gets it from.

The scene in the basement was pure carnage. Smith had already had his niece sent up to the in-house medical clinic to be checked by Curry himself.

Smith was in a corner, talking to both Durante and Kaplan, and though onlookers couldn't make out the low-voiced conversation, the degree of arm waving and finger pointing coming from those three was nearly enough to create a perceptible breeze. One of the door guards who had tried out for the BERTs but quit after a couple of runs leaned over and whispered to his buddy who was staring a blood splash that went all the way up to the ceiling.

"How the fuck does someone so itty bitty do that...?"

He looked down at the arrangement of zombie bodies and tried to re-create the scene.

"I mean, that crow bar is actually *bent*!"

The first guy looked back over at a cluster of thigh-thick gray-water water pipes. Originally blue, they were now liberally painted red and an unidentifiable article of torn clothing as well as a hank of human hair was visibly wedged into a bundle of cabling that ran alongside the pipes.

"I don't know man, just don't piss her off."

"She's crazy, Boss," Durante said, throwing his hands up in the air. "I mean crazy in a good way, but also stone crazy as in 'won't listen to warnings and insists on wrestling with zombies for shits and giggles' crazy. If she was ten years older, I'd be analyzing the hot-crazy matrix as to whether to date her—I mean apart from her idiotic love of HK..."

"Not a time for jokes, Gravy!" Tom said, his face red with anger. "You were *supposed* to find her an inside job that did *not* involve hunting infected!"

"I *did*, Boss," Durante replied tightly. "From my POV she was AWOL from her filing job. I cannot be held responsible if an 'employee,' an underage *child-labor* employee I might add, goes off zombie hunting on her own! And we've all got too much on our plates to spend our time making sure she's not randomly questing for vaccine donors! So, let me repeat, *Mister Smith*, sir: Your fucking niece is stone-cold *insane*! What am I supposed to do? Chain her to the filing cabinet?"

Durante looked away, his cheeks reddening as well.

Smith glared at Kaplan, who was trying hard to control his cheek muscles.

"You! What part of check everyone for an infection even if they don't look sick wasn't clear?"

Smith worked the economics of the city. Dominguez was supposed to be the enforcer. Matricardi was equal parts criminal liaison and vaccine producer. Joanna Kohn's role was to keep the critical bits of the city infrastructure functioning, including the police. However, her control over the remaining police was slipping. The principal lever that she retained was the supply of vaccine. That vaccine had to be used to protect the bits of the city that kept things in motion. Literally.

So far, the recipients had been haggard with relief just to have a vaccine, even a prototype. Sooner or later questions would rise about where it came from. Of course, that meant that there had to be a later. Joanna had kept the flow of the critical drug moving to her invested parties, as well as the teamsters, the longshoremen, refineries, firemen, garbagemen and most especially the uniformed police. Problem was, the latter might have another source of supply.

There were police precincts that were rather far from the flagpole represented by Manhattan. The police in the extreme east and northeast of the city were literally on the other side of the entire jurisdiction from her base of political power. Following the second consolidation of police precincts, the force was down to less than half its original strength. In places, *much* less than half.

Into that breach had stepped Big Mac Overture, the self-styled Caribbean drug lord. He had his own sizable operation. Previously he had limited his growth to the territory controlled by smaller criminal organizations, either absorbing them or eliminating them entirely. Of late, he had become even more ambitious. It was his outfit that was supplying the cops on the east side of Queens and the Bronx. She didn't know how much vaccine Overture was producing, but the unconfirmed rumors were that he had control of two hospitals, all their equipment and such of their staff as he could extort or buy off.

Outside, the smoky gray haze from the overnight fires across the river was still hovering over parts of the city despite the best efforts of the morning sea breeze. The number of fires continued to grow. Firefighters were increasingly reluctant to enter dark buildings—if no coherent language replied to their hails, the new procedure was to allow buildings to burn. Entire blocks were being sacrificed as fire-breaks. Joanna knew that her principal link to the police was ailing. Dominguez was becoming erratic. She'd happily supported the relocation of his family to the high-security building downtown and the greater protection afforded the kids there had stabilized him for a time. The building wouldn't indefinitely be proof against the risks that they faced and her own small "family" was domiciled there as well. Nonetheless, Ding's effectiveness was waning, and his focus was strictly on preparing for an evacuation.

Her private cell rang and she picked up, only to have the call drop. She had recognized the number of her man Schweizer. His placement inside Bank of the Americas would be critical if the bank was going to renege on the deal, but so far Smith had entirely lived up to the bargain. Smith wasn't just attractive, he was also an honorable man, a rarity in Kohn's experience. Pity that he would have to go after things settled out. His traditional thinking and belief in the hierarchy, in "the world as it was" would eventually become a liability.

Moments later the phone rang again and this time the connection to Schweizer held.

"Ma'am. I have the complete personnel lists and bills of lading for all four refuge sites," Schweizer said. His tone was flat and behind him she could hear the sounds of a busy operations center. "There are supply problems for two of the sites but the bank is working to get at least one more completed in the next two weeks. However, the consensus from the intel team is that we have less than a month before infrastructure drops below the threshold to sustain operations in at least two critical points of failure."

"Where does Smith think that the rupture will occur?" Knowing where the bank thought that the hammer would fall first was important to know when to jump.

"Refined liquid fuels probably, but telecom is slipping."

He paused as someone in the background yelled: *"Look at that shit!"*

"Things are getting pretty exciting over here. The NYSE, the NASDAQ and the Chicago Mercantile all followed the lead of the Hang Seng and Tokyo—trading applications have been adjusted so that tolerable latency has been doubled, despite error rates and associated costs. The long bond is negative—no one is willing to think long term. The overnight rate is also picking up an average of ten to twenty bips daily."

Bips, or basis points, were a more finely graduated scale that permitted bankers to subdivide rates more precisely. One hundred bips made up a single percentage point. Usually the rate was lower than that charged to commercial customers. Twenty bips on the overnight rate would have been considered a seismic event, pre-Plague.

Kohn had no problem following her analyst's report. The banks were charging each other more than an extra percent every week. Unsustainable.

"Basically, what you are saying is that we are going probably going to run out of gas before we run out of money or the phones stop working, but it is going to be close?"

"Yes, ma'am."

"Very well," Joanna said crisply. "Keep me informed on any changes. Are we clear?"

"I want to be perfectly clear, Paul."

Smith had his intel chief and ops center coordinator's full attention. Rune was trying for "dutiful and loyal subordinate" but he was worried that it just came across as "scared that I'm going to screw up" with a healthy dollop of "oh God please don't put me in charge of her." There was a little "intimidated as hell" in there too.

"Mail," Tom said, keeping it simple. "Not mail delivery and exploring. Most especially, not mail delivery and zombie hunting. Just. Mail. Above the third floor. Now, you know what I want to hear, right?" Smith was not going to allow for any parsing of his instructions.

"Only mail duties for Ms. Smith," Rune said. "No going downstairs or outside without escort. No getting into scrums with zombies. Check, Boss."

The subject of his concern was sitting in the same conference room. An oversize bandage covered her thumb and she was picking at the tape.

"Uncle Tom, I told you like a million times that I didn't just go zombie hunting. They were just there! All I was doing . . ." She stopped when she looked at her uncle. His normal "face," at least in her experience, had changed.

The benevolent and kind uncle that she had always known wasn't there at the moment. The blond-haired and steely-eyed man who had taken his place was staring at her and it was a bit alarming. Tom Smith didn't raise his voice and he didn't threaten when he spoke, but there was an unpleasant energy in his gaze. It was a little uncomfortable, actually. She looked over at the dark-haired man in the room with them. Although he had answered her uncle's "sort of" questions just as calmly as her uncle had asked them and was sitting normally, he still gave the impression of being ready to jump without warning and escape through the conference room door.

"Faith Marie Smith, I can't stop what I'm doing to watch your every move," Tom said coldly. "I cannot second-guess a person who should already have the requisite maturity to do what she can to contribute to a very serious situation without creating a crisis. I won't dedicate my top security staff to babysit..." His voice trailed off and his eyes slid towards Rune. "Not that they were successful the first time..."

He refocused on Faith.

"I need all the time that I can squeeze out of every day. Time to do things so important that it affects real lives, every hour. I can't afford to worry about you in the interim. So, when I say that you are going to deliver mail and only deliver mail, I need to believe that you are going to do only that."

Faith stared at the stupid thumb bandage. She was rather annoyed by the injustice of it all. It wasn't like she wanted to fight zombies. Well, fight that many at the *same* time. She looked up with a ready retort... and stopped. The "stranger" was still looking right at her. She slid her eyes right for a moment. Mr. Frozen wasn't even breathing.

Sigh.

"Okay, Uncle Tom. Mail. Only mail. Check."

"Moving this much gold is unnecessary, Rich," Tom said. Smith didn't appreciate the distraction and really preferred to be back at the bank. They each only had about a billion things to do and the bottom could drop at any moment.

"Too massy to move, really hard to meaningfully damage, pretty much the definition of corrosionproof. The best choice is just pump the room full of cement and weld the door, then fill the stairway with more cement. Without the right tools, you would be a long time getting inside, assuming you get past the doors from the outside. And in the immediate aftermath the value of gold versus more important commodities is likely to be limited. We'd be better off moving this much volume, or mass, of medicines, ammunition or food. If we *had* this much medicine, ammunition or food available."

Bateman looked around the offsite bullion depository, located well away from Manhattan. The specially built facility was actually in the sub basement of a large, secure and unmarked data center about half an hour outside Manhattan. Standard gold bars, weighing a little over twelve kilos each, were stacked in short neat piles ten bricks high. The CEO looked around at the shin-high piles of gleaming metal that filled most of the medium sized room.

"Can't we stack them higher than this?" Rich asked, kicking a pile. "I actually agree and don't want to move them, but we may need floor space here. I might have a chance to cut a deal with the Met, the Frick and the Guggenheim. They want safe storage for some of their more important items." Bateman leaned down and actually hefted a single bar, making the Bank of the Americas guard twitch a little.

"This depository can handle a load of up to five tons per square foot," the facility manager said. "The issue isn't the concrete. The forklifts that we can fit inside have a ten-metric-ton lift limit. As it happens, stack those bars ten high across a single standard pallet and it weights just under ten tons. With that, we still have to use special pallets."

"Let's not make our staff any more nervous than necessary, sir," Tom said. He reached over and held his hand out for the bar that Bateman was holding. "Each stack is worth about half a billion, give or take."

"I see," Bateman said with a grin, a rare enough sight recently. "I had to see this to understand, and I don't mind being out of Manhattan for a little bit. Let's look at that stack in the corner." He led the way to the farther pile, several meters from the armed guard in BotA livery.

"We are getting direct pressure from Treasury," Bateman said, pitching his voice low. "They know about at least one of the refuges and they are asking unhelpfully detailed questions about capacity and equipment."

Tom Smith thought through the implications, not just of the CEO's statement, but of why he was talking about it here.

"Which one?" he asked.

"New York," his boss replied. "At least that one, maybe the others too. They could have gotten it from almost anyone in our staff, but if they only have the one, then the leak might be on the sell side of the real estate deal, the state deeds office, anywhere. At this juncture, the forensics are nearly pointless."

"Yeah, I can find a way to get more room down here," Smith said just loud enough for it to carry. He kicked the pile of worthless metal and added for the other man's ears, "I'm already moving staff by van to the refuges in small groups. As soon as we think we are within twenty-four hours of losing the roads or the cops, we stop operations and push everything that's left all the way out, okay?"

Bateman nodded.

The location of Fort Hamilton, on the coast of southern Brooklyn, was the place where optimistic colonial artillery had engaged elements of the English fleet on the fourth of July 1776. Although they succeeded in causing minor damage, the cannonade was largely symbolic, and the English went on to occupy Manhattan. During subsequent wars, and repeatedly over the years, the fort's walls had been upgraded and the cannons up-gunned, right up until missiles made harbor defense moot. Then the developers had moved in and planted subdivisions on much of the original fort. The entrance gate to what was left of the last Army installation in New York City stood under the shadow of the Verrazano-Narrows bridge. The atmosphere of the American inner city contrasted with the National Guard vehicles, weapons and uniforms, making Copley feel a little surreal as they rolled towards the fort's main gate.

The security point was typically manned by two bored civilian rent-a-cops, but as the little convoy hove into sight, Copley noted an infantry squad in full battle rattle manning the now reinforced Vehicle Control Point. Backing them up was an armored combat vehicle, a Mine Resistant Ambush Protected truck, or as the acronym mad Army called them, MRAPs. Thousands had been made for the Iraq war, and several different models were fielded.

As the two HMMWVs and Copley's truck passed the VCP, the sergeant could see that this MRAP retained a loaded fifty caliber machine gun in the turret position behind the cab, and it was manned by a watchful soldier. This level of alert was something that had *not* been getting airtime on cable news.

They weren't in Kansas anymore.

The sign read UNIT CHECK IN HERE, but to Copley, who was fluent in nonverbal fobbit-ese after his Iraq experience, the dour look on the colonel's face read "abandon all hope." Nonetheless, Copley came to attention behind the battery XO as they reported in.

"Colonel, Lieutenant Pozzo reporting with the advance party from 1st of the 258th," 1LT Pozzo said, announcing them.

"How many with you now, Lieutenant?" asked the colonel, looking over the officer's shoulder and squinting skeptically at Copley.

"Seventeen, sir," came the answer, as Pozzo handed over a manifest.

"Seventeen whole soldiers?" The colonel's question was clearly rhetorical. "Astroga!" The colonel snapped his fingers and then extended his arm, palm up. A pert brunette private in crisp, unfaded ACUs materialized and slapped a clipboard into his hand. He consulted the papers, flipping a few.

"Your battery has sixty-eight soldiers assigned and this is all you brought?" the colonel asked, shaking the paper at the pair of artillerymen. "The chain of command is taking notice of units that are failing to report in with the majority of their strength. The state of emergency has been declared for a while now and yet a suspicious number of units are late reporting and understrength. Including yours, Lieutenant."

For a second, Copley thought that Pozzo was going to argue, which was generally frowned upon, even among weekend-warrior types. In some cases, especially when dealing with units outside the New York Guard, politely refuting an unjustified or incorrect senior was possible. However, he was getting a distinct feeling that their current situation was closer to the early days in Iraq than it was to a normal drill weekend, or even a routine hurricane response. Thankfully, the battery XO apologized and suggested that the colonel take it up with the battery CO or even the colonel who commanded the 258th.

"Your colonel is still en route, but due to the pressing need for boots on the ground, I'm sending you to reinforce the First of the Sixty-Ninth Infantry. Their headquarters company has the TOC set up at Tomlinson Square Park," the colonel stated, glowering. "Take your detachment and report there. Billeting will be at a local hotel. If you don't already have ammunition for your personal weapons, draw it before you leave. Tell your CO to report to me personally as soon as he arrives."

"Sir, don't forget the updated rule of engagement," the little private said, offering yet another clipboard to the colonel for a signature. "Since these guys actually belong to my unit, why don't I go along to show them the best routes to get through the checkpoints between here and Manhattan."

"Your unit?" the colonel raised an eyebrow, as did Copley. He knew everyone at all three batteries that made up the 258th by sight.

"I was supposed to join HHB the 258th in Jamaica before I got shanghaied here," the private replied, referring to the headquarters component of the arty regiment. "These are our guys."

On Copley's forehead the second eyebrow rose to join the first. He doubted that Captain McCabe or anyone at Battery A would have thought of themselves as "Private Astroga's guys." Whoever she was.

"Fine," the colonel answered, scribbling on another proffered authorization.

"Private, tomorrow or the next day, grab one of the Officer Friendly types and guide this detachment over to the Tomlinson ops center. Whatever it takes to get the 258th off the dime. Lieutenant, you have until we move you into the city to get the rest of your unit here."

The Holland Tunnel exited onto street level only a hundred meters from the historic blue painted entrance to the First Police Precinct. Both the white legend over the lintel and the more colorful NYPD badge logo on the door proclaimed control of the island to the incoming cars as they exited the tunnel into Manhattan.

Pre-Plague, the traffic exiting the tunnel had been very high. Now, the number of cars and trucks serving the city was still considerable, but much less than there used to be, and dropping every day. What surfeit there was consisted of head-high stacks of black plastic garbage bags, lining both sides of the street and occasionally spilling into it.

The traffic and the garbage both reflected the police force's control of the city, mused Dominguez.

Senior staff as well as additional line officers not read into the vaccine manufacture were receiving the weekly operations summaries. As the audience listened to statistics about service call coverage, arrests figures, the numbers of officers reporting for duty and the other routine reports, Dominguez sensed a resignation in his fellow cops. The change in the situation from day to day wasn't catastrophic. The trend was.

The next briefing officer began the threat intelligence briefing. He painted a bleak picture.

"Across the river, Matricardi has effective police control over everything west of the Ninety-Five," he said, highlighting the area on the plasma. "There are still uniforms, but Newark PD is in his pocket, and most of the sheriffs in the northern counties. Intelligence reports they're harvesting infected for illegal vaccine production. Where and under what conditions is unknown. We are denied access to some parts of Newark and everywhere near the airport. The state troopers are pretty much absent—haven't seen them at all."

Dominguez's deputy blinked and looked at his boss, who blandly returned the glance. The source of NYPD's vaccine was publicly attributed to a secret pharmaceutical laboratory somewhere near the pharma corridor in New Jersey. Although some negotiations with the different gangs was a matter of record, detailed knowledge of their underground cartel operation was still closely held.

"The lower number of cops in Newark appears to have led to a very high number of zombie calls," the briefer continued. "That begs the question about zombies getting across the river. In addition, both the Matricardi gang to the west as well as the Overture organization in Queens are reported to have heavy weapons. In a chance encounter, they potentially outgun anybody but the Ajax and Hercules units."

"What do we do to keep them out?" The gruff captain from the Nine-Four spoke up. "We're holding in Manhattan. The Guard is scattered to hell and gone, their armored trucks never leave the car parks and the grunts don't do much more than enforce curfew, even though they're bringing in more zombie chow to replace losses and quitters. We're holding the line in the east, but I can see a time when the island is squeezed from both sides."

The surviving special agent in charge from the FBI field office had unofficially thrown in his lot with the NYPD a few days earlier. Direction from his bosses in D.C. had continued to focus on the goose chase to find the originator of the plague. Whoever had done it was long gone and there wasn't a cure. Better to focus on what could be salvaged than on figuring out how it all started.

"We've got heavier stuff," the SAIC admitted. "And I'm solidly dialed into the Guard. If we had to, we could control the tunnels and bridges—create a semipermeable barrier. Essentially a border crossing for Manhattan only."

Heads swiveled at that.

"Temporary, or permanent like?" A classic New Yark drawl from the back sounded.

"Either," the SAIC replied. "Both. It's part of some of our post-9/11 planning."

"It's a little premature to treat all of the Bridges and Tunnel crowd like zombies," Dominguez said, keeping his tone artificially light and adding a chuckle. "We aren't battling Jersey, Billy. Yet."

All the commuters, whether from Long Island, the boroughs across the East River or worst of all, from New Jersey, were labeled "Bridge and Tunnel" by the full-time island residents. Manhattanites of long standing had ever resented them as not truly being "of the City." However, the ongoing business activity remained utterly necessary for the city-shaped human-colander that was New York. The money that commuters, businesses and visitors left behind after each trip, whether for work or play, fed directly into the financial bloodstream of the City.

Yet, Matricardi represented the worst of the New Jersey crowd. Flashy and cheap, he continued to aggravate the de facto chief of half the remaining cops in New York. As the cops lost strength, the jackals like Matricardi gained in power and reach. He'd have to talk to Kohn about that again.

It might be necessary to keep him out of New York at some point. Or, if the situation in New Jersey went entirely out of control, Dominguez thought that it would be helpful to have a way to close the door.

He scribbled a note to himself to chat with the feeb and then addressed the group again.

"Let's talk security for open spaces like the Park. When do we go to a full curfew? Ideas?"

CHAPTER 11

"... the Cardinal Camerlengo having affirmed the untimely passing of His Holiness, the College of Cardinals was sealed inside the Sistine Chapel to elect the successor to Benedict XVI. Unfortunately, at least one of the cardinals appears to have contracted H7D3, and from the forensic evidence of the conclave ..."

From: *Collected Radio Transmissions of the Fall*
University of the South Press 2053

Tom Smith walked the various security posts frequently, less to check on the attentiveness of his staff—between the obvious severity of the situation and Durante's scrutiny he didn't really expect to find any slack—rather it was the way that he could check on the mettle of his crew as well as take the temperature of the city at ground level. It also helped to just get out of his office. He stopped briefly at the NYPD vehicle checkpoint, which was one of several that guarded approaches to the NYSE a block or so away, and then kept walking in the warm mid-August morning sun.

Two of Durante's team stood outside the underground garage entrance.

"Hey boys," he called to them as he approached. "Did the BERTs already roll?"

"Yes, Mr. Smith," the nearer guard said, offering a

handheld radio. "'Bout fifteen mikes since they left. You need to reach them?"

"No," Tom said. "Just checking. It's all good."

Smith kept walking until he reached the corner at Wall Street. He could see along the front of the bank. The double doors into the atrium were full of the morning rush; even at a quarter of regular staffing several thousand people still had to enter in a short period in order to meet the opening of the market. He started to head back in when a painfully loud crack went off right behind him, like a single beat shattering an enormous bass drum. He flinched again a split second later as what felt like heavy rain struck the back of his suit.

Kendra was in the atrium lobby grabbing a coffee from the local caffeine pusher. As long as the world's largest coffee franchise was still in business in downtown Manhattan, things couldn't be that bad, right? She turned to the sugar and cream station to properly adulterate her daily lifeline in its white and green paper cup.

A very loud boom, the next thing to an explosion and sounding like an anvil being dropped into a dumpster, shook the lobby windows. One person screamed in startled reflex.

She spun towards the direction that the sound had come from. For a moment she couldn't parse what she was seeing.

Several feet from the heavy glass atrium walls a pile of bloody rags appeared to be tangled with a fractured red and yellow Jell-O mold lying on the sidewalk. A moment later, her eyes traced one line of red to the window opposite her. A mangled human hand and a fragment of cloth snapped into focus. Suddenly she could trace all of the streaks of what must be blood back to the point of impact. In the center lay a what looked a dark and greasy bit of carpet remnant.

Hair.

A person had jumped. From her building. While she had her coffee.

Screams, varying in register, began to rise in earnest around her as onlookers realized what had happened. She recognized a member of the lobby security team who ran over and started talking into his handheld radio, his Jersey accent somehow perfect for the scene.

"Yeah, someone else just gave notice," he narrated casually. "Eh, 'bout fifty floors worth. Main entrance. Send the cleanup guys over to the Pine Street entrance and they can work from the outside in. Call it in to Durante, he can pass it up the chain and handle the cops. Nah, we'll have to clean it up ourselves. EMS ain't gonna come out for no street pizza." He paused and looked outside. "Shit, that's the boss. Yeah, Smith is already outside. Shit shit shit. Nah, he looks okay."

Kendra could see Smith gesticulating at the guard, pointing to the employee turnstiles.

The security man watched Smith for a moment, nodded his head exaggeratedly and then keyed his radio before resuming his comms.

She looked outside again, and just outside the densest part of the spatter pattern she saw Smith looking at the body, frowning. His stature was calm, hands folded in front of him, just another day at the office. Just another minor security issue to manage.

He was annoyed.

Annoyed.

Kendra's unwilling attention was broken by the voice of the security man.

"I'll look for an employee badge on the stiff," the security guard's voice grated on her suddenly raw nerves. "You make sure that everyone going up still gets screened. People are running to the elevators."

Disgusted, he started snapping on a pair of latex gloves before looking up and noting Jones.

"Hi Jonesy. Helluva thing, eh? Some folks can't take the heat, amirite?"

She nodded jerkily and forced her eyes away. The elevators were over there, on her right. Kendra turned precisely, and holding herself carefully erect, walked over and pushed the elevator call button.

Then she realized she had about three seconds to make it to an open trash can to puke.

"Smith here."

"Tom, I need you on thirty-two now." Kaplan sounded perfectly calm and apart from using his boss's first name, his delivery was deadpan. "Faith just scrummed with a zombie. Again."

Tom knew that calm was a bad sign.

"She was just *here*, damnit." Tom's answer was equally without inflection. "Is she bit?"

"No obvious marks, but she might have been contaminated with blood through an open wound," Kaplan replied instantly. "I am taking her to decontam now."

Smith could hear Faith talking to someone and an elevator *ding* in the background.

"On the way," Tom said, hanging up.

❦ ◯ ❦

"We got this down to an *art*, Boss," Tradittore said happily, holding his fingers up in an "okay" symbol. "Art."

The early, messy days of vaccine production were behind them now.

Matricardi had purchased a funeral home and after trying out more than a dozen candidates, settled on a pair of experienced butchers, one from his very own delicatessen. Tradittore had loaned the operation his understanding of just-in-time manufacturing, so they didn't have an enormous backlog of confined zombies to manage. Members of the cartel had toured the police-run holding facility in order to "see" how the cops managed the process. Oldryskya thought that "hellish" didn't *begin* to cover it.

She stood with Matricardi and his lieutenant, safely behind the glass of an observation room, as they watched the assembly-line process. Each morning, the previous day's zombies were delivered already dead, usually from a carefully aimed small-caliber pistol shot to the head, which preserved the structural integrity of the skull. Corpses were lined up on gurneys, and drained into the purpose-built blood gutter that ran the length of the large room. She wrinkled her nose at the fecal smell, mingling unhelpfully with the heavy iron scent of the blood already running down the spouts to the trough. The suited and masked pair rapidly incised each corpse's neck and, after separating all connective tissue, withdrew the spinal column and placed it in a specimen tray. Processed bodies were dumped into very large triwall cardboard boxes for truck delivery to a large industrial incinerator.

"We're matching the bank's number now," Tradittore

exclaimed. "Better than seven doses per asset average. Our teams plus the take that we are getting from Newark PD is two hundred zombies a week. Fourteen hundred units per week and street price is at over seven thousand bucks per, cash. Our team is fully vaccinated, and most of the cops that have taken our deal have the first shot. 'Course, there aren't as many left as I'd like, but..."

His snow-white shirt popped into view as he shot his cuffs.

"...not really too surprised. Cops, you know. No vision."

Matricardi grunted.

"Are you making nice with Dominguez?" the boss asked. "That guy is coming unglued."

"Well, nice, sure—but I mean, like you say, that guy is a piece-a-work," Tradittore said, temporizing.

"What did you do?"

"Nothing, I swear," the lieutenant said, holding both hands up at shoulder height. "Just busted his balls a little bit, when he gave me stink eye."

Matricardi sighed, pinching the bridge of his nose between his thumb and forefinger. There wasn't time to sit on everyone, every minute, but he did not need problems with the cops right now.

"And Overture?"

"His teams tried a few sorties near Fort Lee," Tradittore replied. "We persuaded them otherwise."

The bridges and tunnels that connected New Jersey ran the entire western side of New York City. The last bridge across the Hudson was the George Washington in Fort Lee.

"The Jamaican has a very large organization, more

cops, more of everything," Oldryskya said softly. "If he isn't pushing now, he will soon. If the zombies don't eat us all first."

Both men looked at her, startled.

"Don't get your panties in a wad, sugar," Tradittore said with a sneer. "We're on top of this. By the time we finish containing the outbreak, *this* organization, the one that you work for, is going to be controlling the entire shebang. When the feds finally get around to checking on everyone, we'll have our own mayor in the big chair, we'll own all the cops and the city will belong to us. Only us."

Matricardi looked amused at the younger man's vehemence.

"Easy Joey," he said, putting his hand on Tradittore's shoulder. "It's a reasonable fear. She's been working with the fancy money men for a while, and their usual way of life is coming apart, so she sees that part first."

He turned to address her directly.

"But you need to remember your part."

He tapped her shoulder with two fingers.

"Your job's to be ready to plant the idea in Smith's head that he wants to work with us. Just us. His tame cop is losing it and I sincerely hope that he doesn't really think that he can trust that harpy from city hall. She is genuinely crazy."

She didn't quite believe what she was hearing. Did Matricardi really think that Smith would just roll over for anyone? Was no one reading the bank intelligence summaries she forwarded—the military in quarantine lockdown, Asia coming apart?

"Mr. Matricardi," she said, just as calmly, very carefully using American diction. "I like the idea of preparing for a successful defense against the virus, but surely you don't think that we are going to automatically beat the disease?" Her discipline held, and she smiled smoothly and then let her face shift into one of contemplation. "We're still ready to evacuate and then rebuild, yes?"

"Listen to the big thinker, Boss!" Tradittore chuckled. "Look missy, we'll keep the options open, and if..."

"I don't keep youse around like some kinda bank analyst, Risky," Matricardi said. He waved a hand, silencing the younger man. "I keep you 'cause you understand your place and you're good at it. You're useful now because Smith clearly finds you... interesting. You're supposed to be encouraging that. But, remember: You work for me, not the other way around."

He looked back at the men in the harvesting room as one lifted another dripping cord and laid it across the tray.

"I love these guys, Joey," Matricardi said, gesturing towards the glass divider. "They're smooth. Watch! Watch Mikey do this bit. He has great hands. I think this is harder than when he is shaving prosciutto nice and tissue thin—that way it melts in your mouth, see? He's an artist. Another batch almost in the can. Love it."

Oldryskya didn't snort. She supposed that she shouldn't be surprised they had already forgotten that this approach was *her* idea.

"Is there a long-term deal?" Matricardi said. "Sure. We have a deal with GenetiCorp.

"We already took over their security, and they seem

to think that they can start mass producing a protein matrix vaccine in a couple months. One that is safer, cleaner, none of this hacking up zombies. You can give it to kids. Skip the FDA bullshit and presto, we can make hundreds of thousands of doses per week. So, you see, I like Smith's plan to keep 'everything running.' We aren't just sitting on top of New York, but something a lot bigger. We'll be able to expand our...influence. Be untouchable, again. Get back to the way things are supposed to be."

He turned back to Risky and twisted one hand palm up, then palm down.

"Still, we do need Smith for the financial angle," Matricardi admitted. "And I don't mind having him around as a parachute. But...if it all goes *grande confusione*, I am not going to quietly take a few seats on a bus and leave all this behind. We'll just use his setup, but civilized like. The whole plan just takes longer. He is a businessman *and* a family man, right Joey?"

"Sure is, Boss." Tradittore smiled. "My buddy is tight with Smith. Banker-man has a couple of nieces in the city. Heard that one got bit, so maybe only one now."

Tradittore's smile was getting entirely too nasty, in Risky's opinion. As he kept talking, she imagined smearing it across his face with an entirely out of character palm strike.

"But yeah, even with that, we can make a deal," the Cosa Nova lieutenant was confident. "He'll come around. And if he doesn't: not a problem."

Durante stared at Tom Smith who in turn, stared out the window at the darkening sky. Durante had been relieved by Kaplan, who was on the "Faith watch" for now. The newest head of security and notional "Faith-watcher" knew what the pending phone call was about and was grateful that it wasn't his call to make.

It had taken the better part of the day to run down all of the employees who hadn't been visually screened. After Kaplan had reached him by radio, he had turned his BERT around and found Smith organizing a building-wide screening using their stock of test kits for even the most trivial suspicion. Even though they were close to exhausting their remaining supply, it was hard to argue considering how the screening process had failed, again.

He watched his boss stretch his neck and roll his shoulder for a moment, then grab the receiver.

The phone rang only briefly, and although he could only hear one side of the conversation, it was pretty obvious who Smith was talking to.

"Faith may have been infected. She's in decontamination and we're running a test for H7D3 right now.". . . "She had the vaccine primer a week ago.". . . "Steve, she was inside the building, within layers of our security. I had her delivering the mail, security everywhere, I swear.". . . "Um—". . . "An employee turned in an elevator, and during the struggle some blood from the infected may have contaminated an open wound on Faith before she brained it with her mail cart and—". . . "Not exactly.". . . "She AD'd herself with another auto-injector. But, that, that was from before—". . . "The zombies in the basement."

There was a pause in the conversation, and then Smith continued, his voice lower.

"No excuse, Steve. It's on me. I fucked it up.". . .

"Look, Steve. You know your own daughter better than I, but...it's Faith. Barring locking her in a cell, she will find any opportunity to get stuck in the Barney. I had my two best lads riding herd on her. Didn't more than slow her down.".... "Right, I'll send Durante with a boat for Stacey right away."

The bank had purchased two surplus ex-Navy Rigid Hulled Inflatable Boats and retrofitted them with enclosed cockpits. Smith had subsequently arranged low-profile berths near Battery Park. When questioned about the expense Tom had patiently pointed out that Wall Street was located on Manhattan *Island*. Of late, the RHIBS had been used to ferry the Smith family to their yacht, the *Mile Seven*.

Without taking his eyes from the window, Smith trained his index finger directly at Durante. Even though his boss wasn't actually looking at him, Durante still nodded and drew his own phone to warn the boat crew as he headed for the door.

Oldryskya kept the searchlight mounted on the window pillar in motion, alert for any infected. Durante rode behind her because "there is less chance that you can accidentally shoot me from up there." Now that Faith's mom had made it to the bank to nurse her daughter, he had joined the ad hoc BERT crew, displacing the regular lead. Kaplan drove, and for the last half hour he had exchanged quips with his buddy in back.

"I really need to kill something," Durante said from the back seat.

"I really need to not get killed by the boss," Kaplan responded.

"*Credula vitam spes fovet et melius*, Kap," Durante sonorously opined.

"Oh, fuck your Latin bullshit. He'd do you first."

She could hear Durante's grin, even if she didn't turn around to check.

"Okay, what *does* that mean?"

"When he comes over all philosophical, he prefers the original Latin," Kaplan said. "You've got to be fluent in a language to get into SF. He got in on the basis of being fluent in Latin. That one was basically a reprise of Little Orphan Annie. 'There's always hope for tomorrow.' Give us one about time flying and your fancy watch, big man."

Durante's watch was a Rolex Submariner and he was inordinately fond of it. It had been the subject of a few jokes since Oldryskya had integrated with Smith's security team. Something about a Jordanian princess, or maybe an Egyptian crime lord.

"*Cum magnum vigilia Tiberes*," Durante intoned.

"Cum . . . what?" Risky asked.

"Do we really want to go there?" Kaplan asked.

Oldryskya kept her own counsel, though internally she shared the overall sense of frustration that underlay the banter. As the outsider, she intuited that she wasn't yet accepted with the implicit trust a few of the security staff shared. She had asked questions around the periphery of the team about these two. Though clearly Smith's stirrup men—she also guessed that they were something beyond the normal soldiers and policemen that were common in the banks. However, apart from being told that they were from some special military unit, no one had shared details.

Special military unit. That phrase resonated with Oldryskya.

Her earliest memories were of a small village. She had been young when some vague disaster struck. There had been a fire, gunfire and men carried her with other girls to trucks. Sometime later, there had been another fight with many loud and frightening noises but her recollection of the details was hazy. Mostly gunfire, dead bodies and men in black balaclavas with strange accents sweeping through a warehouse, putting rounds into the heads of the men who had been holding her. She had been afraid they were going to kill her as well.

They had not. They were a "special unit" of the "Georgian military" on a mission to find one girl. Instead they had found many.

More vans and buses. Go here. Go there. A doctor. Vague memories of travel.

Eventually, she had been settled with a new family. Her foster father had been an air force colonel in garrison before the collapse of the Soviet Union, transplanted from St. Petersburg. Unable to have children of their own, he and his wife adopted an orphan of the wreckage of central and southern Europe.

The colonel had remained at the air base in Khanabad, after the old USSR was dissolved. The family had made it out of the increasing ethnic violence that accompanied the fracture of the former Soviet republics. The real end hadn't come till much later. Some of the Russian officers had decided to convoy with their families north. The group fell victim to an ambush during which her father died. Older at that point she remembered, too well, her treatment at the hands of the Chechen special unit. And the years that followed.

Her long and painful journey ended in the United
States. During that journey she lost everything she had
ever known, save for a few scraps of nursery songs
and tears for her foster mother: the woman had not
survived the first week.

Risky's experience of the term "special unit" was
a stark choice between "very good" or "very bad."

She maintained her wariness of these two new
"coworkers."

"When do you think that Mr. Smith will tell his
boss 'enough'?" She returned to the present with a
question. "Martial law now for days. We can't secure
the bank forever and most of the staff is already
evacuated from the center of New York. What's keeping him, us, in this dark place?"

"Trade secret," Durante replied flatly. "Besides,
Tom knows about dark places."

"Really? We don't get to know when we're going
to have to bug-out?"

A silence greeted her question, and at first she
thought that they were going to ignore her altogether.
Then the quiet was broken by Durante.

"A person has to decide what part of their word
they are going to live up to," Durante continued.
"Tom's vision of himself is that of a person whose
word is good. If he screws up, he owns it and either
fixes it or pays the price. Simple as that."

"How about you?" she asked Kaplan, while maintaining the scan of "her" side of the sidewalk and
cross streets.

"Like Gravy said, it's simple." The reply was laconic.
"Train keeps his promises, pays me really well and

lets me shoot stuff. Not too many places that meet that description."

"And shooting stuff is important?" Oldryskya wasn't squeamish, but she knew the type of man that lived for violent excitement. Most of the ones in Cosa Nova had a habit of dying off before they actually became as good as they thought that they were.

"Look around, newbie," Kap said with a snort. "You're helping turn sick people into tapioca just to save your own ass. Or maybe you are doing it for a dollar. Maybe something else. But you're still doing it. Right about now, everyone should see that life is cheap. That's something I've known my whole life."

As they passed another alley, she picked up a flash of pale skin.

"Target," she said in a businesslike tone. "Right side. Back up a bit."

Kaplan braked to a sudden stop, chirping the wide tires on the armored six-pack truck. Despite bracing for the expected maneuver, Oldryskya was still thrown against her seatbelt, hard.

Durante already had his feet on their seatbacks, and didn't seemed perturbed at the violent maneuver.

"So yeah, the money is great," Kaplan continued, while operating the shift lever. "And I am pretty happy to have a prepared fallback. But even if I gotta wonder how long we are going to stick around, don't matter. We go when Tom says. Not before."

He backed and then pulled into the narrow side street, flicking on the highbeams. The bright light pinned a single infected, who was crouching over a still form, tearing at the abdomen of the unresisting figure. It was a testament to how much carnage all three had seen that no one turned a hair at the gruesome spectacle in front of the truck.

Play time was over.

"Kap, leave the lights on," Durante said, shifting modes. "On command, Khabayeva and I exit the truck together. I'll cover with the M4, Khabayeva is on Taser and tranq. Kap, you're on the second long-gun from the truck keeping a three-sixty. Once the bugger is down and we check the rest of the area for extras, we'll tag and bag. On command, unass the vehicle together. And . . . execute."

The other two knew the drill, and had been unsnapping seatbelts, squaring away their gear and had a hand on the door handles before he got to the "execute." They slid out simultaneously, as though they had practiced it.

Which they had, dozens of times, during the training that had been required before they allowed Oldryskya to join the team. Every evening, the pre-mission brief practiced the most common team actions. Smith had coined the repetitive training "dirt diving," initially confusing the Cosa Nova transplant. Who would dive into dirt for practice and what did that have to do with fighting infected?

It turned out to be a term from his time in the Australian special forces, she learned. Since talking underwater during a dive was impossible, you practiced on land, on the dirt first, and *then* you did something for real underwater.

The muggy late summer air, rank with the odor of decomposing garbage that had been piling up in the alley, was like a damp, stinking rag slapped across their faces. Once up and on point, they approached the infected who snarled into the blue-white glare of the truck's halogen lights, clearly blinded but unwilling to leave a meal. At five meters' distance, Oldryskya felt that she could make the shot.

"Ready to tase," Oldryskya said.

"Green," Durante responded.

Oldryskya put the two metal barbs into the infected's naked chest, right in the x-ring, causing it to collapse across the dead body, twitching. After locking the thumbswitch in the down position, a little modification that they had made after discovering that the zombies shook off the electrical charge much more rapidly than expected, she transferred the Taser to her left hand. She drew the tranquilizer gun.

"Ready to move."

"Move," Durante replied. The two advanced carefully as she kept the electrical leads from either tangling or pulling from the shuddering infected.

Within touching distance, she crouched to inject the infected while Durante scanned the sides of the alley past their location. Letting up on the Taser power, she injected the infected in the back of the thigh, then hit the Taser again to keep it down.

Durante's weapon light was lost in the bright glare of the headlights, which washed much of the color, but unfortunately not the smell of rot, from the scene. As the infected relaxed into a familiar limpness, she called again.

"Down and tranked."

"All right," Durante replied from over her shoulder. "Let's bag it, then you can drag it back to the truck."

She began the process of putting a Kevlar bag on the infected and used double zip-ties to lock its wrists and ankles together. The now flaccid infected's breath rasped, but at this point Oldryskya had already had the full course of vaccine as a member of the BERT cadre, so an airborne infection wasn't her worry. As she began to drag the infected, the partially consumed body shifted, revealing a Russian designed light machine gun.

"Hey!" she exclaimed. "The dead guy has an RPK!"

"If you like that, you're going to love this," Durante replied flatly.

Concealed by the sharp shadows created by the headlights of their ride, a total of three armed corpses were revealed by Durante's taclight. Two wore the signature dreadlocks of Big Mac Overture's organization. Both were heavily armed, one with the Krinkov SBR that the Jamaicans preferred.

"Whatcha got?" Kaplan called, still several meters away and watching rearwards onto the intersection from which Oldryskya had first spotted their target. She had dropped the unconscious infected and drawn her sidearm, covering towards the dead Jamaican gangsters.

Durante glanced at her approvingly.

"We got three dead guys with serious guns," he replied. "Looks like they belonged to Overture."

"Infected?"

"Don't think so," Durante said. "Oldryskya: Go check the other guys. Covering."

Oldryskya moved forward in the gliding step that she had learned during their practices. It did work to reduce the amount of motion imparted to her gun, improving aiming.

She studied the two bodies, then looked at Durante with one raised eyebrow.

"What do you think?" he asked.

"They're dead?" she answered, deadpan.

"Ha-fucking-ha Khabayeva. What else?"

"Definitely not a scuba-diving accident."

She knew that the dirt diving thing would come in useful at some point.

"I swear to Christ that you are worse than the asshole back at the truck. How about answering my question, newbie?" Durante's voice didn't sound any more tense, but Oldryskya decided that she had pushed it far enough.

"First—bullet holes," Risky said, pointing at a visible entrance wound. "They died first, then the zombie fed. Two, no bullet casings near the bodies. They never got a shot off, didn't expect a fight. Last, look at this." She picked up a stiff card from the second corpse's chest, glad for her Kevlar biteproof gloves. The edge of a purple surgical glove peeked above her wrist. Holding the card so it was illuminated by the headlights, she tried to avoid smearing the blood further.

"It's a tarot card," she explained to Durante. "Sort of a fortune-telling device. This one is the Emperor."

"What does it mean?" Durante asked.

"Means different things," Oldryskya said, trying to remember. She hadn't studied tarot in years. "My foster mother used these to tell the future. Emperor can mean 'unyielding strength.' Depends on context."

Durante panned his light around.

"Are there more?"

They found a card near each body.

"Let's load this guy and clear the location," Kaplan said. "I don't like being stopped for too long. Someone is gonna come looking for those guys. Not to mention police response to an active crime scene and, oh yeah, zombies."

Oldryskya nodded to Durante and tucked all three tarot cards into her tacvest.

"Any day now." Kaplan didn't sound nervous, but suddenly Oldryskya felt a little tingle of apprehension.

If both of these former "special" soldiers felt that it was time to move, she fervently agreed.

"This shit ain't right," Durante said as they drove away.

"That can't be right."

Kendra frowned at the summary across the top of the page. Thirty-seven zombies in a single incident? Except for the scene with her boss's niece in BotA's own basement a few weeks ago, no one had seen more than two or three zombies at once, and usually one of those had just been turned by direct blood contact from a bite. The second page of the report dispelled all doubt; there was a high-definition image of a literal stack of dead infected, messily arranged between the stairhead and the intersection of Lexington and East 96th. She printed the e-mail from her contact at MetBank and looked around the bullpen.

She spotted her boss, who had just exited a conference room with Smith and Durante. As Paul Rune walked over she thought that she noted a slight pallor under his normally dark skin.

She handed the him the report and gave him a verbal rundown.

"That's a lot of zombies in one place," he said. "MetBank had one man shot, and the Overture guys lost two or three, right? This is going to impact the cartel operations. What about other groups of infected?"

Kendra shook her head. She had begun tying her

shoulder-length hair in a ponytail, and the flippy motion caught Paul's eye.

"So far, this is the only group of multiples," she said. "At least known. The infected were emerging from the Four-Five-Six subway station near Lexington, just a block from Credit Suisse."

"Okay, that's not good," Rune replied. "Show me."

They walked a few steps to the wall maps, stopping in front of the one offering a top-down view of Manhattan.

Kendra placed her finger on the intersection representing the incident.

"Here's where they came out. Nobody is sure where they came from."

Both intel professionals looked more closely at the different colors of subway lines on the map. The green line representing the Four-Five-Six subway ran south all the way downtown, directly past the bank. One stop was only a few blocks away, literally named "Wall Street."

"Yeah, not good at all." Rune repeated.

He looked back over at Jones, who was still staring at the little subway symbol next to the map icon for Bank of the Americas.

"You have reached the personal voicemail of Captain Dominguez, commanding Precinct One of the New York Police Department. Please leave a com—"

Smith grimaced, disconnected and hit another speed dial number.

"Office of Emergency Management for New York City, how many I direct your call?" a nasal voice answered on the second ring.

"Commissioner Kohn please, this is Tom Smith from Bank of the Americas."

"Iyamvereesorrysir," singsonged the admin. "Is the commissioner expecting your call?"

Smith almost snarled an answer, but constrained himself to a simple, "Yes."

Several heartbeats later Kohn came on.

"Mr. Smith."

"Ms. Kohn," Tom said without preamble, "we have a situation. Are you aware of the bank and contractor involved shooting, with casualties, during an encounter with a very large group of infected earlier today?"

"I am aware," Kohn said.

"I'd like to call a short notice meeting for all of the cartel players in two hours," Tom said. "I would prefer it be at the Elevated Acre. Given tensions and the implications of the zombie count on Lexington I prefer a bit more space to see threats coming."

Smith really didn't want to be in a conference room unarmed, again, when someone turned.

"Understood," Kohn replied after a moment's thought.

"Reaching to Matricardi next," Smith continued, his staccato delivery betraying both his haste and shift to "operational" mode. "Haven't been able to connect to Captain Dominguez. Are you in communication with him at this time?"

"I am not in communication with Captain Dominguez." Tom could make out tapping in the background as Kohn continued. "I believe that he is now unacceptably unreliable. The acting deputy mayor has informed me that he will be at the meeting that you referenced. I have intelligence that the shooting may have been part of a botched attempt to build a stronger set of ties to Overture. A plan already in motion."

Tom stopped dead in his mental tracks. While the original four cartel members had edged around the topic of police control being diluted by additional relationships, Kohn was clearly signaling the possibility of something more dire.

"Joanna, I need a plain answer," Tom said, slowing down. The answer to this question could signal the end and his knuckles whitened on the phone handset. "Is the NYPD still supporting the cartel agreement?"

"The answer to that question is provably up in the air, Tom," Joanna said calmly. If she was nervous, it wasn't apparent from her voice. "Were you aware of another infected related contractor shooting on the West Side?"

"If you mean the three dead Overture goons, then yes, I was aware," Tom replied. "Unless there was another on top of that. Some of my people found the bodies. We recovered items. Specifically, tarot cards. Ring a bell, Joanna?"

There was silence on the line for several long moments. Tom let her have them.

"I see the connection," Kohn said. Apparently, her assessment matched his. "If we lose Dominguez and the leadership of the core Manhattan precincts, I will neither control the vaccine production nor protection for some critical city services. This becomes end game. Find Dominguez or his second."

"I have Tangarelli," Tom said, working to stay as calm as Kohn sounded. "He's trying to reach his boss. The problem is that Overture is not going accept the murder of his teams. He's got to respond in order to keep his own organization under control. Expect something to pop at the meeting. I gotta go. Find Dominguez."

"Tom. If I can not keep the police onside, we either complete the evacuation procedures, or we are likely to lose the ability to leave the island," Kohn responded. "I kept our bargain. Will you?"

Smith didn't like her. But he had made the deal. "Yes."

The BERT prep room was full of banter, some music and a generally relaxed feeling. Smith's security team relaxed when they felt in control, and the operations had been proceeding well, although there had been a strange drop off in collections given the increase in reported infected.

Oldryskya's phone rang. She looked at the caller ID and walked outside the BERT team room where the crews were performing maintenance on personal gear and generally waiting around for the evening mission brief.

In the hallway, she picked up.

"Khabayeva."

"Boss says to come back to the office." The Cosa Nova lieutenant didn't waste time. "Shit's going down."

"Define?" Oldryskya said.

"There is a big powwow happening this afternoon between the banks, the cops and the businessmen." Tradittore sounded a little excited, his words coming fast. "One of the banks shot up an Overture team, or some shit. Something next to fifty zombies came out of the subway. Overture is pissed, the banks are pissed and everyone is freaking out about the zombies."

"I heard," Risky replied. "But it wasn't fifty, was maybe three dozen, and it was the Overture team that shot first."

"Are you listening?" the gangster said, irritated. "Does it matter? The boss said to shake your ass and get the fuck back to the office. Period. Go ahead and argue, be late. I'd like to see what he does to you."

The connection broke, and she looked at her phone for a moment. Could she stay here? Would they even have her? She could hear the laughter coming from the team room.

Oldryskya took off the loaner plate carrier, leaned it against the hallway wall, and headed for the elevators.

Paul stood with Kaplan and Durante while Tom sat on the edge of his desk, facing his remaining department heads. Between the implications of a large zombie cluster, the fall off in reliable intel and the knowledge that things seemed to be coming to a head—Paul didn't feel too guilty about being on edge. Kaplan and Durante were relaxed, as usual.

"I set up the cartel meet at the Elevated Acre," Smith began. "We can see for miles there. Things are delicate right now. There is a power play happening in the PD, and I don't know if our cops are going to come out on top. Those tarot cards you found point to some of Dominguez's crew, or Dominguez personally, killing Overture's team. Overture isn't going to overlook that and I expect him to make a play—take the bigger and better deal that he has offered on the other side of the East River and pitch it to the current interim assistant deputy mayor."

"What *is* the play, Boss?" Rune asked as Tom's pause lingered.

Smith shook his head, lost in thought for a moment.

"Bateman isn't ready to pull the handle," Tom said, gesturing at a wall covered in status reports. "The Fed, the NYSE etc.—they are still functioning, after a fashion. We have reports that the city is supposed to get an additional large National Guard contingent. Maybe we can hold another week. Maybe that's enough. Maybe."

He faced the window.

"Doesn't matter. We don't pull yet. So, we're going to have to ride out the meeting, regardless."

"Overture's guys are loaded for bear, Tom," Paul objected. "We've got credible firsthand reports that they are running belt-feds in addition to rifles. They also have a lot more teams than we do, at least a dozen, maybe more. If they want to focus us down at the meeting, they can."

The tall Australian kept looking out the window while Paul asked the question.

"I don't really expect Overture to initiate open hostilities against us, yet," Tom said. "I think that he knows it wasn't the banks that killed his team. But."

He turned to face them again.

"Gravy, remember that Marine general in Iraq... Morris, Mattingly, something like that. You said he was the only Marine you met you could see working with. Recall what he used to say?"

"'Be polite, be professional and have a plan to kill everyone you meet,'" Durante quoted. "Wasn't the first guy to say that, but that the one?"

"That's the one," Tom said, turning back to the window. "Set it up."

∽ ⊖ ∽

"This feels like a setup, Boss," Copley said, looking at the depressing scenery in Manhattan. "It's a lot worse than I expected."

The city traffic was slow, even though the number of vehicles was down, even compared to suburban Newburgh, where Battery A was located. Despite reduced overall volume compared to before the Plague, the number of roadblocks and checkpoints made up for it. Accidents had been bulldozed onto the sidewalk to keep traffic lanes clear, and the soldiers could see entire blocks cordoned off by concertina wire and gas-mask-equipped cops armed with rifles.

Pozzo had waited in vain for the rest of the battery to show, and eventually decided to push into the City. Copley drove, but the XO kept Astroga in his HMMWV to help navigate the still congested city. They also had an NYPD cop.

"What's with all the VCPs, Private?" he asked Astroga.

"Mostly to show the flag, let the civilians see that we're here, you know sir," replied the private. "Sometimes they see someone about to turn and they help restrain them till the cops or one of the contractors shows up to take them off our hands."

"Contractors?" Copley asked, sniffing. The windows were permanently up on this model of HMMWV but the smell of smoke drifted in through the firing cupola.

"Left at da next block," the ride-along cop said in a thick Brooklyn accent, before answering Copley's question himself. "Army AR-OH-EE iz still less than lethal. The depahtment and some contractors we highyed are da actual baggehs and taggehs. The contractahs call demselves Bialahgical Emergency Response

Units—BUHRTS—an' dey take any zombies offa aw hands and transport dem to da Handling Fahcility, see."

"Baggas and taggas?" Copley followed up, struggling to understand the cop's speech. "Baggers and taggers? Oh."

"What do they do with them?" asked Pozzo, drawn into the conversation. "The zombies, that is."

"Yeah, dat's wuhna da questions youse learn not t'ask," replied the cop. "Right on Tird Av, we're goin' north."

"So how bad is it, really?" asked Copley, as they were waved by another VCP manned by two soldiers, backed by another uniformed policeman. The trio managed to look simultaneously grim and bored.

"'Feecially, da toin around iz raht around da corner," replied the cop. "Un-offeecially, da numbah cops not comin' back to work every week iz going up. Da city has some vaccine, but it's unofficial. Stickin' 'round to gettit iza big reason dat we got cops left, at all."

"Vaccine? You get vaccine?" Copley said, sniffing some more and looking at a scorched low-rise building. "Man, there sure are a lot of burned-up buildings."

"Yeah, well, the firefighters don't have the same deal as the cops," Astroga spoke up. "And we don't either. TOC is up here a couple more blocks."

CHAPTER 12

"I don't understand why you are so convinced that existing viruses can't be weaponized. Your finest specialists are convinced that it's just too hard to make a reliable weapon that can be made stable enough for storage yet hardy enough to survive delivery in a shell or bomb. I keep telling you, I've already done it!"

—Cold War–era Soviet defector, as translated
during debriefing in an undisclosed location

From: *Angels and Devils: The Practical Response to H7D3*,
David Curry, M.D., Ph.D.,
University of the South Press 2055

Paul didn't have a military background. Intelligence analysts, however skilled, have a lot more in common with the average financial services broker than with line troops, or even military cooks. Intellectually, he understood that his skills were best suited to what was actually an important part of the overall success of the bank's crisis response to date: gathering information, placing it into context for decision makers and more recently, managing the Security Operations Center, or SOC.

That didn't keep him from wishing that he could contribute a little more directly.

Inside the darkened SOC he could see the meeting on the Acre taking shape on the various video feeds shared by the city. Known to him but not readily visible were three teams placed by Durante. They had taken the really large equipment cases from the ad hoc armory and most of the picked security staff and set up in a few different places, including at least one rooftop overlooking the meeting location. A skeleton crew of security staff remained at the bank proper.

His job was to keep his watch standers alert for obvious signs that Overture was going to "go kinetic" at the meeting. *Kinetic* was popularly used by the military brass during the Second Gulf War to refer to operations that made loud noises, blew up buildings and shredded people. It preserved a false sense of precision and neatness, by design, falling into the same category of labels such as "surgical strike" and "smart bomb."

Kinetic events tended to end up pretty damn messy.

Paul agreed with Tom, though. If the remaining city bureaucrats and cops showed, the Jamaican should be disinclined to start a shootout. Overture seemed to be playing a long game whose timeline was even more protracted than that of the banks.

Named for the largest privately owned public space in the City, the Elevated Acre was originally a scheme between the builder and the city to allow the consolidation of four adjoining city blocks in downtown Manhattan. More acreage equaled more profit. Who couldn't get behind that? The resulting building, though only some fifty stories tall, was one of the largest office buildings in the world, with as many square feet as the much newer Liberty Tower. The large outdoor space was set forty feet above street level and featured low landscaping and generous views along the perimeter streets and across the East River, which was just across FDR Drive.

On screen, Paul watched the various delegations

congregate on the upper deck. Noting the police caravan, he keyed the desk microphone and spoke directly to the on-site personnel equipped with earpieces.

"Okay, the cops are pulling up," Rune said, counting units. "Five cars. The ground party is under ten, they are leaving a significant group with the vehicles." Paul used the optical zoom feature on the mast mounted camera to scan faces closely.

"I don't see Dominguez. Looks like the third or fourth guy to hold a deputy chief spot, instead. Only light arms in view."

A few double clicks on the speaker informed him that Smith, Durante, their team leads and drivers were all hearing him clearly.

Oldryskya wasn't wearing the tactical outfit that she had come to prefer. The decision was not hers.

"You don't need body armor and boots," was Tradittore's least profane comment. "Put on something nice. I don't want anyone thinking that we have a thing for cop chicks."

Matricardi had endorsed his objections. Neither had ever been aware of the details of her experience prior to leaving Central Asia and neither particularly cared about the recent polish applied by the BotA's security team.

The late summer sun kept the rooftop park from being too chilly, but the thin material of her cocktail dress combined with the breeze off the river wasn't helping. She remained in character, playing the part of the dumb bimbo. It let her ignore Tradittore, who so far had managed to spend most of his time leering. She wasn't going to give him the satisfaction of seeing just how much that made her skin crawl.

On the roof of the Acre, matters developed quickly.

Risky had been to her share of meetings, but none had devolved as rapidly as this one. Overture's goons began pointing fingers at the team from MetBank, whose BERT had tangled with both a very large number of infected and Overture's BERT early in the day. The kicker was a moment later.

Tom Smith knew that his team was on overwatch. It didn't stop him from feeling like he was missing something, somewhere.

During their last call Kohn had connected him to the mayor's office. The current deputy assistant was on point for the meeting. Nominally three levels down the hierarchy, he was the seniormost official who remained in the city. He wasn't particularly delighted with the situation either, and was happy to have Smith kick things off.

Tom heard Rune's commentary, and he heard Durante check in with his teams' status. Since Tom had been the one to call the meeting, it was his to start.

"Everyone, please take your seats," Tom said. "I have talked to His Honor the Deputy Assistant Mayor Sphalos, and he has graciously allowed me to expedite this meeting. There will be only two agenda items, a summary of the MetBank and Overture BERT response on 96th and Lex and a discussion on what we are going to do differently to ensure further safe operations. The term the U.S. military uses is 'deconfliction.' We need to smooth things out on the subject of the encounter and ensure we don't conflict in a similar manner again."

He had planned to skip the usual preliminaries in order to get straight to the point. Immediately after his introduction the general yelling and mob scene started. Everyone was tense and everyone started shouting and pointing fingers at once. That wouldn't do.

He moved his microphone closer to one of the speakers mounted to the forward edge of the table, generating painful squeals of feedback.

"There will be a complete discussion of the tactical situation, the Rules of Engagement and discussion on asset territory," he said, looking around the table. "That does NOT mean a shouting match. As the largest financial services BERT operator here, may I confirm that this agenda suits Mr. Overture. Sir?"

He looked straight at Overture, who was frowning at the painfully loud sound.

"Sure, sure," he said. The big Jamaican was digging unproductively in one ear with a spatulate finger. "As long as you get clear on why da fuck there so many zombi and why my boys got shot!" At the mention of the shootings, more yelling started in Overture's group, quickly matched by MetBank and other groups.

More amplified feedback.

"Fuck, stop yelling already!" yelled Overture. This time it sounded a little more heartfelt, and his group instantly quieted, followed eventually by the rest.

Tom allowed himself a single, internal smile.

Ah, there we go, back on track.

Paul kept scanning the group, which was adding people even as the meeting started. The rooftop was about as full as they expected. He saw a number of people clap their hands over their ears just as the slightly delayed audio of distorted feedback sounded in his headset. Paul smiled. He had seen Smith use the same technique during a testy Occupy protest.

He counted the number of people in each delegation. Overture's group was nearly as large as the rest of the meeting, combined. He passed that along on the shared channel.

The pan-tilt-zoom camera that he was using was really good.

"Hey Durante," Paul said as he double-checked a familiar face in Matricardi's little group. "I spotted your buddy Khabayeva. She is back to playing for her team. I think that I like this outfit better than I liked the one that you picked out for her."

"You see her?" Durante came back right away.

"Yep," Paul said. "Third row, behind Matricardi. Next to the guy with the suspiciously large exercise bag hanging from his shoulder. Which he has declined to set down."

"Ah. Yep. Copy. She doesn't look happy."

Kaplan was with Smith.

"Could we spend more time on the 'suspiciously large bag,' please?" he asked.

"Don't get your tits in an uproar, Kap." Durante's laconic voice both reassured and irritated Paul. "There are at least three guys in that meeting carrying bags big enough and heavy enough to be holding a belt-fed. Each of them is going to be dropped in the first quarter second if someone starts a drama."

"Wait," Kaplan commed. "Did you guys catch that?"

By prearrangement, Tom asked the MetBank Chief Security Officer to give a short rundown on the incident that had yielded massive numbers of infected. The CSO didn't get very far before objections and profanity from Overture's contingent drowned him out. One stood up and started yelling, but sat again when a more dapper man stood and addressed the crowd.

"We are sure sorry that one of MetBank's people got shot," the well-dressed ganger said reasonably. "I used to work there, I know those guys. But you know, I am even sorrier that I lost *two* good men because the MetBank BERT couldn't and wouldn't coordinate their operations, although I tried to talk to their lead several times."

Tom recognized a pitch when he heard one. This wasn't a spur of the moment speech. The Overture man continued.

"I am sorry that their team lead, standing right there, had one of her boys, also standing right there, put a bullet in the head of one of mine, without checking the diagnosis of infection," the gangster continued. "I am sorry that their lack of capacity placed everyone at risk. The good news is that we are ready to completely coordinate and 'deconflict' the city wide BERT management."

"Boss, the guy speaking and waving his hands is Gutierrez." In his ear Tom heard Rune's calm voice. "Army vet and the tactical brains behind Overture's BERT organization. Used to work at MetBank. I think we are about to hear the real reason that Overture looks so smug."

Tom nodded his head as if acknowledging the speaker. Several others tried to drown Gutierrez out.

"No, please, let him finish," Smith said after he overrode them with the microphone. "Everyone just hold on for the moment. Mr. Gutierrez, please continue."

∽ ⊖ ∾

"I don't see Dominguez," Matricardi whispered to Tradittore. "Do you know the cop next to the guys from the mayor's office?"

"No," Tradittore replied, scanning from side to side. "I don't see Kohn, either. If Smith wasn't sitting there, as exposed as we are, I would say that this is a setup."

Khabayeva agreed. Their little group was far outnumbered. She was scanning the crowd and briefly looked at Smith. She couldn't tell if he recognized her or not. She rather hoped that he hadn't, but the impossibility of her situation prevented her from even articulating why that was.

In front of her, Matricardi palpably stiffened. Tradittore spoke a single phrase under his breath.

"Porca troia!" He must have keyed his radio because his next comments were even lower, but distinct. "Ralph—get the car running. Georgie—be ready with the big gun. I think we are going to be leaving in a hurry."

She snapped her attention back to the meeting. One of Overture's goons was talking now.

"Our organization will oversee and coordinate all the BERT efforts," Gutierrez continued. "We can embed NYPD observers from the NYSI into our operation center to provide top oversight."

"We recognize that we have been harvesting more... raw materials for the critically needed medicines that all of our organizations and indeed the entire city must have. We propose to sell your companies up to thirty percent of our total production at cost if we can directly manage *all* of the BERTs and are given access to the facilities *and* staff at Mt. Sinai."

Tom didn't let his alarm show on his face. If the NYPD agreed, then it was the end of the cartel, or at least of the bank's ability to steer it. It also meant the loss of control over their own teams.

Not good.

Outwardly, Tom remained relaxed and replied. It was time to end the meeting, which had spun entirely out of his control.

"That's a very interesting offer, and provides a lot of things for us all to think about," he said with a polite nod directed towards Overture. "However, speaking for the financial services groups now present and for those whose proxies we hold, I think we need a day to confer with our regional officers and respond authoritatively."

Overture agreed and waved expansively even as other teams protested. Tom picked out one manager that he knew and tried to reassure him. He really wanted to hear what Overture was saying to the mayoral contingent, but missed most of what was said.

The details might not matter as much as what seemed clear. Overture was in. The cartel was out.

He spoke into his radio.

"Gravy, as soon as we get back in the car and roll, break down the teams and get back to the barn."

"Look, Sergeant, I'm ready to get out there," Astroga said. "And you're down two guys. I need to get outta this TOC," she added, referring to the Tactical Operations Center that was surrounded by tall sandbag and concrete barriers.

"I know that I'm a seventy-three Lima," she added. "But I've got the soul of an eleven Bravo."

Copley and his depleted team were thirteen Bravos, which was Army speak for artillery specialists. Astroga was a clerk-typist, and while Copley was willing to concede that she was the most un-clerky private that he had ever met, it was a long stretch to bringing her on a presence mission under the worsening conditions. And between a few unexplained absences and yesterday's casualty, they were shorthanded...

"Who got you guys the best rooms at the Hyatt?" asked Astroga, pursuing her perceived advantage. "Who kept colonel whatshisname from dragging your team even further uptown by losing the paperwork and radio traffic? Who scrounged up some extra ammo?"

"All right, Astroga, all right." Copley was tired. "You can come. But you stay close to Randall, see? And you keep your chamber empty and don't shoot anything unless he or I say to shoot. Got it?"

"You got it, Sarge!" Astroga said happily. She pulled a partially rigged plate carrier out from behind her desk while Copley stomped out.

In the background, Randall grinned. He had been sharpening his personal knife, working on the oversized blade with a funny bend in the middle. Randall had previously defended his preference for an honest-to-god Himalayan kukri, winning every argument with his sergeant. As a result, he had a good sense for Copley's temper and patience and had seen noncom's capitulation coming from a mile away. Some days it was good to be part of the E-4 mafia with none of the headaches of a sergeant.

"Hey Specialist Randall, how many mags do you think I should carry?" the irrepressible private asked. "Three or six? I've only got three."

"'I brought too many bullets,' said no one ever," replied Randall. He fished around in the large para bag at his feet and slid four more magazines over to her before returning to his chore. "One extra to keep in your rifle."

"How are you carrying your CamelBak?" Astroga went on, referring to the water bladder with a drinking tube that troops could use while staying in motion, without fiddling with a belt canteen and pouch. "Is it worth the weight?"

"Ditch the shoulder straps and clip it directly to the back of your carrier," Randall said, stropping his knife, still smiling. "If I don't need it, I can dump it. After ammo, water is the second thing that you can't have too much of."

The private began manipulating her rig before bothering Randall again.

"You got any extra MOLLE clips?" she asked, pronouncing the word for the Army's standardized attachment system like the common girl's name.

Randall dipped back into his bag and tossed Astroga a ziplock filled with black plastic clips.

Astroga shoved magazines into the pouches on the front of her carrier before fiddling quietly with the back of her plate carrier and her drinking bladder. Next she looked at her issue bayonet, which was much shorter than the kukri that the larger man was honing. Then she looked back to Randall. Her eyes gleamed.

"Hey, Randall, can I borrow your knife?"

Randall suspended smiling instantly.

"No."

"No, I *can't* suspend at this time, Tom," Bateman said, frowning.

Richard Bateman was torn.

He trusted his managing director for security. Tom had been right to initiate Zeus when he called and Bateman, now, knew it had been...unwise to throw Tom to the sharks instead of supporting the security decision. And he knew that the situation had gone from bad to worse. Everybody knew that even if they didn't have the details.

Still, the bank was running. The entire system was still lurching along. He had his own contacts in the government. Just last spring he had hosted both New York senators to a very nice sit down at Per Se, where table reservations ran out weeks in advance. Just this week, that same pair and others in a position to know assured him that the CDC was on top of a vaccine that didn't involve "processing higher-order primates."

He hadn't shared the fact that he already had a vaccine, of course.

Still, the extra National Guard troops, the relatively smoothly functioning backup trading sites, the manageable drops in the major indexes—things were still survivable. Not good, mind you. But not apocalyptical.

"Rich, it's time to go." Tom Smith replied, making it plain that he didn't agree. "We no longer have visibility into what City Hall is going to do next. We can surmise that Overture has the whip hand and is in control, or about to be in control, of both the remaining police and the National Guard. That means they will control access to roads, rivers and heliports. If they salvage the situation, which I don't think is likely, then I don't want us to be the public example they make for 'bad guy who made a vaccine.' Someone else can have that honor."

He grinned, the wry expression suddenly taking years off of his age.

"And if they don't salvage the situation in time to prevent a complete break, then I still don't want to be caught in the city without an assured way out.

"Either way, *we* don't want to be here."

"What do you recommend?" Bateman said thoughtfully. "I mean, the details."

"We do this per plan, in phases," Smith replied. "The last noncritical staff, such as had stayed, were released on paid leave last week. All remaining personnel move out of Manhattan and Jersey City and immediately shift to a combination of the two complete refuges and the alternate trading sites. The remaining market volume can be handled from the those two, anyhow. Tomorrow we pull the handle, and you, the family, the remaining leadership and staff all get out."

"Are you *sure*?" the CEO said, still pensive. "Because, Tom, you need to be *really* sure. I look out the window, and sure there are fires, but not any more than I remember from last week, or the week before that. I am still reading fresh copy from the NYT and the FT. Most importantly, the Fed hasn't issued an official caution yet."

He referred to the U.S. Federal Reserve, which was part of the government system that oversaw financial markets based in the United States. During times of crisis, the "Fed" could suspend markets temporarily. During periods of expected interruption due to extreme weather, for example, they could issue a "caution" that they might intervene in normal trading as the result of an emergency.

Smith shook his head decisively and pointed out the window, where the glow of a large fire was visible, miles away on Staten Island.

"Rich, that fire has been burning for *three days*," Tom said, dropping his hand to his side. "It looks the same cause it's slowly consuming half of Staten Island. No one in City Hall is even mentioning that it exists. If we tried to get a Gold call it's even money that the secure phone bridge wouldn't hold because telecoms are screwed. The CDC updates have been a cut and paste job for the last two weeks. The National Guard commander went back to Albany 'for consultations' and the local deputy has withdrawn his troops from anything but 'presence patrols' near their laagers. What else do you need to know?"

Rich Bateman could sense that his man Smith began to push the discussion and then deliberately paused. This was his first time dealing with "Train" Smith in full "go" mode. While he watched, Smith appeared to reach an internal decision and picked up a red intelligence binder.

"Boss, the few sources of information that we retain will be gone in a day or three," he said, dropping the binder on the table, making a slapping sound. "Those sources of information drive our ability to monitor the expiration date of the very expensive evacuation option that the bank has purchased. I can guarantee that tomorrow I'll still have access to the means for us to evacuate. The day after, I can't. Using the option now costs you a little margin. If you wait, the option will expire, and that could cost us *everything*."

Bateman listened carefully, his hands steepled in front of him. He looked out the window too, and noted the same fire that Smith had highlighted.

"Point," Bateman said with a sigh. Even from a distance of several miles, the fire was bright enough to leave a mirage on his eyes when he looked away. "It would be stupid to have invested in all the risk controls and then fail to use them. I'll notify the board members tonight and recommend immediate and total withdrawal from Manhattan. We'll maintain operations from the recovery sites and be ready to move back right away if things improve. We leave tomorrow morning. What's the term you use? 'Pull the handle'?"

He looked back to Smith, who seemed perceptibly more relaxed with the decision made.

"What are your plans for your last night in New York?" Bateman added.

"Faith, my niece, is out of the woods." Tom actually smiled. "I plan to send her family back tonight. They're evacuating independently."

"The staff call her the 'zombie killer.'" Rich grinned broadly, his mood mirroring that of his subordinates. "The picture of the dead basement zombies would have been hilarious if they weren't our own staff. Anything you want, give them a sendoff on us."

"Thanks Rich," Tom said, heading to the exit. He paused at the door. "She's been saying that she feels recovered enough to want to eat something. I thought that the bank could stand to buy her family a nice dinner. I know a good restaurant that's still open. Hell, there's even a regular concert in Washington Square Park..."

∽ ⊖ ∾

The dark bedroom smelled of cigar smoke, even though Matricardi had quit lighting up in his private rooms months ago, after she complained about the smell permeating her clothes and hair. He liked to read, so bookshelves lined the wall. Biographies and history mostly. Initially, Oldryskya had been surprised to see that the head of the Cosa Nova was a bibliophile. She was horrified to learn that he routinely annotated his volumes and worse, the better or more important the book, the more he scribbled in the margins. She learned that he regarded the books as tools, nothing more.

"They're just books, not the Grail," he answered when early in their relationship she mustered the courage to ask him to stop defacing them. "I don't keep them because they are special—I keep them because the knowledge in them is something I can use."

Still, the wide variety of books provided a riot of color on the wall and a nice contrast to the usual gangster furnishings.

Somewhat like Oldryskya herself, who was watching her boss and sometime lover. He was alternating between a book and glancing over at his computer, occasionally clicking on his browser.

She broke a long silence.

"You don't seem as worried now as you were at the meeting."

He looked up at her from under his brow, then back to his computer.

"Well, it would be a lot harder for Overture or his new friends in Manhattan to hit me now, wouldn't it?"

"If Overture has control and we can't stop the disease, we should be talking about getting out, no?" That seemed the logical question to Oldryskya.

"Look, missy," Matricardi said tightly. "I told you to leave the thinking to me." He looked up again and smiled to take the sting out of the mild rebuke. "You did all right with the bank guys. Not your fault that Overture was smarter and luckier than our guys on the force. I figure Dominguez is gonna get hit tonight, and Kohn with him. Smith will be all right for now, but Overture will get around to making an example of someone, maybe Smith, maybe someone else. But I think he's right. This disease? We can beat it. What's pretty handy is how it's really screwing the big boys. We can still use that."

They hadn't slept together in months so she wasn't in his bedroom as often as she used to be. Still, he genuinely seemed to like her company. That extended to indulging her questions as long as she didn't make him lose face, or his temper.

"So, what's our play?"

He didn't look up this time, but talked while he clicked.

"We are going to have the ports, the medical companies, a bit of manufacturing and lot of the food here in Jersey," Matricardi said. "Tradittore has been a great help with that—college kids have their uses. Once the city government is completely broken, Overture's boys still can't push across the river. They will have to deal with us. Manhattan ain't got nothing for production or food. Everything has to come in, *capisce*? Which means coming from *us*. Meanwhile, I'll keep consolidating south. Atlantic City, anyone?"

"You seem pretty confident that we can brush everything else out of the way," Risky said, ticking off the list of other players. "What about governor, military . . . ?"

"You see them around anywhere?" he said with a chuckle. "They have their own problems, starting with not getting vaccine in time. Oh, there will be a military, but they are going to work with us, and Port Elizabeth, and Newark PD and whoever else they have to. But we'll win. Boy scouts aren't going to make it through this plague, and the ones that do, they'll either deal or lose."

"I don't think Smith can give up," Risky pointed out carefully. "He has good people and preparation. Is more prepared than a *boy scout*."

Matricardi sat up so he could look her straight in the face.

"Oldryskya, you and me, we're not so different," Matricardi said, lowering the lid of his notebook a few inches. "I had to scratch and claw to get this far. You wouldn't have made it to the point where that asshole tried to sell you to me unless you were a survivor too. Smith? He is a college boy in a bank. And if he ain't? He works for a college boy. And you know what? Most college kids from good homes will lose their first real fight against anyone who isn't another college kid. They're still thinking in terms of limits, what's going to get them in trouble, worrying about getting a good GPA and avoiding a criminal record."

Matricardi chopped the air, gesturing decisively.

"The first ex-con that they swing on has already given all that up. He could kill them in two shakes, if he wants. Overture, he's the con. He's already playing beneath street rules, let alone *banker* rules. Smith's still thinking about honoring deals with the cops on the losing side even though he knows that the situation is dicey. Mark my words, Overture's gonna move against everyone in Manhattan who he hasn't already recruited, and soon. He will gobble up all the college kids who ain't directly useful. At least my college kids are out. They decided to set themselves up down south. Smart kids."

He held her gaze and then his inbox chimed, catching his attention.

Oldryskya got off the bed and walked over to his desk, her long nightgown swaying. A year ago, Matricardi would have paused and watched her. Now, he was preoccupied or indifferent.

Or both.

She laid a hand on his desk.

"How would you do it?"

"Ah, lotsa ways you could do it," he said, waving a hand idly, side to side, as though he were painting a wall. "You need an excuse to really drop the hammer, and you need to give the people who don't particularly like you something else to fear, which they have—zombies, you know? And you gotta give them something to hate. All I'd do is find a way to give them someone to hate more than me. Turn them against each other."

"So why don't you do it, then?" Oldryskya said, a touch angry. "You can be the strong one, can rebuild the city or help defend it. I've scratched in the dirt to live and this"—she gestured around the room—"is a lot better!"

He paused and sighed, setting down the book and taking off his glasses.

"I'm one to talk about boy scouts," he said, maybe a touch rueful. "I got limits too. There's a reason why I killed that prick what was selling you girls. Life is cheap, but everyone has a bottom and I know what mine is. I deal in a lot of merchandise, an' I ain't no angel—but Frank Matricardi don't sell people. Kill 'em? Sure. But selling women and kids, hurting them? Nah. I ain't a fucking animal. This crew ain't gonna touch that shit, long as I am breathing.

"Just chopping people up gives me the stomach, you know?" he continued, looking off into the distance. "Overture's going to move. When he moves, a lot of the boy scouts are going to die. Maybe I've still got limits there, too. Just killing the boy scouts won't be enough to take control. You gotta target *families*, too.

"Smith, he's got family. His brother, his nieces. He cares about them. You don't threaten *Smith*, you threaten that *family*. And if threats don't work, they gotta be offed, and offed messy and public, so the next guy knows you're serious. All you been through, Risky, you won't want to be one of those girls when Overture gets aholt of them.

"It ain't actually moral or nothin' but I'll let Overture do that work. That guy, he's got *no* limits. Then we make a place for ourselves. Keep things mostly running while the disease burns out. By the time Overture realizes we've got the real cards, the bio-corporations, the food, the water, hell, the fuel, he needs, we'll be in a position to take him if he can't deal. And my boys won't have to be the ones killing the families. That'll already be done for us."

His smile gleamed, contrasting with the shadow of blue-black stubble.

"Now do you mind? I got shit to do. Read or do something, willya?"

Oldryskya watched him work for a few moments

longer. She knew a little more than she let on. As a young girl, she had watched what happened to the states of the old Soviet Union when central control failed. Allegiances could switch overnight. Some who kept the faith overlong stood to lose all the money they thought they had saved. Some lost even more.

Like her foster father.

While she worked at Bank of the Americas, Smith's staff had been gently probed by Overture's agents, ready to offer a bigger and better deal to anyone who might waver. The subtle inquiries had all been rejected and reported, as far as she knew.

But.

The meeting at the Elevated Acre was a setup. Overture knew too much. Someone in City Hall, someone among Dominguez's cops or someone in the cartel had taken the deal. Maybe all three?

Risky continued to watch her boss scroll and click. Tabbing between reports, e-mail and pay ledgers.

Big Mac Overture paid well. He could afford to recruit anyone with a price. The deputy assistant mayor and the deputy chief didn't think of it that way of course. They were still thinking about his supply of vaccine, the number of BERTs he operated, the security he had claimed to have brought to Queens and eastern Brooklyn. Lastly, they were favorably impressed by the surprisingly informed professional proposal to operate from hospitals and mass produce vaccine.

Presented in familiar terms by an erudite MBA with experience on Wall Street, it connected them to the "old" way of business.

This was not an accident.

Sure, working openly with a criminal who had

sold drugs was unusual. Weren't these unusual times? Confident that they could control the terms, they seriously considered working with Overture, on some introductory basis. Their lack of understanding of what Overture really wanted and their desperation to hold onto some familiar framework made them suggestible. Their perception of reality hadn't shifted yet.

However, their ignorance didn't change the reality. Oldryskya knew better.

She agreed with her boss's summation. She appreciated that he had limits; after all, those limits had kept her alive and unsold. Instead of working in a worsening series of cribs until she was discarded or disappeared, she had only had to service Matricardi, which rapidly became light work. She didn't love the man, but she respected what he offered, and understood how much further she could have fallen.

Her boss *and* Smith's man agreed: life is cheap.

She was pretty sure that Overture hadn't limited his outreach to just the cops and the banks. If they didn't take Smith's plan, would they be able to keep their organization together, here? Was it already too late?

Oldryskya pulled her gown a little tighter. The pistol under it suddenly seemed to weigh a great deal and behind her, Matricardi's mouse clicked occasionally.

The two cops waved their badges to the gate guard, a younger man who had joined the force only months before the crisis began.

The unmarked gray police sedan was the right model and correct color. The rookie could see a glowing NYPD mobile data terminal screen between the driver and passenger.

The car didn't stir suspicion; it was a real police car, after all. The rookie diligently looked at the credentials and matched the accompanying photo IDs to the men's faces. The badges were perfectly genuine, having previously belonged to two of New York's finest, now deceased. The IDs were genuine as well, or near as no matter, and the photos matched the car occupants perfectly.

There was no reason why they shouldn't, since the images were only a day old.

The men parked in the secure car lot and styled a relaxed saunter as they stepped across the lot and into reception. The desk sergeant barely looked up from the YouTube channel on his PC as the men ran their access cards through a magnetic reader, which chirped and obediently lit a green LED. His glance took in the suits, haircuts, creds, the issue pistol visible under one man's jacket. The other man flipped a hand in a casual wave.

Everything was normal.

The men walked past the lobby area and made as if to go into the first floor bullpen and temporary briefing rooms. As soon as they lost the interest of the desk officer, they stepped around the corridor and into the stairwell. After ascending four floors they exited into the corridor adjoining that floor's elevator.

The laser-printed sign opposite the elevator doors had an arrow pointing left and the legend DEPENDENT HOUSING. The men headed left and opened a door marked CAREGIVERS.

As they stepped inside a well-lit room whose walls were liberally covered in amateur macaroni art and rainbows, the four women inside watching TV looked up. The youngest and closest stood and smiled.

"Hello gentlemen? Are you dads? Isn't it a little late for a visit? The children are all down for the night."

The first man, obviously younger than the other, waved both hands at shoulder level in an "I surrender" pose and smiled in return.

"Not me, miss!" His grin revealed a very white and attractive smile. "I'm not even married! I am just giving my friend a ride. He wanted to look in on little Juan." The nannies in the room smiled back. What a good friend to come with his friend, the single dad. Attractive, too.

The older man looked a little bleary. He handed over his ID to the woman.

"No need to disturb the kids. I just wanted to make sure that my boy is okay. Did he do well at school today, that kind of thing. The last name is Gutierrez, and his first name is Juan. I haven't seen him for a week."

The nanny still standing replied.

"Well, let me check the summaries." She walked over to a desk whose backboard was hung about in clipboards as the others settled back down, returning to their TV program. The one holding a clipboard looked back up when she simultaneously heard a quiet *fut* and felt a sharp poke on the side of her neck.

Her mouth made a little O of surprise as the tranquilizer dart took her between the ear and shoulder. She stood stock-still for a moment and by the time she crumpled to the floor, all three remaining women were darted, the report of the compressed air pistol lost in the sound from the big screen TV.

"All right, work quick but for chrissake don't poke yourself." The older man reminded his partner. "The tranq is good for two hours. We gotta hit at least two more rooms."

Suiting actions to words, he loaded a new magazine in his tranquilizer pistol. The pneumatic system operated the weapon without recoil, but still required fresh ammunition.

"Yeah, yeah—sharps precautions, I get it." The younger man wasn't smiling anymore, but his hands were steady as he rapidly donned puncture-resistant gloves and then removed a hinged, flat black plastic case from one suit pocket. He reoriented the textured surface to maintain a better grip and then operated three small combination wheels with exquisite care. The case cracked open along the edge with an audible pop, and the man withdrew an ordinary syringe that appeared to be filled with deep red blood.

He knelt and injected the first woman's neck, neglecting to first swab it with an antiseptic. Working swiftly, he visited the other still bodies, depositing five ccs of the payload into each before replacing the empty syringe in the case next to its four full brothers.

"Let's put this one on the couch, like she is sleeping. We'll drag the others inside once we are done. And don't forget the special."

He turned to the next door, labeled CHILDREN'S DORMITORY.

Perfect.

CHAPTER 13

"Biology is technology."

—Robert H. Carlson

"This is a bad idea, Tom," Paul said. He rarely mustered the will to flat out oppose one of Smith's decisions, but this one was easy. "I strongly recommend that you not go out for dinner. Let me order in, you can treat Faith and your family to all the trimmings up on Forty-Five."

The uppermost floor of Bank of the Americas' New York City office housed the C-suite. Named for the chief executive officer, chief operating officer and all other positions starting with the letter *C*, it also commanded the best views and featured an opulent dining room.

"I promised Faith a nice dinner," Tom said. "I called ahead to Matricardi's place. Fattore himself will serve and you know that everyone there is going to be armed. As are we. Durante has security and we'll take the two armored Mercedes or the cleanest truck that we have."

His teeth flashed as he smiled a little paternally at the shorter man.

"We'll hold the fort here," Kaplan said. "Seems

like a pretty quiet night. Still planning to pull the handle tomorrow?"

"Bateman is on board," Tom said. "A lot is predicated on how the remaining board votes, but with Bateman committed, I think that it's a lock. If the Fed suspends activity, then it becomes a no-brainer. So far they are still riding it out. We can stay in the market from the alternate trading sites, and if it all goes for a ball of chalk, we'll evacuate those too."

Tom looked back at the clearly skeptical intel lead and tried to reassure him.

"No worries Paul," Tom said, his original accent drifting in. "Safe as houses."

Later, Paul would reflect on his boss's statement. He would remember everything: the chalk stripe Armani suit that he was wearing, the faint smell of the hand sanitizer that everyone was practically bathing in, even the color of the office carpet upon which they stood. He would consider Smith's optimism, the offhand confidence and that smile.

He would remember that feeling crawling up his spine and would then swear on his medal of Saint Joshua, patron saint of all intelligence officers, to never, ever ignore it again.

For the moment, he limited his response to the basics. It wasn't a CLD he was worried about. He simply recognized what Smith looked like in full "Train" mode.

"We also serve who only stay behind and monitor the VHF," he said with a dutiful smile. "I'll also keep the SOC land line clear in case you need to call in. Bring back some takeout, would you?"

∽ ⊖ ∾

Losing an argument was not entirely an unknown to Joanna. However, failing to convince the deputy assistant mayor to even temporarily defer his intent to explore the possibility of collaborating with Overture was a clear signal. She was out. The agreement between her and the actual mayor was almost two months old and for weeks he hadn't responded to e-mails or phone calls.

From anyone.

Apart from him, only a few critical OEM staff outside of Schweizer and Gauge, and of course Dominguez's cadre of loyal Manhattan based police officers, no one else was briefed on both the origin of the vaccine and her role in producing it. However, Joanna was a master of detecting shifts in the political winds.

And they had shifted. That meant someone was going to be the designated victim. Since it wasn't Joanna's hand steering the new course for the City, she had to assume that she herself was at risk.

Rather than attend the Overture-led meeting, she had moved her personal coterie out of the secure housing area and into a new apartment, even though they had to leave many of their things behind. Her own information analyst had delivered a stunning update on the situation in Washington D.C. and other capitals.

Although there was still a federal government issuing communications, the basis for economic activity had effectively ground to a halt. His sources suggested that unknown even to the banks, the Fed was going to suspend activity while major trading operations were relocated away from the large cities. The number of commercial aircraft still flying had dropped to less than five percent of normally scheduled flights. Where flights still operated, there was no Federal security apparatus visible.

She had actually found a sliver of humor in the thought that the blue gloved goons of the Transportation Security Agency were gone.

Tomorrow she would ask Smith to accept her remaining staff for immediate transport, right after she gave him the nonpublic information regarding the Fed's plans.

That should do it.

The desk sergeant looked up when he heard the first scream echo from the stairwell. He was well trained and decisive, so his first action was to activate external door locks, securing the physical envelope of the building from outside infiltration. The second, louder scream convinced him that this wasn't a drill, prompting activation of the building security alarm.

That woke everyone up.

On the fifth floor, where groups with at least one parent shared converted offices, adults jerked awake. Off-duty cops armed themselves and looked for the source of the emergency.

A twelve-year veteran with two small kids of his own stepped into the center hallway and, hearing screaming from the stairwell, cracked the door in order to see its origin.

His eyes opened and he hesitated for a single, fatal moment before he raised his pistol. His wife, who had followed him as far as the lobby door watched as the door appeared to open the rest of the way by itself. Small figures, some in the remnants of pajamas, swarmed out of the stairwell, knocking the policeman down.

His pistol sounded twice, but the first zombie to reach him fixed its teeth in his throat and started shaking back and forth hard enough to jerk the man around on the tile floor. The infected was joined by several others. His wife echoed the earlier screams as she saw her husband literally dismembered in front her. Scores of children, some keening, some growling, pelted towards the first person they saw.

She flattened herself against the door, as though to bar it with her arms. Her own children were behind it.

She survived her husband by less than a minute.

The door to the next sleeping area was breached well before that.

The staff in the Security Operation Center for Bank of the Americas had joked among themselves that once the head of security and his nieces went to dinner, his intelligence chief would keep his hand physically on the land-line handset, the better to instantly call his boss if the security situation changed.

That was a base canard. At some points during the evening, Paul Rune was as much as thirty feet from the command desk and its hotline to the boss. Which was the distance to the nearest bathroom.

The truth was that duty in the darkened SOC was boring. The usual twenty-four-hour news feeds had been reporting the same slow moving zombie crisis for weeks. Even the large flatscreens that allowed watch standers to click from viewpoint to viewpoint within the city were boring when there wasn't much activity to monitor.

In addition to the shared video take from the Domain Awareness System, or DAM, Paul kept an eye on the aggregate bank building video feed and one ear cocked to the three different BERT related channels where the different units operated by the banks and contractors coordinated, reporting on collection numbers, street hazards and other routine matters.

He paused and held his hand up as a panicked voice sounded on the desk speaker.

"Any unit, this is MetBank Zero Three. We are at Union Square with three infected in the back. We have three Overture trucks boxing us in, and lighting us with spots. Need immediate support!"

A few transmissions blanketed each other, but Paul heard a clear reply from another BERT as the different first responders started calling in. He turned to the watch standers.

"You!" He stabbed at one person with a blunt forefinger. "Get Union Square up on the map screen. Get me a distance from Fattore's. You!"

He picked a second person.

"Call the boss, give him a sitrep, tell him we need to extract him from midtown."

He leaned over the desk and pressed the intercom button for all of the security stations.

"This is the SOC," he grated out. "Button up the building. No one in, no one out without permission from the SOC."

He turned back into the radio chatter just in time to hear the Goldbloom Chief Security Officer, Smith's peer and a personal friend, go radio dark in mid transmission.

That was not good. Very not good. He turned back to the communicator.

"Have you reached Smith yet?"

∽ ☉ ∾

Ding clutched a small piece of bloodstained blue fabric. It was the top half of a pajama shirt. The laundry tape inside the neck read "Dominguez." He, Tangarelli and several other cops from Manhattan precincts had fought their way from room to room.

Clearing zombies.

Killing their children.

Once, there was a brief internecine firefight when one father saw his infected child shot by another cop. It had taken precious minutes to resolve the fight, which left several cops dead and as many wounded.

During the fight to reach any dormitory areas that might have been unbreached, one of the Ajax units had arrived in response to the desperate radio calls. Six big men in complete Explosive Ordnance Disposal suits had stepped up to the front line, three carrying military issue M240 belt-fed machine guns, and three more carrying heavy satchels of linked thirty caliber ammunition, boxed in green-wrapped containers of two hundred rounds each. Each shooter was accompanied by a single ammo bearer.

The pairs stepped up to the doors that demarcated the furthest points of advance reached by the pistol- and rifle-equipped cops and tried, as selectively as possible, to shoot only confirmed infected. Twenty horrible minutes later Dominguez was standing in the fourth-floor dormitory shared by the kids of single-parent cops.

A lot of the cops were single parents.

He was surrounded by a sea of his bloodied, deafened and sobbing brothers and sisters.

Dominguez couldn't even form the words. How could this have happened? The security was tight—all the adults and teens were vaccinated.

In the nannies' office he found one of the caregivers. She seemed to have died with all of her clothes on, unlike nearly all of the infected in this catastrophe, child and adult alike. Her body was only partially eaten, mostly the exposed soft tissue on the face and neck.

He looked away, even more sickened, and squeezed his eyes shut as he wrung the bloody pajama top between his hands. He could feel a scream building inside him. When it broke, the world would end. He would end it. No one should have to live in a world with this much pain.

He opened his eyes, and found that he was staring at a blood-splashed art display.

Pinned in the middle of a large macaroni smiley face was a single, perfect white carnation.

His eyes widened.

Paul was frantic but successfully maintained a professionally calm exterior.

The cell phone network appeared to be completely down, which was impossible. The redundant systems that made up the grid in New York City was supplied by redundant, overlapping service providers. Cell towers were equipped with battery power enough to last days in the event that the grid went down. The only way that cell coverage could be interdicted was if a large-scale, very powerful military jammer operating across and on both sides of both the 3G and 4G LTE bands was stepping on all transmissions or if the city and state government implemented the antiterror protocols that suspended cell operations at the trunk level. What was more, VHF radio calls to the cars had gone unanswered, perhaps jammed.

Only the mayor's office, acting through OEM, and the local FBI field office, acting together, could do all that.

The land-line call to the restaurant reached Fattore, who explained that the Smith party had left to hear some music. Something about a French philosopher or artist? Fattore didn't know.

Paul carefully did not tear at his hair, not that he had enough to rend, preferring a slick scalp. He calmly addressed the entire SOC staff.

"Does anyone here know about a music performance by a French philosopher somewhere in midtown?"

The hammering of keyboard keys announced the sudden, furious googling by some watchstanders. However, among a sea of completely puzzled looks, one hand went up, from the youngest of the crew.

"Sir, do you mean, um, do you mean Voltaire?"

Tom had to admit, he had been a *leetle* bit optimistic. Dinner was delicious. Faith had in fact learned that some Italian dishes which she would have previously considered outré were in fact amazing. Steve had unbent enough to allow the girls a glass of red each. Stacey had been charming, and flirted gently with the maître d'. Sophia had been, well, sophisticated and thoughtful. He had even successfully steered the dinner table talk away from most mentions of the ongoing zombie apocalypse.

However, when he succumbed to Faith's wheedling to go to a concert in Washington Square Park he had probably allowed his niece too much leeway. When he assured his brother that it was going to be fine, safe even, he had definitely been overly optimistic. Touch of hubris, actually.

On the other hand, it was his, Tom's, family. It may not have been "safe," but it was, probably, manageable.

When Durante called out "Company!" and Tom saw the number of infected rushing towards the crowd in front of the stage, he didn't automatically start shooting. Shooters he had. What he needed was the cars that they came in. It was time to depart, taking billy big steps in any direction but the zombies, which were rapidly blocking his egress route.

A glance at his mobile phone revealed zero bars of reception.

Joy.

He looked at the number of infected closing on his family's location and told Durante to go hot.

"I'm going to go with 'I told you so,'" his brother said.

Steve and Stacey were back to back, using their pistols on any leakers that Durante and Faith missed, focusing mostly on the party's flanks. As the first rounds went out, a familiar ringing started in Tom's ears.

Tinnitus my old friend, I've come to sing with you again . . .

"Cell service is out," Tom announced flatly. He looked right and saw more zombies loping towards the crowd who had been enjoying the music to that point. "Engage at will."

"Already on it," Faith said, drifting right. Durante went wide to support her movement, which spread their front enough to cover Sophia, who appeared to have been arguing with a pair of grungy bohemians in skinny jeans and plaid. The concert goers appeared oblivious to any threat.

A pair of shotgun rounds went down range with their

characteristic booms. Then as clearly as if the thirteen-year-old was standing next to him, Tom heard Faith:

"*Fuck* Tasers," she said. "*This* is how you handle a zombie apocalypse."

Behind her Durante grinned and serviced targets.

Tom's ears continued ringing, despite the foam plugs he had provided to all for the concert. He tried to spot the cars, but between the crowd and the infected there wasn't a clear path to where he thought they had parked.

He really didn't want to walk all the way downtown. He rechecked his phone, which had finished rebooting, as a very hot shotshell casing bounced off his face.

In the background, amazingly, the concert kept rolling.

Tradittore's phone was still quiet when someone broke squelch on the Push To Talk handset racked against the wall. He was scanning the weekly activity summary in the Jersey office Cosa Nova conference room, reflecting on the mundane requirements of a life of crime. Paperwork, logistics, personnel reviews. Personnel reviews! The radios were his idea, though. Tradittore had persuaded Matricardi that a little communications redundancy was a good thing, and since the PTT network was served by far more than the usual carriers, it was an additional bit of insurance against ridiculous cell charges. It didn't hurt that PTT was harder to track than cell phones too.

"This is Nova Two. Anyone there?" The voice belonged to one of the team leads in a Cosa Nova BERT. Tradittore recognized the voice and then picked up and keyed the handset, which looked like a slightly chunky smartphone, albeit it with a monochrome screen.

"What's up, Tony?"

"Ah, hey!" Tony said, sounding nervous. "Sorry to bug you on the radio Joey, but the damn cell phones are down. We're working the Island late shift tonight, and there is a big ass road block on West Fifty-Eighth, not too far from Columbus Circle. The cops are checking every car. Anything I should know about? Over."

The lieutenant's frustration almost peaked. He looked at his cell phone screen and saw the crosshatched symbol where the reception bars should have been.

"Since when do you bother me about a roadblock?" he shot back. "The cops are probably just doing checks for infected."

"Well, we just watched them divert another contractor truck into the closed lane, and throw all the riders in the back of a cop van," Tony said. "This ain't normal, Boss. I mean, we're a few cars back and this sure as hell doesn't smell right."

Tradittore thought for a moment.

"Can you turn around, over?"

"West. Fifty. Eighth. Means one-way," Tony responded sarcastically. "Even if there wasn't a butt-to-bumper line of cars, just where would I turn around?"

"Show them your creds. Keep the radio keyed so I can hear. Worst case, pass the radio to the guy in charge there."

Hand holding junior gangsters. As if Joey didn't have better things to do. What he would give for decently competent subordinates.

Although there wasn't anyone to see it, Tradittore sighed theatrically as he walked over to Matricardi's exclusive humidor and opened the lid, selecting a custom Cohiba with a nice maduro wrapper. He sniffed it appreciatively as he listened to the cab chatter on the other end of the line. Finally, he heard Tony again, addressing what had to be a cop.

"Good evening officer, how can I help?"

"Put the phone down, keep your hands where I can see them, and when I tell you, get the fuck out of the car, shithead!"

Tradittore's spine straightened as he kept listening.

"Whoa, whoa, officer, please aim that somewhere else! I am talking to my boss right here, on this radio. Your boss and my boss have an arrangement. We are legit contractors, see? Here are my credentials."

"Keep your left hand on the wheel, and give me that."

There was some rustling sounds and then a new voice sounded.

"This Matricardi?"

"Number one, that's Mr. Matricardi to you," the Cosa Nova man bit out. "Second, my name is Tradittore, and I handle the assholes so my boss doesn't have to. Third, we have a deal with the deputy chief of police—do you need me to call Captain Dominguez to straighten your ass out, or are you gonna apologize and let my guys go do their job?" Tradittore relaxed his finger on the mic button.

There was a low, mirthless chuckle from the other end.

"Tradittore. Yeah, I remember you. You were the dickhead in the sharkskin suit who was busy fellating Matricardi every five minutes. You'll do. My name is Dominguez, and I have a modification to our deal that I want you to run and tell your boss about as soon as I hang up. Are you ready?"

As a combination of anger and confusion battled inside him, Tradittore could hear Tony and the other Cosa Nova man starting to babble in the background.

"*No man, no need to point that here. Chill man, it's all . . .*"

Modern radios and cell phones automatically dampen very loud sounds to protect both the handset and the listener, so what Joey heard wasn't deafening. However, the unmistakable sound of guns firing next to the radio cut off every other sound for several seconds. Ironically, the new technology and software filters were good enough so that as soon as the shots stopped he could hear the brassy tinkle of a few spent cases rattling on the concrete for a few moments.

Then the channel went dead.

The cigar snapped in Tradittore's hand.

"The guardsmen say that they have radio contact with higher," Durante yelled. "And maybe a ride out!"

Tom couldn't really call the zombie battle a firefight when only one side had guns, but it was as potentially lethal as any fight he had ever experienced. Although his entire party had been vaccinated, the number of zombies was sufficient to physically tear his group apart. The dark treeline had continued to vomit out groups of infected that charged the fans, who seemed insanely, or perhaps stonedly, relaxed about the rush of zombie cannibals. As a result, there were a few who had been brought down and lethally mauled, despite the accurate shotgun and pistol fire.

Voltaire continued to wail into his microphone and play lead guitar, the sound of which seemed to attract the infected towards the main mosh pit area and away from the bank group.

Small mercies.

During a magazine change, he had heard gunfire

with a slightly different timbre and looked over his shoulder to where Faith and Durante continued to anchor the right side of group. Across the open area, nearly on the other side of the concert, three guardsmen in heavy ponchos, gloves and MOPP gear had been laying rifle fire into the increasingly heavy infected pressure when they were swarmed. Sophia, Durante and Faith had automatically begun supporting them and Smith's group thinned out the infected enough for the Army detachment to shake off the remaining infected.

Tom leaned over to his brother, who was in mid magazine change, and pointed out the biggest of the three soldiers. The man had let his rifle hang on its sling and was still chopping at infected with a distinctively shaped oversize knife the size of his forearm.

"Faith is going to want her kukri back now, sure as a gun."

Steve glanced over and then back towards the threat axis, keeping his pistol at the low ready.

"No bet," Steve said. "And I'll give it to her, New York City police regulations be damned. Down to two mags, by the way. We need to do a flit."

"We need our wheels, if they're still there," Tom replied. "If not, I'll talk to the Army about a ride. The cell network is down but maybe they have radios we can use."

They were mostly clear of the immediate scrum, as zombies continued to head for the stage. Over his shoulder, he could see the guitarist swing his guitar, the white instrument liberally blotched red. He glanced ahead, across 6th. The road was clear in both directions and well lit. Good conditions to perform an extract.

"Let's get this cluster organized and moving. At least we still have lights."

As if on cue, the entire city went dark.

Paul was alternately monitoring the active radio channels that he could find, and repenting for all his sins, both imaginary and realized. His greatest fear was that if they lost the Smith party entirely, it would be up to him to complete the evacuation from Manhattan.

Now that would be a nightmare.

It could always be worse. At least he wasn't managing any of the trio of borderline sociopathic cartel "partners" that Smith had climbed into bed with.

"SOC, Post Two," one of the radios crackled. "Need the watch commander, ASAP."

Smith had recognized that a plurality of his security and intelligence staff already had either military or law enforcement experience, so it was simpler to retain the communication brevity codes that most already knew and have the rest learn it rather than to create another protocol that would be entirely new to all. Paul was one of those who had learned from scratch and he still felt awkward referring to himself in the third person on the radio.

"This is SOC Actual, go." Paul simultaneously acknowledged the call and communicated that he was the actual SOC lead, not just the shift manager.

"SOC, we have a big SUV with City plates at the Water Street chicane. Driver states that he's carrying a Ms. Kohn, the director of OEM. Driver further states that Sierra Actual has cleared the visit. Request instructions, over."

Rune's brain didn't actually stutter, but he felt like

it did. He reviewed the bidding. Kohn had a deal with Smith that hinged on getting a ride out should it all come a cropper. Which appeared to be happening. However, it wasn't a carte blanche deal. Rune knew that the stated limit was up to three primaries and two "plus ones" per.

"Two, SOC Actual. How many souls?"

"This is Two. I count eight." The post clearly anticipated the question.

"Copy." Joy, joy, joy, at least eight more pax to move by helo. "Tell the driver that they will be allowed through, then searched for weapons, and then passed into the parking area, to be accommodated until Sierra Actual returns. No information on his position is to be shared, and they don't talk to anyone but our staff. Clear?"

"Crystal, over."

"Right, I'll be down in five and meet them in the garage."

When they buttoned up the building, the SOP was to have all staff in response equipment, so Paul had somewhere to put the radio. By the time he reached the garage, Joanna and her group were in a small briefing area. They wore blue Bank of the Americas' visitor badges emblazoned with the legend "Escort Required."

Although Kohn was as cool as Paul had ever seen her, some of her group were visibly unsettled.

What Paul wanted to say was "Ah, Joanna! What news on the Rialto?" but somehow he doubted she would appreciate the classics at the moment.

"Ms. Kohn, a pleasure to see you," he said, instead. "We are, unfortunately, in the middle of an operation and Mr. Smith is unavailable. However, if you wish to wait, we'll be happy to accommodate you here until his return."

Joanna, clearly tired but unrumpled and erect, smiled back warmly.

"Hello Paul!" Her eyes didn't crinkle as authentically as another might have done, but it was a credible performance. "We will be happy to wait. But if you would not mind, I have some information that you might appreciate having right away. There is a specific reason we are here. Now. Perhaps we could talk separately?"

Paul bowed slightly as he gestured to the door, but he was confident that he wasn't going to like what came next.

A uniformed patrol cop was in a maintenance access space that ran adjacent to the eastbound roadway of the Holland Tunnel. Another group was on the westbound side. The dingy illumination of the battery-operated emergency lights sufficed to guide his efforts with a nail gun, pinning green canvas satchels to the concrete wall. There were two more cops with him, one holding a sleeve of hardened nails to reload the gun, and another festooned with three additional satchels.

An older detective whose suit jacket was missing, revealing a bloodstained white business shirt and a custom shoulder rig, spoke up. He sniffed the mixture of car exhaust and musty sewer smell that permeated the tunnel.

"Damn, this place smells like ass," he said, sniffing. "You gotta wonder why the Feds had a few tons of explosives in Manhattan."

"Don't much care," his partner with the nail reloads replied. "What I am thinking is that we ain't gonna drop no tunnel with no measly eighty pounds of C4."

The uniformed cop on the ladder finished anchoring the first bundle and reached for the next one.

"No shit," he replied. "I didn't do eight years in EOD to have some detective state the obvious."

"Fuck you, uni, and fuck your Marine Corps. What's the point, then?"

The nail gun chunked rhythmically, adding a second M183 charge to the first.

"Ding has a plan, asshole," said the uni, his balance wobbly as he grabbed the next bundle. "We don't need to blow the tunnel. These things are proof against anything but a nuke, anyway. All we got to do is break up the roadbed a bit, make cars slow down to almost nothing. Meanwhile, the other guys are gonna blow the four ventilation towers, each side of the river. Anyone comes down here and spends more than ten minutes is gonna pass out, see? A little obstruction and Bridges and Tunnels, including that murderous asshole Matricardi, come to a halt and choke out on their own fucking exhaust. Ding has some other guys rigging the Expressway the same, and some more working the Washington. After we finish here, we head north to the Lincoln. Them as make it in before we call the shot are stuck on the island, with us. We trap all the right rats in the all the right places. Poetry justice."

It was dark enough that his face was in shadow. The other two echoed the grim smile that they could hear, if not see.

The cop at the foot of the stepladder passed a third haversack up.

"Poetic, Joey," he corrected. "You mean that it's poetic justice."

"But poetic justice would be turning all of them, and their kids, into infected," the first cop pointed out.

"We'll get around to that."

CHAPTER 14

"The following is a message of the Emergency Broadcast System at the request of the Washington Office of the Federal Emergency Management Agency. As a result of interruptions to critical supplies for major metropolitan areas, officials in major cities have advised FEMA that they are recommending the start of an orderly evacuation process. Residents are advised to prepare to self-evacuate by collecting water, food, medication and clothing and await directions specific to your area . . ."

From: *Collected Radio Transmissions of the Fall*
University of the South Press 2053

"This feels unfortunately familiar," Copley heard one of the civilians say.

Riding in the back of an overfull MRAP, lurching along in a surprisingly rough ride, was a lot like being in the 'Stan.

Copley was trying to get his head around what had just happened. A full-blown firefight in New York City's Washington Square Park wasn't what his team expected at the start of their afternoon "presence" patrol near the midtown Apple store.

Thank god that rules of engagement had changed. The MRAP gunner who had used the 240 to fire up a large group of zombies during the extraction of their small group had also passed along the change in ROE. When Copley asked for details, the gunner had waggled the machine gun towards the zombies and bits of zombies spread across Fifth Avenue and looked simultaneously annoyed and preoccupied.

Usually they had a ten-page binder of when and under exactly what circumstances they could use specific levels of force. "Redeployment for active clearance" appeared to mean "see zombies, shoot same."

God, he hoped that's what it meant, otherwise his ass was going to be in a sling. 'Cause they'd shot a lot of zombies.

Copley's team of three and the contractors that they fell in with at the concert fracas amassed more than a hundred kills in the first hour of heavy contact. No one seemed too worked up about it, not even the hyperactive, hyperviolent teenage girl who was bumping into her fellow passengers as she wiped down a weird-looking Kalashnikov.

She turned to the hulking brute sitting next to Copley. His plate carrier and oversize BERT patch were liberally splashed with blood.

"See, Gravy, this is why I like shotguns. Love, love, *love* shotguns. Shoot a zombie, they fall down go boom, easy-peasy."

The big guy was leaning against the bulkhead, chimped down and relaxed. He just grunted and, noticing that Copley was looking, raised an eyebrow.

Copley nodded and returned to ruminating on the ROE.

"Redeployment for active clearance" sounded pretty neat. Strong, and in control.

Riiight.

Copley knew what the change in ROE really meant.

The reserve two-star running the National Guard operations in the five boroughs had decided that he was done losing teams, and nonlethal was not going to cut it. In other words, the general finally accepted what even his juniormost soldier had known for a week: it was time and past time to just plain kill zombies.

Fuck Tasers.

U.S. Northern Command, NORTHCOM, was supposed to be coordinating with NYPD and DHS. Copley figured that in the beginning it may have even worked that way. He suspected, hell, he knew in his heart, that after the concert everything had changed. For starters, his chain of command was notably absent. Nobody was getting anyone above a sergeant on the radio. And a bunch of callsigns simply weren't answering. Either they weren't there anymore, the zombies got them, or it was every man for himself.

He fought down his fear—not for himself but for his little team and for his family. If it was this bad here, how about Reenie and the kids out west? If the trains stopped running, how was anyone getting back? Who the fuck was in charge?

He looked over at Randall, who was carefully cleaning the blood from his kukri. Despite the ribbing he had given Randall, he was ready to eat a little crow and get one for himself. It seemed to do a good job on grabby zombies, of which there was an overabundance.

Covertly taking a deep breath, the guardsman focused on trying to make something out of the hash of intermittent radio traffic emanating from the speaker.

Overall, the MRAP ride from the concert wasn't too bad. The last team to be collected had to ride on the outside of the hull until they joined up with a second vehicle. Then they squeezed a few more inside under armor. Copley was glad that their unit was using the later MRAPs. These had three axles, more armor and interior room for fifteen, if you tore out the litter racks and didn't mind painful overcrowding.

Copley had spent most of the ride continuing his effort to reach higher in his chain of command. The tactical radio net was the only functioning communications that anyone seemed to have, except for the really short-range Fox Mike handhelds used by a couple contractors. A few seats down, he could hear the contractor team lead trying to use his own radio. Inside the big city, their useful range was only a few blocks.

Apart from increasingly fragmented directions to the armored vehicles that were trying to collect teams, there were no coherent orders. "Their" Forward Operating Base, located inside John Jay Park on the East Side was off the air. The MRAP that they were in was from an entirely different unit.

The patrol sergeant was feeling lost. Looking at some of the faces inside the dimly lit interior, he saw he wasn't the only one. The civilian woman they pulled from the concert was quietly sobbing into her hands.

The vehicles paused to drop off most of the passengers at another FOB, this one farther south. Looking around Gramercy Park, Copley saw only a few uniforms. Two other vehicles were in view, and a pool of yellow light illuminated soldiers frantically turning wrenches on the power pack of one MRAP. He motioned to his two troops to stay put. A few contractors hopped out and huddled, while others maintained an alert posture, weapons out.

"Find fuel for the MRAP," Copley said, addressing Randall. "I'm going to go talk to the bank people and the truck commander. Take care of Astro. Drink, eat..."

"Take Motrin," Randall finished. "And change your fucking socks."

"Just take care of Astroga," Copley said, looking around and shaking his head. "What the fucking fuck?"

Inside the TOC, the roar of the generators was muted. There were rows of folding tables and chairs, some green-painted field desks and several open notebook PCs. However, the TOC, if that's what it was, was severely understaffed.

A private had his feet up on the table and appeared preoccupied with a paperback book. At the other end of the work space, a paunchy captain doodled on a clipboard. The radio blared briefly and Copley watched as the captain busily logged the radio calls.

In a zombie apocalypse.

The guard sergeant walked up and saluted, reporting in with a party of three, but the captain, whose name tape read FLAMENCO, held up one hand as he transcribed a radio transmission that was mostly static and screams.

"So, where do we get fuel for the MRAP?" Private Astroga asked.

"In a situation like this?" Randall said. "Grab anything that's not nailed down."

"So...we loot the Humvee?" the private said.

"What Humvee?" Randall answered, looking around.

The vehicle in question was an uparmored version of the HMMWV, called an M1114. It was making its way through the serpentine roadway in a random fashion. It would nearly hit one of the concrete barricades, then swerve at the last moment, stop, jerkily back up, move forward, stop, turn . . .

"I think the driver's drunk, anyway," Astroga said. "We probably should drain the tank for his own safety."

The reinforced vehicle made the last turn, accelerated dangerously in the narrow space leading towards the headquarters and then stopped abruptly. An Army officer stepped out in Class As, a much fancier uniform than their own stained and bloody ACUs. The ribbon rack hung slightly askew and the coat was misbuttoned. The officer made a sincere effort to neatly adjust his uniform while carefully inspecting his surroundings. He carefully avoided making eye contact with the two dumbfounded enlisted personnel.

"Holy fuck," Randall whispered, spying the gleaming silver star on the officer's blue epaulet. "Ten Hut!" he added, throwing a parade ground salute.

The brigadier general waved absently in his direction without, again, making any eye contact.

"Duh fuck is a general doing here?" Astroga whispered as she dropped her salute.

"Where's his aide?" Randall asked, referring to the aide d' camp that always followed generals around.

"Eaten?" Astroga suggested. "Turned?"

"May we assist the General, sir?" Randall said, walking over to the officer who seemed frozen in place.

"I require the presence of an officer or NCO on a matter of urgent business," the general replied, not looking at the specialist.

"Uh, yes, sir," Randall said, looking around. Copley had wandered off with the banker people so he wasn't available. "Astroga, go get the captain."

"Roger that!" the private said, hurrying off without asking who the fuck Randall meant.

A brief flurry of motion caught Copley's eye, and he watched Astroga rush in and start frantically yanking drawers open before seizing a sheaf of papers. Captain Flamenco had just begun speaking, so Copley looked back at the officer, ignoring the obvious sounds of a keyboard tapping and a laser printer humming. It was taking the captain a long time to say exactly nothing.

Nope, no idea where you are supposed to be, Nope, not in contact with higher. Yep, you can shoot zombies now. Yeah, you can have fuel, if there's any left. No, I don't know if there is any left, didn't I just say that? No, there isn't any ammo. Now go away and let me do my job.

Copley looked towards Astroga again but kept his peace as the private scribbled on the paperwork and snapped it to a spare clipboard before running out again. Mr. Radio Watch finally wound down as he completed his litany and returned to his own radio.

What the fucking fuck, Copley said to himself, looking around for anything useful.

Glancing over at the lone private who was reading at the opposite end of the tent, Copley noted that the book was a trashy sci-fi paperback with a chain-mail-bikini-wearing elf on the cover. He couldn't compete with that, so Copley made a quick decision to try the officer again.

"Sir, I know that you're very busy, but I need to report about the civilians that we had to shoot, and the huge number of zombies," Copley said. "And the banks are fighting each other and the cops are shooting the bankers and..."

"Do I look like a banker, Sergeant?" the officer said angrily. "Do I look like a policeman? *Do I?* No, no I do not. I have one job and I'm doing it. I'm guarding this channel and recording the hell out of this radio traffic. Now get the hell out."

"Sir, yes sir." Copley answered, saluting.

He looked back over at the private, but that wise man had only raised the book a little higher, blocking any view of the room.

It was time to move on down the road.

"May I assist the General in the meantime?" Randall asked.

"I do not speak to specialists," the general replied.

Randall started to open his mouth, then closed it before pointing out that the general just had. They waited in silence until Astroga came running back with a clipboard in her hand. She circled behind the general then held the clipboard out around his side.

"General, sir, some important paperwork, sir," she said. "Promotion orders and a fuel delivery order, sir."

The general signed the papers without looking.

Astroga then stepped around, ripped the specialist rank off of the velcro patch sewn onto Randall's armor and slapped on a sergeant rank. It was slightly askew, in keeping with the overall fuckedness of the situation.

"May I present Sergeant Randall, General?" Astroga said. "Recently promoted."

"May I assist the General?" Randall repeated.

"I require a piece of string," the general replied, eyeing the sergeant's new patch.

"String, sir?" Randall croaked.

"The order seems clear enough, Sergeant!" the general barked. "Get me a piece of string!"

"Yes, sir, General, sir!" Randall barked in reply, snapping to attention. "Private Astroga!"

"Specialist," Astroga said, slapping his old rank on her armor.

"Specialist Astroga," Randall continued. "Secure a piece of string for the general!"

"Roger that, Sergeant!" Astroga said, snapping a salute, then scuttling off.

"Where are you from, Sergeant?" the general asked, still standing at parade rest and looking into the distance at nothing.

"Plattsburgh, sir," Randall answered, trying not to think about his family back home.

"Good town," the general said. "Lovely people. How has your day been?"

"We fought our way out of Washington Square Park last night against heavy resistance, sir," Randall replied. "Had to go hand-to-hand to break contact. Met up with the MRAP and picked up a few more survivors, General."

"Good to hear, Sergeant, good to hear."

Randall realized the general wasn't really hearing a word he said. He wasn't even sure the officer was on the same plane as the rest of them.

"Your string, General," Astroga said, trotting up. The white nylon string was internal line pulled from parachute cord and about a meter long. "I hope it's long enough, sir."

The general took the string and inspected it.

"Good job, Sergeant," the general said, careful to

only address Randall. "I would write you a commendation but time precludes that. Ask me for anything but time, as Napoleon said."

The general turned, and with the careful deliberation of a drunk who was determined to navigate a perfectly straight line, navigated back to his vehicle. The clunk of the driver's side door punctuated the night as he climbed back into his Humvee. He started the truck and nearly backed over the twosome before negotiating his way through the barricades in an equally bizarre fashion.

"What. Just. Happened?" Randall asked, carefully. "In all of the questions I've got about this little scene, near the top is where did you find promotion papers on an instant?"

"They were in the database in the TOC," Astroga said. "There really was a captain there, but he was busy ignoring Sergeant Copley so I had to improvise. Remember, you guys are arty: I'm admin. And I got us authorization for ten thousand gallons of diesel," Astroga continued happily. "If we can find a fuel point, that is."

"Ten thousand?" Randall said incredulously. "Ten thousand!"

"Generals never look at paperwork," Astroga said. "We can probably trade it. Hell, we can probably trade the *authorization* for something."

"There's no way that this promotion is going to stick..." The new sergeant shook his head.

"Sure it will," the new specialist replied. "I've got the signature of..."

She squinted at the signature.

"Brigadier General William Bickel, deputy commander, JTF Empire Shield. Even if we make it back to 258th, they're gonna have to respe—"

"What the fucking fuck?" Copley said, walking up and looking at Randall. "Why is your rank sideways? Why does it say 'sergeant?' And when did Astroga make specialist?"

"Want to be a staff?" Astroga asked. "I've got two more blank signed promotion orders."

"WHAT THE FUCKING FUCK...?"

The eastern sky was starting to lighten as they turned the corner from Broadway onto Wall Street. Though littered with abandoned cars and debris, the roads had been mostly deserted, apart from the occasional group of infected. They had also passed a heavy firefight between two groups of unknown actors.

Both Copley and the TC had looked to Smith, who had just shaken his head. Operating on NVGs and IR headlights, the combined Army and contractor group had mostly ghosted by. At one point the MRAP had taken some fire but it was an MRAP. The light rounds had just bounced off as they drove by. That really brought home the feeling that something important had shifted. Their "presence" mission was well and truly screwed. And if the City was this bad, how bad was it back home?

Ahead, yellow lights blazed, creating an island of normalcy.

Inside the perimeter, everyone exited the MRAP, and most of the contractors headed down a ramp into a brightly lit carport under the skyscraper.

"Too much!" Astroga looked at the logo on the side of the building and laughed. "My dad has an account at Bank of the Americas. I wonder if the ATMs are up?"

"Stick a sock in it, *Specialist*," Randall said. "Worf,

what are we gonna do now? Do we stick with the truck, stay here or what?"

The bank's security had set up a strong point by completely blocking streets at a one block radius from the front doors of the bank. Generators were running floods that had half blinded them as they drove in, and there was a degree of purposeful bustling that reassured Copley.

In the background, the junior specialist was scribbling in her green notebook.

"Item number twenty-three," Astro muttered. "The specialist shall not attempt to make ATM withdrawals during a zombie apocalypse."

"Don't let Astro wander off," Copley replied with a grimace. "I mean, seriously, sit on her. She's got the attention span of a baby duck. And stick close to the corporal running this rig. It doesn't roll without my say. Threats of violence are authorized."

A string of suppressed rifle shots, still recognizable as outgoing fire, popped from the barricade and all three troops spun towards the sound.

"One infected," a voice announced from a speaker. "Clear."

Randall and Astroga pivoted back towards their sergeant in unison, looking the question at him.

"Yeah, I know," he said with a grunt. "Just stay frosty and keep the truck here."

"You've always wanted to say that, haven't you?" Astroga asked. "'Just stay frosty, Astroga.' Or, wait, am I that Hispanic chick...? Does that mean...?"

"Just keep the truck here till I tell you," Copley said with a shake of his head.

∞ ⊖ ∞

Tom Smith got out of the back of the Army vehicle and counted heads. His brother ducked low as he stepped out, but his tall niece still managed to knock her head again. Her heartfelt cursing was more colorful than he would have guessed, even after all that had transpired so far.

"Motherfucking son-of-a-bitch fucktards suck!" Faith said, holding her forehead. "This is why I said we should bring fucking *helmets*! Where's the helmet store, Gravy?"

"If you weren't the Jolly Green Giant it wouldn't be a problem," Sophia replied. But even the mild harangue sounded tired. It had been a long day and night.

The bank security leader motioned to Durante, who was trailing the little family group walking down the ramp.

"Get everyone inside, do a gear and ammo check," Tom said. "Grab some food and stand by. I need to check status."

"Jump time?" the sanguine security specialist replied.

"Maybe," Tom said, assessing the new people in view. The National Guard members, and the truck, were potentially useful. "I need to check with Bateman, and I want to talk to the PD. I think that Matricardi, hell—all the players, will be in motion after last night. Did you see who was in that scrum we passed?"

"Overture's people for sure," Durante said, looking thoughtful. "Couldn't tell about the others. Check out the plates on that Suburban." He hooked a thumb at a strange SUV in the bank's garage. The plates had a three-digit number under the legend "NYC Official."

Before Tom could respond, Rune trotted up, looking

both immensely relieved and annoyingly cheerful. He was wearing an equipment belt with pistol, machete, Taser, reloads and a radio over his suit. Instead of an M4, he was wielding an iPad and a thermos.

"Welcome back, Boss! How was the concert?"

"Voltaire was great," Smith said with a crooked smile. "The mosh pit was a little too intense, though. In order, I simultaneously need coffee and a SITREP, then a bathroom and a change of clothes. After that I'll wing it. And no, you can't say 'I told you so.' My brother beat you to it."

"Never crossed my mind," Rune said, smiling back broadly. "At no point during the entire disaster that was last night did I ever even once *think* the words: Told you this was a very bad idea, Boss. You have a priority message from Bateman, you are supposed to call the second you return. You also have Joanna Kohn on the premises, asking for evac. She bears... interesting news. Short version is that the secure police area got hit last night and casualties among the families are very high. We've got her and her crew stashed in training room one."

Rune looked over Smith's shoulder at the hulking six-wheeled armored vehicle.

"Nice ride. Can we keep it?"

Tom looked meditative as he accepted a thermos cup from the shorter man.

"Going to try," Tom said. "Find out who is senior and bring him over. I think there is a sergeant in charge."

Rifle fire popped a short distance away, and a verbal all clear sounded. Smith recognized the voice as belonging to one of his department.

"Zombie clearance on Wall Street," Tom reflected aloud. "Might be *that* time."

"We're out of time!" Bateman's voice was coming through clearly on the speaker phone. "The damned bitch just turned, right in front of me. She had been vaccinated and everything. The driver is dead, and garage is full of zombies—you can hear them right through the steel, growling..."

To Tom's ears, his boss sounded more annoyed than scared, but the whimpering in the background suggested that not everyone forted up in the Park Avenue townhome shared his equanimity.

"Roger, Boss," Tom replied. He waved a hand over his head to get the attention of his team. "I'll flush a pickup team in some armored trucks to come get you right now. There have been some serious developments and I need to run the main effort from here. I can brief you in detail when you get in, but you need the top line information now. Ready?"

"Go," the CEO replied.

"Power grid is down," Smith said, sticking to basics. "Not temporary loss. Down.

"There was an attack on the NYPD secure compound last night where their dependents had been secured and it's chaos right now. There were very confused gun fights last night, cops versus cops, cops versus contractors, gangs, you name it. As far as can be determined, city government and the Army have collapsed. I am looking at e-mails that say the Fed announced that we are suspending trading on the NYSE, the NASDAQ and the Chicago Board of Trade. Indications suggest London and Frankfurt are already there. Nikkei and Hang Seng no longer respond to inquiries. No responses worldwide. I urgently recommend that we get out. I can start the ball rolling while we extract your family. How say you?"

Tom waited while Bateman digested that. Finally, Rich replied:

"Handle is pulled."

"Pull the fucking handle! Pull that motherfucker!"

Matricardi usually didn't yell at his subordinates. But if ever there was a time...

The world had come apart around him, beginning with his own building in Newark. A bunch of "his" cops had actually had the nerve to try to force their way into his building. The guards reported that the cop in charge was spouting some fairy tale that he, Matricardi himself, was infecting the families of the police on Manhattan.

Matricardi had needed a few minutes to put the frame together, but the damage was already done. He mentally nodded to acknowledge Overture's maneuver. Whatever arrangements that the Sicilian had on Manhattan were effectively dissolved, and his control of the New Jersey troopers was equally erased. His own cops were there to kill him!

Unfortunately for them, they hadn't been fully aware of his precautions. The two dozen or so Newark PD who entered instead encountered his security staff. One side had better training and motivation and the other had numbers, heavier armament and the benefits of the defense. It was very nearly a wash.

In the end, the good news was that Matricardi remained un-arrested and alive, though his team paid dearly. Newark police had fought their way through much of his security, killing many of his expensively acquired and trained staff, and damaging or destroying most of the mob's heavy weapons. The somewhat better news what that the cops had stopped trying to apprehend him, having retreated in numbers insufficient to muster even a corporal's guard.

The bad news was that the entire population of East Orange appeared to have been infected and then elected to congregate around his building. Realistically, Matricardi knew that the zombies couldn't coordinate; they were just two-legged beasts. The loud gunfire and the generator powered lights in his Clinton Hill compound had likely served to attract them. However, the result was effectively the same.

Hundreds had beelined towards his facility. Maybe more than that.

There were already enough infected inside the perimeter of the fenced and belatedly darkened compound that movement outside the building and vehicles was dangerous. If they waited until more appeared, or until the police returned in greater numbers, the position would be untenable.

Matricardi looked around at the expensive facility and mentally shrugged. You couldn't take it with you, so it was time to move.

Abandoning the compound meant that they would have to evacuate the immediate area. Matricardi had a plan for everything. In this case, the relationship with Bank of the Americas was about to pay off, so evacuation eastwards seemed to be in order.

Loading had proceeded mostly to plan, and the remaining two score Cosa Nova personnel were distributed among four large vans poised to depart, led by Matricardi in the foremost vehicle. There was the predictable last-minute backing and filling, cross loading and delays associated with any zombie apocalypse. Now the infected were trying to prevent the rear door on the boss's van from closing.

If it wasn't one thing, it was another.

Since Matricardi's vehicle was number one in the convoy, it was blocking the gateway outside, and the remaining vans could neither pull around nor offer assistance to the current issue.

"Put your back into it!" Matricardi understandably wanted to leave without any infected in his vehicle. Oldryskya certainly didn't agree with all his opinions, but that one seemed pretty solid.

"I can't close the door, Boss!" replied the junior mobster. "Their fingers are jamming the latch!"

Despite the danger of being pulled out by the infected, perhaps motivated by the very real risk of the lethal disapproval from his armed boss, he was really putting some effort into closing the door. However, he couldn't open it wide enough for a really good slam without risking the loss of control and having it swing all the way open. The zombies, some at least, were actually *pulling* on the door. Oldryskya could see the grasping hands and wrists being damaged, even deformed by the frantic thudding of the heavy door. However, the infected weren't yielding.

The growling and screaming at a distance of inches wasn't helping anyone's mental state, either.

A second Cosa Nova gunman looked frantically for anything that would work. Lying on its side was an automatic grenade launcher. Oldryskya saw his searching look pause on the Mk19 and as he reached it, she slid forward and used her appropriated police Benelli shotgun to sharply rap his fingers.

"We're *way* too close to use that, idiot! Give over!"

Without waiting for him to move, she leaned over him and the semi auto bucked as she fired it at point blank range. She emptied the magazine with rapid shots that chopped at the hands and arms protruding around the edge of the rear hatch. The high-pitched whine of partial deafness immediately overlaid all other sounds in the van, including the previously overwhelming snarling and growling. Some of the zombies fell away, but were rapidly replaced. The door still wasn't shut.

Risky heard an engine rev, and then looked up in time to see the van behind them lunge forward, crushing the infected between the two vehicles and smashing the rear hatch shut. Most of a severed hand flopped onto the thigh of the overmuscled guard who had been frantically trying to close the back of the van. He let out a manly yip and shoved it off.

Oldryskya heard Matricardi laugh immediately after the crunch of sheet metal cut off some of the growling from the infected.

"You gotta like it when your people think on their feet," the crime boss said. "I positively love subordinates with initiative!"

He waved to Tradittore, visible riding shotgun in the vehicle that had "helped" close their door. Tradittore smiled and waved in return, his mouth working as he said something to his driver.

"All right." Matricardi smacked the driver's shoulder. "Lincoln Tunnel to Wall Street. Let's go."

∽ ⊖ ∾

Tom Smith looked up from the pile of reports. Events had moved rapidly between dinner at Fattore's and his return at dawn. The primary evacuation contingent still at the bank was fully vaccinated and boosted. The lab was packed out and Curry flown to the most secure location that Smith had. The move to the completed refuge had begun incrementally days ago and continued now. The alternate trading floors were already operational and starting to absorb the staff that Tom was shuttling out of lower Manhattan via hardened buses. The air bridge out of the city, though short on capacity, was running smoothly and his contingency watercraft were staged and guarded.

Rune brought over one of the guardsmen. Divested of his ersatz zombie rig, the man in front of him was only middling size and middle aged, but still broad across the shoulders. His name tape read "Copley" and the stripes read "sergeant." He looked about as tired as Smith felt.

"Have a seat," Tom said, gesturing to a chair. "My name is Smith and I run security, all sorts, for Bank of the Americas. I wanted to chat, especially to say thanks for helping us extract from the Park. Real shit show."

"Thanks, and you're welcome, sir." Copley didn't quite flop into the office chair. "Maybe you can help me with a problem."

Looking around the deeply carpeted office, the guardsman in his stained utilities clearly felt out of his element.

"We're orphaned," he admitted. "I can't reach anyone who knows what we're supposed to be doing, or where we are supposed to be. Can't find my chain of command. The only officer I saw last night seemed pretty unconcerned with taking my report about hundreds of zombies in Washington Square Park, and I sure as shit didn't want to sit around waiting for him to experience a rush of blood to the brain and have an idea. You seemed like you had your head on straight. So here we are. Do you have a brain?"

Tom leaned forward, shifting his weight onto the elbows that he had planted on the desk.

"I'm in a tearing hurry, Sergeant Copley, so please consider this SITREP your prep for the frago that follows, but one that you can take a pass on, if you prefer."

Tom chose the lingua franca in which both he and Copley were wholly fluent. Fragmentary Orders, or fragos, were the operational communication by which a field commander gave his subordinates just enough information to carry out the mission at hand, in the context of the greater situation, without overwhelming the unit with detail. It was tacitly understood that fragos were delivered by the senior and carried out by the junior.

That context was going to be critical to any future relationship.

"I think that this city is already dead, but the different bits of the body are still ignorant of the fact."

He gestured to the pile of reports, the maps pinned to the rich paneling of his office walls and the view from the office window.

"Any activity we see out there is just the nervous system of a big animal, twitching. There's effectively no city government, no city services, no centrally controlled police force and to the extent there's any cop force at all, it has gone insane, and now, now we've got no solid contact with any higher in military."

As he listened, Copley slowly leaned forward, till he was perched on the edge of his seat, matching the taller man across from him.

"Is there a plan?" Tom continued. "Yes, there is. I'm charged by my employer to get all of the critical financial and technical staff out of this city in order to have enough of an economy to jump-start whatever is left once we fall back to our refuge points."

Copley's ears grew points.

"I've sent most of my people forward already, and now I'm understaffed for a few emergent missions that I must, *must* complete before we can finish the evacuation," Tom said. "So, I need trained and armed personnel and god help me, a little more armor wouldn't hurt either. I need you."

"Sir," Copley said carefully, "we all still fall under UCMJ. And somewhere there has got to be someone in charge."

"Look out the window," Tom said. "Do you *see* the fires?"

Dirty columns of smoke were rising into the dark morning sky from several points in the city. More than one skyscraper was visibly aflame.

"They're spreading because there aren't any firemen to put them out. Did you see any active formed units fighting in the last twenty-four hours? You see how the Statue of Liberty's torch and crown are lit and nothing else? That's because those are the only lights whose generator still has enough diesel to keep running. That's it for city services. Do you have contact with higher on your military circuits? You already said you don't. Before, this bank was tied in to DHS, NORTHCOM, STRATCOM, you name it. Now we're getting zero. Not even *'sauve qui peut'* from higher. The radio from FEMA is just repeating 'stay in your homes.' We got a message from SEC that trading was 'temporarily suspended' and now we're getting diddly."

Tom took a breath and stretched his shoulder a bit.

"I'm so short of people that I'm going to ask my brother and his family, you know, the overarmed hyperactive teenage *girls*, to help me retrieve my chairman from his house in midtown. It will be a hostile extract. ROE is up to me, and ROE is 'go hot.' Not an issue with the thirteen-year-old. *Keeping* her from going hot has been the issue."

"Thirteen?" Copley sputtered. "Which one?"

"Saiga," Tom replied. "The semiauto shotgun."

"Son-of-a—" the sergeant said, shaking his head.

"I'll sweeten the deal," Smith said. "Is your team immunized?"

Copley's eyes narrowed.

"You've got vaccine?" he asked cautiously. "Where from?"

"And booster," Tom said, ignoring the second bit. "It's a two-part series. Join my team until we finish the evacuation or for forty-eight hours, whichever comes first, and I ensure that you and your colleagues get the first shot now. Stick with us during the entire evac and you get the booster. Once we reach our fallback point, I'll work to put you in touch with higher, to the limit of my ability, and in the meantime, you can draw on our stocks to resupply water, ammo, parts, et cetera."

Tom sat back while Copley digested the offer.

"The truck isn't mine," Copley pointed out. He didn't fidget, but looked at Smith intently, and then down at his hands. "I can only speak for my team. To swing this, I need the same deal for its crew."

"I can do that, but if they evac with us, the truck stays behind."

"How are you getting out, sir?" Copley didn't think that was an unreasonable question.

"Need to know, Sergeant, and unless you are on board, you don't need to know," Tom said, standing up. "However, I have to get a mission underway."

Smith plucked a handheld radio from the charger on his desk and slipped it into a pouch on his plate carrier. He added freshly filled pistol magazines and some spare batteries. That done, he looked back up.

"I need your answer."

He waited until Copley began to answer and then deliberately cut him off.

"If you take this deal, you accept my authority without question for the duration or until we connect with competent military authority. You're all the way in. I don't have time to renegotiate every couple hours. You take our salt, and you commit. Clear?"

Copley stood.

"I know the term, sir. Ready for the frago."

CHAPTER 15

"... maybe the southern route will work. The I-15 and the 40 are both fully stopped. People are trying to drive around the wrecks and getting bogged in the sand. It's the Mojave in summer, for chrissake! They're starting to die of thirst and there's fighting ..."

From: *Collected Radio Transmissions of the Fall*
University of the South Press 2053

"This is Ding. What's our coverage?"

Dominguez was looking at the front of the mayor's building. His smile didn't reflect happiness. Just satisfaction. The dead BERT operators were hung by the ankles from the building's dirty gray facade. Some bodies bore the dreads from the Overture group, more had Cosa Nova polo shirts and a few were otherwise nondescript but still wore bits and pieces of tactical kit. Only one body was suspended above a much larger pool of blood than the rest, apparently hung there before the body's former owner had finished the messy business of dying.

The granite over the bodies was splashed with a white-painted legend: RETRIBUTION.

Over two hundred police still stood with him. Ding didn't have anything like the thousand or more cops that had survived the clearance operation on the dependents' housing. Hundreds had disappeared through the night.

Attrited by the fighting that yielded this monument to their dead, trapped by one of the growing number of zombie mobs that were spreading outwards from the parks and subways or simply dead from self-inflicted gunshots—his family of loss had shrunk.

A spattering of shots rang out nearby, followed by a cop calling out "Clear." Dominguez never turned his head. Instead, he raised the radio to his mouth and spoke, still looking at the corpses.

"C'mon, what's our coverage?"

"The take from the city cams is still pretty solid, with a few holes. Central Park is crawling, and I mean crawling, thousands of infected, maybe more than that. The Army survivors pulled out to the east. There are few spots of organized activity, but mostly the civilians are trying to get off island or just get groceries, not that the traffic is moving. Zombies are starting to congregate in midtown, mostly in green spaces and subway entrances."

The voice of the remaining Domain Awareness Systems operator scratched at Ding's mind. In reality it was uninflected, but Dominguez heard it as brittle, cold and full of malice.

"What kind of bank activity are you seeing?" he asked.

"There isn't a BERT operating anywhere in Manhattan," the DAS man said. "There are burnt and wrecked BERT trucks in a few places though. The midtown banks have pulled security back inside, or maybe all the way off the island, no way to tell. Downtown, the Goldbloom complex is intact and they have set up a cordon outside their front doors. Bank of the Americas has a one block perimeter, using the DHS chicanes downtown. Both

are still shuttling helicopters. There was a convoy that
headed north a while ago, out of BotA."

Ding's smile grew feral. Bank of the Americas. Kohn
would be there. Matricardi, the mongering whoreson,
might be there. Smith would be there for certain.
Ding would give him one chance.

He turned to the FBI special agent who had moved
his family into the police dorms.

"Can you turn off the jammers and reactivate the
trunk lines now?" Ding asked. He waggled his smartphone to make the point. "I want to make a call and
I need to reach the right guy."

The feeb was exhausted, but his eyes were fever
bright. His vest was soiled, the agency lettering smeared
with red.

"Yeah. I can do that. Also, we brought the special
weapons. Where do you want 'em?"

"Load them in the truck."

Paul Rune watched the little convoy navigate the
barricades, squeeze past the guarded exits and head
north on FDR Drive. Consisting of the MRAP and
two BERT trucks, one recently repaired, it carried
Smith's scratch CEO recovery team. The cell system
was still down, but at least they would be able to stay
in contact now that the radios seemed to be working again.

"Seems like you left this a little late, Boss. Is the
FDR still clear?"

Tom was rapping out orders on his handheld, and
held up one hand as he finished a conversation.

"Bravo Eight, this is Sierra Actual. Go for SITREP."

"SITREP follows—we delivered the package to *Mile
Seven*." Kaplan's voice came through clearly. "Our

alternates are loitering nearby and I'll be leaving the dock shack in ten. They will follow as soon as *Mile Seven* gets underway."

Some of Tom's tension visibly eased, and he settled his weight back on his heels.

"Great. Get back ASAP. I'll pass the word if we head your way, but otherwise tuck the RHIBs back into the shed and lock up. Break, Bravo Ten, this is Sierra Actual. Eyes on the FDR."

Another voice came back this time. Bravo Ten was a spotter team on the very top of their fifty-story building. Besides eyeball, the team was running hobbyist quad-copters since they'd lost access to the citywide surveillance system.

"FDR is mostly clear—there appears to be at least one lane open from Battery to nearly Roosevelt Island. A few zombies in view but no mobs. Saw a couple BERT units, contractor unknown, crossing the Williamsburg bridge eastbound, otherwise just occasional civilian traffic, but not much of that. Couple of random firefights earlier but that seems to be settling down. Lots of traffic outbound. Over."

"Sierra copies, out."

"Stacey and Soph are back on the motor-sailer," Paul said. "We have a fast boat with shooters within a few hundred meters if anyone thinks about screwing with them. Harbor traffic is light, most of the boats have trickled out over the last few weeks."

Paul watched his boss take a slow breath, unwinding a bit more, and spoke.

"Still shuttling the airlifts. All the birds are up. After the ground fire last night, the helos are departing straight out over water before they gain altitude and then head north and west. But we got a situation. Kohn and her team are still cooling their heels in training room one. I chatted with her staff and they are hinting that she wants to bring more people out."

"She gets her four seats and that's it," Smith said.

"Well, she has more information, and she wants to trade."

"What could she know that is worth more than a seat out?"

"What's this thing worth?" Faith said, excited. "How cool is it that we stole an Army tank!"

Faith rapped the armor of the big six by six with the muzzle of her Saiga, yielding a boring *tap, tap* sound. Armor should *ring*, damnit.

"We didn't steal it, Faith," Steve Smith countered. "Your uncle negotiated to *borrow* it. And it's not a tank. By the way, and not to be repetitive, but can you move in all that?"

Her father sounded skeptical, even if he did approve of the full protective coverage that they had improvised for the bank personnel on the mission. Even though she was vaccinated, Steve appreciated that Faith was trying to avoid getting bitten. Missing fingers and eyeballs wouldn't grow back, even if she was no longer directly at risk of turning into a zombie.

To that end, all the shooters wore a variation on the same theme. The Smiths had matching marine foul weather coats over 5.11 trousers and long-sleeved shirts. Faith had been impressed by the bite resistance of Specialist Randall's gloves, so they went shopping for some, zombie-apocalypse style.

For values of the word shopping.

Someone else might call it a smash and grab on a closed sporting goods store where they found, in addition to the gloves, some knit caps as well as ski goggles impregnated with antifog. Faith also bore ten magazines of 12 gauge for her Saiga and several magazines for the HK that she wore on an antique drop holster.

And her kukri. Most especially her kukri.

Her father made do with a rifle borrowed from the bank and his original pistol.

"Lots of armor?" Faith tapped the side of the MRAP again. "Big gun on top? Super noisy and smooshes things? S'tank." She wiggled in her jump seat. "And yeah, I can move fine—I am zombieproof! Finally. Wish I'd worn this when I was playing mail-girl." She added a little dance in her seat by way of illustration.

"I need you to be able to move, Faith," her father said seriously. "I'm using you and Astroga on the entry team. There are females in the evacuation party and your presence might reassure them."

Faith raised an eyebrow skeptically.

"Reassure them how?"

"You know, you're a female, they're females, we aren't going to be there to hurt them, that kind of thing."

Durante had been listening, and judging from the sudden cloud on the face of the Smith girl, he didn't want any of *that* pending conversation.

He turned to his other side where the predictable pre-mission bull session was underway. The junior soldier, who he could have sworn was a private but appeared to now be a specialist, Astroga, was sitting to his immediate right. The big security contractor listened for a bit. He thought that the young soldier was posing an interesting question to the other riders.

"Imagine it's your last few minutes. Who're you gonna call? You know you're about to die when the zombies break in. But you have time to call just one more person. Should you call your mom to let her know how much you love her? Or your siblings to let them know that they're strong and can go on without you?"

Durante began to answer but Astroga cut him off with a raised knife hand.

"But . . . Bill from the Quartermaster's office really pissed me off last week. He didn't believe me that I legitimately had a crowbar destroyed in service! He said I just lost it and it had to come out of my paycheck!"

She made telephone sounds and narrated.

"*Ring, ring.*

"Bill: 'Hello? Hello?'

"Hey Bill? I'm about to die in this stupid zombie apocalypse and I just want you to know you're an utter pool of cold, spilled toss for not accepting my Report of Survey!

"Bill: 'Whaaat?'

"Fuck you, Bill!

"See, that way I could die feeling like I had lived a life well lived," Astroga finished, leaning back in contentment.

The other two Army types laughed. Durante just stared at her.

"I thought *I* was fucked up," he offered. "*Did* you lose a crowbar?"

"Hell, no!" Astroga said. "It was destroyed in service!"

"How does a crowbar get destroyed?" Faith asked,

chiming into the conversation. "They're pretty tough to destroy."

"Hello, Bill?" Astroga continued, holding a "phone" to her head. "You there?

"Your Report of Survey said that the crowbar was eaten by termites," she added in a deeper voice.

"Yeah, so?" Astroga said.

"Crowbars are steel," she continued in her Bill voice. "Termites don't eat steel crowbars."

"Wait," Copley said, shaking his head. "You actually turned in a RoS that said that crowbar you dropped in the sewer was eaten by *termites*?"

"Bill's right, you know," Durante pointed out. "They don't."

"You're saying I'm a liar when I'm about to die in a zombie apocalypse?" Astroga asked, gasping in disbelief.

"Yes, yes, I am," Durante said. "I'm going with Bill on this one."

"Fucker!"

Up front, the driver announced, "This looks like it."

Matricardi's convoy had made it into Manhattan safely. After first light, the remaining Cosa Nova staff cautiously emerged from their vehicles. Laagered in a triangle, all of the reinforced vans showed bloody collision damage on their front quarter panels and bumpers. After discovering that the infected would run towards headlights, they used parking lights to navigate the streets, often hitting the zombies that loomed unexpectedly in their path.

Oldryskya hoped that they had all been zombies.

One shooter per vehicle faced outwards while the

interior doors rolled back, permitting conversation that didn't require shouting. Turned out that the infected really *were* attracted to loud sounds.

"Why didn't we just roll up last night?" One of the remaining Cosa Nova shooters had been grousing all night, but now he had a broader audience. "We could have taken one of the bank's planes and already be out of the city!"

Oldryskya knew the answer, but Tradittore beat her to it.

"You stupid dumbass," he couldn't yell but he managed sarcasm just fine. "Did you not see all the fucking zombies? Did you not hear all the shooting? Did you see the crashed BERT full of holes? What do you think happens if we roll hot into Smith's security? We attract more zombies than we can shoot and we die. Or maybe we scare Smith's security and they light us up outside the walls and we die. Or maybe the cops are there already and they shoot us as soon as they see us and we die," Tradittore spat. "Shithead."

The goon wasn't hired for his intelligence, but he subsided, demonstrating judgement better than Oldryskya expected. She was actually glad that his linear thinking kept him from thinking too far ahead. Where he thought they were going to get a "plane" in downtown Manhattan was impossible to guess. She looked over at Tradittore and then at Matricardi. Cosa Nova was still over the authorized count of evacuees though only three of them knew that. Besides, Matricardi wasn't planning on keeping the deal anyway.

"Okay, here's the deal," Matricardi said. "We stay here, we stay quiet, and look for our shot to get inside the bank. Tradittore will pick a couple of youse to scout, careful like. We're only a few blocks away and we don't want to bring a whole mob of zombies along with us. When we spot a chance, we reach out, peaceful like. Anyone that doesn't like that can leave and try their luck on their own. Takers?"

There were none.

"Oldryskya, once we know the way is clear, you'll approach Smith. You'll see if he is going to let us in, peaceful like."

"Mr. Matricardi, maybe we should make sure that we send someone else along, to help remind her that she works for you," Tradittore interjected. His eyes slid over to Oldryskya. "Last time, she had the distressing habit of forgetting, sometimes."

She straightened her spine as the head of the Cosa Nova looked at her appraisingly.

"Another good idea, Joey."

Joanna didn't like to wait. She had watched her team settle in and suppressed her impatience. She was reasonably confident that Smith would honor his bargain, but regardless of his intent he would need to move quickly if he wanted to escape. Joanna looked around the dreary classroom for the twentieth time and again restrained her impulse to escape, somewhere. If she didn't get out, she would die too. She took a few breaths, repeating a cycle that she had repeated several times during the wait. It was just a matter of burying the apprehension more deeply. Fear would trip her up. Destroy the vision.

As the situation in New York—indeed, globally—had become worse, her thoughts on how to improve the fundamental structure of the city had begun to come together. However, it would be difficult to remake the world if she was dead.

Gauge walked up and offered a bottle of sparkling water.

"It's been three hours," she said nervously. "Why are they keeping us waiting?"

"They are very busy, Sarissa," Joanna replied with a forced calm. "We need to talk to Smith, and until he is available, we will wait patiently. We are not going to get what we want any more quickly by aggravating our hosts."

That much at least, Joanna believed. She had selected the group that filled her evacuation party for intelligence, political commitment and personal loyalty. Her partner had questioned her approach. He was no longer accompanying the group. His sort of distraction was . . . replaceable.

Although the end game was accelerating uncomfortably fast, Joanna could see advantages to the existing system eroding to a point where someone decisive, with the right vision and the right positioning, could lead a recovery. The next step would be to reach that place.

The door swung open, revealing the trim young man with the ridiculously blue eyes.

"Mr. Smith can see you now," Rune said with a smile.

Joanna's return smile was almost entirely genuine.

"That's a fuck ton of zombies, Da," Faith said. She and the rest of the MRAP riders took turns craning their necks to look out the front windows at the growing mob of infected in view.

Steve Smith agreed. However, there was still a way to make this work. He addressed the driver.

"If you don't worry about knocking over railings or scratching your paint, can you put the back of this thing up against the doors of that building?"

The corporal looked skeptically at the structure, featuring the typical Central Park East walk-up entry.

"Close to it, anyway. The steps are an issue."

"Right," Steve replied. "So, what we do is back all three vehicles up so that we create a barrier between the rest of the street and the doors. We use the firing slots to light up the zombies we trap against the buildings, and then breach inwards till we get to the principal. Grab the family, reverse our way back into the truck and head back. Easy-peasy."

Everyone looked at him like he had grown a third eye.

"What?" Smith sounded aggrieved. "This is a great plan. What do you think, Sergeant?"

Copley considered the zombies through the bullet-proof glass. Several were clawing ineffectually at the MRAP's armor.

"Dunno sir," Copley replied. The sergeant tried to count the infected. "It isn't the craziest idea I have heard today, but that's not saying much. Probably work. Worst case we scratch the trucks up a bit. Can't use frags though, wouldn't want to flatten the tires. Fine on the MRAP, not so good on the civilian vehicles."

"Right, no punctures please," Steve said. "Sergeant, brief the other drivers. We'll game it out in here, then you line us up."

The looks he noted still clearly suggested that he was stone crazy.

"So, you are saying that Ding has gone crazy?" Tom asked his guest.

"Homicidally detached from reality," Joanna stated flatly. "His wife was dead already. Now the children are dead. In fact, most of the unaccompanied dependents at One Police Plaza were turned, and those such as survived the experience were shot dead by their parents or their parents' coworkers."

"Jesus. So, homicidal, irrational, and he blames...?" Tom wondered.

"He thinks that Matricardi did it." Kohn tapped one fist into her palm. "I expect that he is not feeling too cozy about us, either."

She held up a hand to forestall the obvious retort.

"Yes, I know that there is not a logical reason for Matricardi to do it, but logic is not at the fore at the moment. Dominguez is certain enough that it was Cosa Nova that he has cordoned the city everywhere that I can reach. He has killed any of the Matricardi organization that he can find. His anger is unsatiated as is that of the hundreds of cops who are raging to kill those responsible for the death of their children. Which target list, at this point, is pretty much... everyone. At least everyone of importance."

She paused.

"How the hell did whoever did it actually do it?" Smith was still thinking through the problem.

"Somehow some zombies got into the children's dormitory, undetected," Kohn replied. "Yes, I know that does not make sense. It looks as if they were deliberately planted."

"Overture."

"Probably," Joanna said, her tone impatient. "*How* is not immediately relevant. What is important is that Dominguez knows that you have a deal with

Matricardi. He is going to call you. I do not want to be on the island when he does. You stated that if my information was good, you would honor our bargain. I want to be evacuated. Now."

"Your information is . . . valuable," Tom ceded reluctantly. "I'll place you on the evacuation list for a lift in the next couple hours. We only have three helos, and we are planning on driving most of the rest out in a couple of hardened buses as soon as the last people are gathered up—which is happening now."

"And my additional staff?" Kohn insisted.

"Somehow I don't think that Matricardi and Dominguez are going to be using their spaces," Tom said drily. "So, yes, I'll accommodate your extras."

The ringing in Steve Smith's ears was continuous now, ear plugs or not. That meant that everyone was nearly yelling to be heard, especially given the background of howling zombies. The mob outside was thinned by the belt-fed, but new infected continued to appear, drawn by either the suppressed gunfire or the idling vehicle engines.

Things inside were a little . . . sticky.

After creating a barrier with their high-sided vehicles, they had used the limited firing arcs of the gun ports on the MRAP to finish the zombies that the trucks knocked over. The first shooters to unass the MRAP immediately discovered that although the ground clearance on the BERT trucks was low enough to prevent zombies from easily crawling under them, the MRAP's axle height was much more generous. After a few tense moments of shooting under the truck to pile up enough zombie dead to inhibit easy passage, they all caught their breath before Smith and Durante organized the door entry and the team cleared its way to the bank CEO.

Steve flipped up his night vision. The interior of the residence was lit with battery powered lanterns, and the bright white LEDs precluded the use of NODS. Rich Bateman had been briefed on their arrival, and recognized the Smith family resemblance.

Even though the family seemed glad to see them, there was a new wrinkle. Several extra wrinkles in fact. As the group reversed its route and paused inside the front door, Steve repeated his headcount, twice, before approaching Bateman.

"Sir, we planned enough space for your family and household, totaling nine people," Steve said carefully. "You've three times that many."

Steve was staying calm, relying on his master's degree in "Nothing Ever Goes Strictly to Plan," earned at the University of "No Shit, There I Was."

Bateman wasn't relaxed, exactly, but he wasn't panicking. The same couldn't be said of his party. Beyond Mrs. Bateman and the two children and their nanny, his regular driver and his regular driver's family, there was a group of in-laws, their children and some hangers on, including more mid level bank officers and *their* wives. The volume of what Steve assumed were complaints was steadily growing. He was letting Durante handle that.

"Steve, right?" Bateman said, trying for normalcy. "Call me Rich, please. How many can we take in the first go, Steve? Some are friends of Nancy, some just short of showed up."

"There might only be one lift... Rich." Steve's scalp

itched abominably but he didn't want to screw with the straps to re-don his head gear. "The presence of infected is getting heavier and we all need to get off the island, post haste, so shuttling between here and the bank is going to be dicey. It's easier since we have the armor, we now know which routes should be clear and there aren't any more zombies in the house. If the streets get blocked there is no way we'll get back on foot. Then there is the matter of the vehicles themselves. They are . . . less than comfortable."

"Steve, I don't care about their comfort," Bateman replied.

Steve had been filtering out the background chatter as he simultaneously talked to the CEO and mentally shaped a loadplan that would stack people like cordwood in the MRAP and BERT vans. Yelling and then screaming loud enough to overcome the thumps, growls and occasional gunshots coming from outside finally broke his concentration.

"How dare you celebrate murdering my husband, you horrible, evil little girl! I'll have you arrested, and your Neanderthal boyfriend too!"

The screamer was a well-kept woman in her late middle years. One of the strap hangers had made it inside the house before she turned, and had bitten one other person. Both of the zombies were now down and dead, credit one each to Faith and Durante. When the last door opened, the uninfected rescuees had caught the pair exchanging a high five. It turned out a newly deceased zombie had left a widow who felt pretty self-important. Judging from the screeches, she was a former Mrs. ex-senior financial services executive.

The CEO grimaced at her yell and tried to keep

talking, but Steve watched for a moment longer as Faith performed her patented teenage eye-roll maneuver and muttered something that her father couldn't quite make out. Designed to overcome her father's notoriously strong sangfroid, this display of insolence was overkill for the matron, who was sufficiently outraged to scream and leap for Faith, optimistically trying for a slap.

Steve didn't really think that Faith had actually tried to physically provoke anyone, but if the teen was surprised by the response, it didn't slow her reaction. She ducked under the slap and pulled most of the power of her return butt stroke to her attacker's stomach.

"Oh no you don't," Faith said as she levered the woman the rest of the way to the floor in an arm bar. "Da said that I can't kill anybody 'cept infected, but that doesn't mean you get any freebies."

Bateman, Smith and Durante all lunged to intervene and then halted to avoid a three-way collision. The woman's teenage son was yelling, but carefully not touching Faith and equally carefully watching Durante, who had taken a half step back while laying his hand on a holstered Taser.

"Let her up, Faith!" Steve ordered. He really didn't need this.

Faith immediately released her hold and backed away a step, pacifically raising her arms to shoulder height in an "I give up" motion.

She immediately ruined the gesture by looking side to side and asking the group, "Are you not reassured?"

"I feel reassured!" Astroga chirped. Astroga and Randall had slipped in through the door to help with loading.

Randall promptly smacked the back of her helmet.

"Deep breaths everyone," Steve ordered in a loud voice. The woman's son led her to the opposite side of the room, where she sobbed and flailed, but otherwise left the team alone.

In the background, Astroga whipped out her little green notebook.

"Number twenty-nine: The specialist shall not encourage the homicidal teenager to slap around VIPs. Even if it is reassuring."

Steve shook his head, closed his eyes and made Daffy Duck noises with his mouth for a moment.

"*Roight*," he said, opening his eyes again. "Let's see how many we can fit in a single lift, *Rich*. You and Mrs. Rich are first. Then we shall load the vehicles for our scenic tour of Manhattan as follows..."

CHAPTER 16

"If the pot is boiling over, use a long spoon. If the house is on fire, warm yourself."

—Unattributed Prohibition-Era Mafioso

"How many people do we have left?"

The evacuation had been running steadily all night. The massive building was largely empty. The security outposts had thinned, and suppressed rifle fire was common as zombies came into view singly or in small clusters.

"Bateman and his wife left even before the second lift of evacuees were all on the trucks. Everyone's back; in fact, your brother has probably already reached the family boat. We are loading the last of the civilians on the three birds on the roof. Speaking of which, there was another situation with Faith . . ."

Tom looked up sharply.

"Faith is fine, everyone is fine, no casualties," Paul said soothingly. "However, the sister of the lady that objected to the shooting of her zombie husband objected to the cleanliness of the BERT trucks. To be fair, they smell a bit high, but Faith stuck a pistol in her face and offered to turn her into vaccine if she didn't get in the truck."

"You know, I can't really muster any outrage for that." Tom just rubbed his face for a moment. "How's security?"

"We're holding the building with a skeleton now," Paul said. "All the buses are flushed. I figure that as soon as we drop below the current numbers of shooters we can turn off the lobby lights, seal the doors and hold from the roof."

"Roger that," Tom said. "Tell Kap to stream the birds as they return instead of sending them in flights. You're on the next lift. Take Kohn with you. Split her party up, I don't want her with an intact cadre at any refuge. You go with her to Site Blue and I'll catch up."

The radio sounded again.

"*Smith.*" A different voice, a voice familiar to Tom called his name. "*You listening, Smith?*"

They looked at handset for a moment and then Smith picked up.

"Tom Smith. Station calling, please identify, over."

"*You know me,*" Dominguez said without preamble. "*Do you have Matricardi?*"

"Captain Dominguez, is that you?" Tom tried for dialogue. "What's your status? Over."

"*Smith, I want Matricardi and all of his people. Do you have them?*"

"We haven't been able to reach you," Tom replied, ignoring the question. "Most of the comms are down and I heard that there was a zombie outbreak at your building. Talk to me."

"*Outbreak?*" Dominguez's voice was a rasp. "*You heard about that? I guess that means that you have Kohn there, too. Keep her. Or don't. I don't care. I didn't hear you say that you don't have Matricardi—so he's there. Good. Give me that asshole, and you are out of this. I'll even give you time to get off this island before everyone and anything on it dies."*

"Whoa, Ding, wha—"

Tom knew crazy when he heard it. He was trying to cut through the crazy but Dominguez cut him off.

"If I gotta ask you more than once when I get there, you might not get the same deal. I'll be there in a bit. Have that murdering scum ready to give to me. That's all the negotiation that you are going to get."

The channel went silent.

"Ding, this is Tom. Come in."

Tom repeated the call but the radio stayed silent. Tom stared at the radio in his hand for a moment before passing it back to Paul.

"Wellll . . . that was unhelpful," Paul offered. "What now?"

"Run the airlift. Shorten the perimeter. Come up with something to satisfy Dominguez."

"We don't have what he wants, though."

"That doesn't appear to matter."

The entire group had overheard the radio, and Joanna's OEM staffers awaiting their flight out of Manhattan were edging closer to panic.

"Remain calm, everyone," the OEM director said, as soothingly as she could. "The aircraft are very nearly ready for us."

She watched as one of Smith's attack dogs walked over, to be met by Gauge. They conferred momentarily before Kohn saw the man whose name tag read KAPLAN raise both hands palms up and shrug, before he turned without a second look and walked to the open door leading up to the heliport.

She couldn't hear the words but she knew what "take it or leave it" looked like. Joanna motioned Schweizer over as Gauge returned.

"We are to spread out people across the next three aircraft," Gauge stated, gesturing vaguely upward. "Kaplan says that they are refueling now, and that they can take three of our people in the first two helicopters and the last two after that."

"Which site are we going to?" asked Schweizer heatedly. "We need to stay together as much as possible."

"I don't know which site," replied Gauge, ignoring her colleague and instead focusing on Kohn herself. "Do we let them split us up, ma'am?"

Out of the corner of her eye, Joanna saw two more of Smith's key personnel enter the assembly room. The handsome dark-complected intel officer, Rune, was delivering a locked black case to another bank employee, a woman with a haunted look.

"Ensure that our remaining pistols are quietly distributed as evenly as possible Ken," she directed Schweizer. "At least one member of our team on each aircraft should be armed. We aren't in a position to argue with the bankers. Yet."

Rune looked up and met her gaze. He really did have the most beautiful eyes, Joanna reflected.

Schweizer noted her gaze and saw Rune.

"What does that asshole want?"

"Wait, ma'am, you want to hijack a helicopter?" asked Gauge wonderingly.

"Nothing that dramatic, I hope," Kohn replied.

∞ ⊖ ∞

"Welcome back, miss," Tom said evenly. "It isn't quite 'long time—no see,' but you did leave rather unexpectedly. We could've used your help at the Acre. Of course, you were also dressed for the mission, then."

The head of security and Durante stared at Old-ryskya at close range. Her presence was a bit more than unexpected, especially since she appeared to have materialized on foot. Also, she was immaculately coiffed and made up, down to the high heels more suited to an evening out than picking her way among the dead infected that littered Wall Street.

As the number of personnel who remained shrank, Durante had withdrawn staff from the forward positions that had previously kept the infected at least a block from the actual building. The current security point was just outside the front doors of the bank, which explained how someone could just walk up, provided that they weren't dragged down by the infected. Although no mobs were in view, the perimeter staff were briefed to shoot any that approached, and had done so to the tune of several per hour. The dead zombies had really started to mount up.

Risky and two Cosa Nova shooters had very carefully shown themselves and asked to see Smith or whoever was still in charge. Durante knew better than to say anything, but even an atypical Wall Street hire like him knew that her clothes were . . . zombie apocalypse inappropriate. She strode all the way to the front door, while the two Cosa Nova men stopped short. One turned about, facing outwards, while the other stood behind their spokeswoman and continued to face the bank. The group was very obviously trying to signal that they were not a threat.

"I gotta ask ya', Risky." Durante added his two cents. "How did you manage to save that outfit and complete a sunkissed look in the middle of a zombie apocalypse?"

Smith delivered a withering glare, but Durante appeared unrepentant.

"Well, it isn't natural!"

She smiled, showing one cautious dimple.

"Trade secret," she said. "Let's just say I've walked in some dark places."

Durante grinned in appreciation.

Oldryskya glanced up at the roofline fifty stories above as a helicopter disappeared from view, settling onto the roof. Normally, the sound of the helo would be lost at street level, buried in the New York metro noise. Now, it was clearly audible.

She smoothed her hands down her dress and looked back to the reception committee, composing her face in a neutral business mask.

"Mr. Smith," Risky said, nodding. "Mr. Matricardi sends his respects. I *am* still dressed for the mission, which currently is to safely approach your bank. In this dress, I'm clearly not hiding any weapons, yes?"

She had on the same tight black number from the first restaurant meeting. Tom very carefully didn't look at the dress. Much.

"My companions are for my security," Oldryskya continued, noting his gaze. "My boss thought that you might be less ready to shoot me if I wore this instead of one of Durante's tactical rigs. The Elevated Acre meeting *was* tense and I was recalled to assist Mr. Matricardi. I'm sorry that there wasn't time for more discussion."

"And?" Tom replied.

"And Mr. Matricardi wants to come in," she added. "He isn't sure where you stand."

Tom and Durante exchanged a look, before Tom spoke.

"The cops want me to deliver your boss to them, giftwrapped," Tom said flatly. "They think that Cosa Nova killed a bunch of their children. Both of Dominguez's kids are dead. I can't finish my evacuation for several hours and the cops are coming here, maybe right now. So, you can see that I have a problem."

One of the Jersey men swore softly, but didn't turn around.

"And what do you plan to do?" Risky asked calmly. "We have a deal. Mr. Matricardi lived up to his side. We have adhered to the terms, perfectly. The police who are hunting our organization are the ones who have broken the compact."

Tom continued to look her directly in the eyes.

"Did Matricardi have anything to do with the attack?"

"No." Risky's reply was vehement. "We had nothing to do with it. It was a frame, not even a good one. It convinced the Jersey cops. They came last night with the same story and wanted to kill us. We escaped but it was expensive. Afterward, we didn't have the resources to push south or west on our own. Instead of running away, we ran here. For the evacuation."

"Boss! Heads up!" Durante called. Both Cosa Nova men turned to face outwards.

Three blocks away, but clearly visible from the sidewalk, a police special response Atlas truck turned onto Wall Street from Broadway, followed by another. Diesel engines growled in the opposite direction.

Tom looked left and he saw a third black vehicle pull into view from the East River end of the street. He decided quickly.

"You three inside the lobby!" he said, motioning to the Cosa Nova contingent. "Gravy, alert the teams on the third floor. Stay with these people but no shooting. Pass the word and make sure that the Army guys know."

Tom and the original bank personnel stayed put when, minutes later, the black, hulking armored truck stopped in directly in front of Tom. The other two stopped a football length away in each direction. Dominguez stepped down from the truck's running board and walked up to where Tom and Durante waited.

"Smith," Ding offered by way of a greeting.

"Captain," Tom replied.

"Matricardi is here," Ding said, scanning behind Smith. "I saw some of his people scamper inside. I want them all. Now."

"How long to get there, Paul?" Kendra asked.

The flashing black rotors on the big helicopter spun faster as the craft prepared to depart the roof of the bank. There was room for up to six helos at a time, but half the of space was occupied by a highly illegal, unlicensed collection of fuel blivets. A second helicopter was also spooling up while a third, recently landed, was refueling.

Paul placed himself on the same aircraft with Joanna Kohn and allowed her only one personal staff member on the same flight. She'd chosen her male aide and sent the next pair over to the adjacent helo. Paul conveniently neglected to mention that the various flights were not all converging on the same destination. He'd manifested six passengers on this trip, well under the maximum possible. In addition to Kendra, he'd also brought Sergeant Randall and Christine, the female refugee from the concert. Smiling, he scanned the cabin again. Across from him in the cramped space, Kohn smiled back, mistaking his meaning.

He consulted his wristwatch to conceal his expression, but tangled his wrist in the headset cord. Even in a luxury model rotocraft like the big Airbus EC155s that they had on long-term charter, the interior noise was sufficient to require hearing protection and all the passengers wore cranials that were plugged into the ceiling panel.

There were only a few score staff remaining at the bank. Those left at this point were mostly pure security and a few comms personnel. Unsurprisingly, Smith insisted on being the last out. Given the round trip flight time to the refuges, BotA could button the front doors and have the last personnel out of Manhattan by dinner or a little after.

If Dominguez didn't interfere.

Paul's eyes moved to Kendra. She was looking out the window, a black, locked case covering most of her lap. He'd made it clear that she had one job until they arrived at the refuge and the case, stenciled with a white number 2, was it.

"Even a big bird like this can barely reach our Pennsylvania refueling point with a light passenger load," he replied. "That's why we haven't maxed out the seats. Figure three and half hours to refueling stop, and then another hour after that. Then lather, rinse and repeat for each remaining lift."

The pilot eased the collective and they lifted upwards smoothly.

Tom looked steadily at Dominguez. The tall cop was gaunt and his face bore new, deep lines. He wore his uniform under the tactical equipment harness but apart from the sidearm, no weapons were visible.

Yet.

"Captain Dominguez, I don't have Màtricardi," Tom said carefully. "A few of his people approached me a short time ago and they are under my protection. Further, I do not believe that Matricardi was behind the attack on your families."

Dominguez didn't immediately reply. He looked upwards. The patchy gray cloud cover allowed the late summer sunlight to filter through, lighting the scene without shadow. The engine noise from the helicopter was clear. Still looking up, he raised his right arm, then pumped it once.

In his peripheral vision, Smith saw doors open on the more distant vehicles and cops pile out. A few more trucks pulled into sight.

"Last chance," Dominguez said. His tone was the utter neutral of madness. "Give me Matricardi and any other Cosa Nova and you can keep running your operation. You can give them to me or I'll take them. If I have to take them, I *will* kill everyone in the way. No one will leave this place. Your call."

"Ding, you know me well enough to understand that I'm not going to turn anyone over to you to be executed," Smith said, almost as neutral in tone. "Let's all get off the island and settl—"

"No." Dominguez smiled like a death's head as he

cut off further discussion with a wave. "I was rather expecting that. Businessman reflexes. You think that everything can be talked out. You've two minutes to reconsider. If I see you send them out front, I'll do the rest."

He turned and walked back to the idling armored vehicle, reaching for his own radio as he did so.

Oldryskya watched the exchange through the glass front of the building, which filtered the light into a urine yellow color. Behind her the two Cosa Nova guards were unsuccessfully fumbling with their radio. She turned her head towards Durante, who stood with his feet apart and arms crossed.

"Do you think Mr. Smith will take the deal with Dominguez?"

"No," the taller man said, rubbing a hand through his brush cut. "That would be the smart move, no offense. But Tom made a deal, and he is pure hell on deal breakers. This is gonna turn into a fight. We're short on shooters and light on heavy weapons, so I figure we button up, retreat up and defend down. They're gonna have a hell of a time fighting their way up fifty floors as we chopper out. Meanwhile, the zombies come in behind them."

Durante smiled suddenly.

"Tell you this much, I wouldn't want to switch places with them."

"Can we hold them long enough for the helicopters to get here?" asked the gangster, radio clutched in one hand.

"Yes," Durante said, unslinging his rifle. The former special operator was clearly back in his element.

"We're lucky we don't have to break out. *That* would be a stone bitch. We just have to see what the cops choose to do."

They all watched Smith stride back in the front door. Smith stopped, looked at the group and sighed.

"What we have here, mates, is a failure to communicate," he said, his native accent thickening.

"Time to do the dance," Durante said, his face breaking into a broad grin.

Then he flicked off his safety. Wasn't going to need it any time soon.

The presence of the cops around the bank had changed the departure profile of the airlift. Each helicopter spiraled straight upwards, gaining altitude sufficient to make ground fire a lesser risk.

Kendra watched the city recede as their helo leveled off and turned west. The bank rooftop was clearly visible. Around her, the various passengers were clearly occupied with their own thoughts, most clutching a small bag, all that they had been allowed to retain.

She spoke on the shared intercom.

"I thought it would be faster than this."

"Even with fewer passengers, we are really heavily laden with fuel, so it takes longer to climb out," Paul replied, not looking up from his tablet. "This isn't the movies where everything happens at once."

With a final tap, he looked back for the final time.

"Oh, shit."

That got everyone's attention, despite his flat tone.

A white contrail was arrowing up from the ground level of downtown and in a moment it reached the next Bank of the Americas helicopter, just as it climbed away from the roof. From this distance, it wasn't obvious if the missile actually contacted the bird, or just exploded in close proximity.

Not that it mattered.

After the craft reappeared from the initial gray puff of the explosion, it began to spin, slowly at first but accelerating as it descended.

In their helicopter the pilot blanched and pulled up on his collective, burying his turbine RPM needles in the red as he clawed upwards, trading speed for altitude.

"Those things have a slant range over three miles and we are *way* too close!"

Hands clutched arm rests. Behind them the stricken helicopter impacted on the landing area it had just departed.

A small explosion bloomed orange. Less than a second later, a much larger explosion obscured the entire roof.

Tom had relocated the security checkpoint to the third floor, the highest level of the mezzanine that ringed the lobby from the inside. The decorative planters that served as a railing were made of Italian marble. Between the stone and the soil, they were adequate to stop small arms fire, should it become necessary. If Dominguez really tried to fight his way inside, his assault teams would first have to clear the lobby while taking direct fire from hardened fighting positions. The butcher's bill would be high, and the cops would have to pay in blood for every floor they wanted to ascend.

Fighting up a building was manpower intensive.

Tom felt pretty confident that the NYPD didn't have the personnel to buy their way up the entire tower before he could evac everyone from the roof.

Still, standing alone at the doorway, watching the cops watch the building, Tom really hoped that it wouldn't come to that.

But it had been two minutes.

At the railing above him, Durante lowed the handset and got Tom's attention.

"We got two birds aw—"

Pop.

Tom spun around at a half remembered noise, but then the implication hit him and he dropped to the ground, banging his jaw on the hard marble floor.

"Incoming!"

As a loud whoosh registered, automatic fire began shattering the lobby windows. Tom frantically low-crawled over to the escalator and laid as flat as the steps permitted while the lobby filled with glass and bullet fragments. Before he reached even a third of the way to the landing, his building shuddered slightly.

That didn't feel right.

Oldryskya dropped to the floor as soon as Smith yelled. One of her guards also went prone, as did all the bank staff. The glass sheathing of the lobby blew inwards and down as quickly as a venetian blind yanked off its fasteners by a sturdy toddler. Ricochets howled off the marble that clad much of the lobby. She heard a meaty slap and a simultaneous grunt as the building perceptibly shook.

She glanced over at the sounds to watch the second Cosa Nova shooter fall to his knees, then onto his face, a blood pool spreading quickly from an unseen wound. She rolled him over to check his airway but the missing scalp and exposed bone rendered the point moot. Instead, she helped herself to his carbine and worked on getting his plate carrier off. It would be large, but it was a hell of a lot better than an LBD in a firefight.

Moments later, the digital whooping of the building fire alarm added to the cacophony, and a few orange safety lights pulsed as they rotated overhead.

The incoming fire continued. At least two heavy machine guns were chugging, absolutely demolishing everything on the ground level.

"Good instincts," Durante said, laying a hand on her arm and placing his mouth close to her ears. "But forget it. Boss had me save yours. Keep the rifle and strip him of the mags."

At the very end of his sentence the fire stopped, and his last words echoed loudly.

Oldryskya looked around the edge of the planter to survey the damage. Drywall dust filtered down, and a small fire smoldered at the wooden reception desk area, ignited by a tracer. Paper and glass covered the lobby floor, but there were no cops in view.

Smith leopard crawled over, body nearly flat to the floor, face turned sideways to lower his profile even farther. It didn't look like the heroes in the American movies, but then again, he wasn't shot either. She made another mental note.

Outside, a loudspeaker blared.

"Smith! Smith, we get you?"

Tom watched as Durante wormed his away across the floor to the control panel on the third floor and punched few buttons, silencing the profoundly irritating alarm. The orange fire lights still blinked sullenly.

Someone broke squelch on the radio net.

"Gravy, Thunder, this is Kapman, do you read, over?"

Durante slid the radio across the floor to Smith.

"Kap, go for Thunder."

"MANPAD took the second bird," Kaplan reported, using the shorthand term for a Man Portable Air Defense missile. "It crashed into the refueling station and took the last helo and everyone inside with it. The top two floors are fully involved and spreading. Lost the comms shack, the UHF antenna farm and both radio guys. I don't even have a corporal's guard, let alone enough people to attack a liquid fuels fire, over."

Tom digested that for a moment. That big thud *had* felt wrong. Oh, so very unpleasantly wrong.

"Copy. Looks like the way out is going to have to be through. Come down to three, over."

Tom heard a sigh on the channel.

"That's what we figured," Kaplan said. "Tell Durante not to get his ass shot off till I get there. If he does, I got dibs on his watch. On the way."

Tom looked around. Counting Oldryskya and the extra Cosa Nova man, they had eleven armed people on the third floor, maybe another half dozen coming down from the roof. If that many. Oh, and the fire.

The fire. Well, that was just perfect.

"Hey!" came an amplified voice from the street.

Over the persistent and newly refreshed ringing in his ears, he recognized Dominguez's voice on the megaphone.

"I said, are you all okay in there?" Ding sounded positively upbeat. "Hey, Smith!"

The crunch of booted feet on glass was plain as police tac teams deployed just outside the bank walls.

"Oh yeah, we're all good," Tom yelled back. "No worries, mate. Howzit with you?"

"That's the first laugh that I've had in a while, Smith," the cop replied. "Thanks. That big boom you heard? That was my FBI guy using a Stinger to shut your private rooftop airport down. Looks like quite a fire up there. You weren't illegally storing a lot of aviation fuel up there, were you?"

"You just killed a bunch of innocent people, Ding," Tom said, his voice hard. "*My* people."

"How many of them were kids, Smith?" Dominguez's replied instantly. "Give me Matricardi and you can still walk before I close every route off this bitch of an island. I know that you have some of his people inside, so he's either with you or nearby. Either way, they don't leave."

Tom looked around again. Oldryskya's mouth was pressed into a firm red line. Durante had his usual game face on, which was indistinguishable from any other face he made, and as Steve watched Durante exhaled a huge yawn. The rest of the team varied between manic grins to a "I think I just shat myself look" on the lone mobster. Tom waved the entire group back down to the elevator area where they could at least stand.

"Hey Ding, if you try to fight your way inside a burning building full of people who know how to fight back, you are going to lose everyone," Tom said, attempting math. "It doesn't add up for you. You might kill us, but you're going to die. Every single one. I'll make sure of it."

There was a pause and Dominguez answered, a little more quietly this time.

"No, Tom, no we won't. You see, we already lost everyone. We're already dead, every mother's son. Give me Matricardi or no one gets off the island. That's the final word."

Tom looked down at his marine radio and switched channels. He took a deep breath.

And yelled.

"Fuck the motherfucking First Precinct and fuck the NYPD."

He keyed the radio.

"*Mile Seven*, this is Thunderblast," he called.

He heard his brother Steve respond.

"*Thunder*, Mile Seven."

Tom took a breath and made the call.

"Code is Goose, say again, Goose."

Every spring and fall in Ireland, migratory geese pass through on their way to their feeding grounds in the south or their nesting grounds in the north. Working the harsh and stony lands of the green aisle, Irish lads of old would watch the geese fly and wonder what lands they sought.

When those same Irish lads left home to seek their fortune, it was assumed they'd never return. Few did. Irishmen had scattered their bones on every continent on Earth. And when they left home, as so many had, they called it "following the wild geese."

With the helos gone all they had left were the RHIBs, which had very limited range. The *Mile Seven* was Tom's last more-or-less secure exfil. But it was less than likely that Tom would make it out of the building, much less to his brother's boat. And if he kept his brother waiting, they might not get out either.

It was time for Steve and the Smith girls to follow

the wild geese. Let someone make it out of this hellhole.

Most of Steve Smith's last transmission was lost in a loud rumble outside the bank, but he made out a few words.

"Roger, Goose. Good luck."

It was enough. Tom looked down at the trashed lobby and rolled his shoulder, unconsciously easing some of his tension.

Now, to cases.

They watched the bank burn as Paul's helicopter loitered in a lazy circle above Upper New York Bay, five miles from downtown. The pilot tried fruitlessly to raise the ad hoc rooftop control tower.

His comment to Paul was superfluous.

"I got nothing on UHF."

The initial gabble of conversation on the intercom had died, so his words rang in everyone's headset accompanied by the background whine of the engine.

"Jesus!" Into the silence, he added, "The bridge, lookit the Brooklyn Bridge!"

Small puffs of dirty gray smoke hung alongside the aged suspension cables that supported the roadbed. A few stopped cars were visible. They watched cables part, first on the inbound and then the outbound lanes. The roadbed twisted back and forth, the rotation increasing in amplitude as the balance swung first one way and then the next, till the concrete and steel roadbed fragmented, raining down into the bay. Immediately adjacent, they watched the spectacle repeat on the Manhattan Bridge. In the far distance, smoke enveloped the Washington bridge, obscuring any damage.

An awed voice echoed on the intercom.

"Motherfuckers blew the bridges. They blew the fucking bridges."

For several more moments they surveyed the destruction. One by one, the passengers looked up at Paul while the pilot continued to maintain altitude, swearing softly.

Paul gazed around the faces about him. Fear and shock dominated, but there was at least one completely composed face.

"We can not set down in the fire, even if we could see through the smoke," Joanna Kohn said into the silence. "And they might have more missiles, correct?"

The pilot replied while Paul gauged her words.

"Fucking A," the pilot replied. "You can find someone else to fly this thing if you want to land there. That is a non-LZ."

"Just so," Kohn replied. She looked at Paul. "Even if we could land, what would we do? You told us we were at the maximum safe load to reach our way point, yes?"

"Yes," Paul said tightly. "Fuck, fuck, fuck, fuck, fuck. Anyone down there is on their own. And we're burning fuel."

He leaned forward and tapped the pilot's shoulder and then shook his head in response to the query on the pilot's face. Paul pointed outwards and leaned back.

The aircraft straightened and flew west. Paul kept his head turned to watch the black smoke from the bank mingle with the darkening haze from the other fires around the city.

CHAPTER 17

"... there are persistent, broadly distributed fires consuming every city with a population of over two hundred and fifty thousand. Nearly universal power outages, the complete gridlock of every major highway leading to population centers, and the absence of organized law enforcement have effectively suspended anything resembling the rule of law. The Department of Defense is in slightly better shape. With regard to the Strategic Nuclear Deterrent..."

—Extract from the Presidential Daily Brief,
August 26, 2012

Frank Matricardi and Joey Tradittore watched the white finger of the Stinger reach up and swat the helicopter back onto the roof of the bank even as the echoes of automatic fire rang along the concrete canyons of lower Manhattan. The older man tried to count the guns from the sound and failed.

"What the fuck was that?" exclaimed one of his shooters.

"Fuckin' missile is what," Tradittore replied.

"That's a lot of fucking guns," the boss added.

Inside the cluster of vehicles, the remaining men exchanged nervous looks but otherwise kept watch.

"Still nothing on our radio, either," Frank mused. "Got to be the cops."

"This is looking pretty thin," Tradittore said. "We

could still get out of here." He looked in the direction of Wall Street. The column of black smoke from the bank grew.

"And go where?" Matricardi asked sarcastically.

"Maybe the house upstate?" Tradittore said, shrugging.

"One thing's for sure, we aren't flying from there, or anywhere, as long as the cops have missiles," goon two offered, demonstrating his mastery of the obvious. "What do you think, Joey T?"

"I think we do what the boss says," Tradittore replied.

A few minutes later, they heard deeper, rumbling explosions. None of the bridges were in direct line of sight, but they watched an explosion bloom from the side of a tower on a pier projecting from the opposite shore in Jersey City. It began streaming a plume of brown smoke. Tradittore jerked his head backwards, like a man who had just been slapped. He glanced around, checking for any live zombies.

"Back in a sec."

Without waiting for permission, he moved from the vehicle to look around the corner of the adjacent building fronting the river and nodded. He trotted back, a little out of breath.

"Yeah, they got both of them," Joey said, slumping into the seat in defeat.

"Both of what?" asked Matricardi.

"The Holland Tunnel ventilation towers," Tradittore huffed. "They feed fresh air and power down there—no towers means that anyone trying to get to Jersey is going to suffocate before they get too far."

The rumbles continued in the distance.

"I'm betting that they didn't just blow the Tunnel, neither," Tradittore grumbled, crossing his arms. "That'd be da fuckin' bridges. Assholes."

"The cops think we killed their kids, their women," Frank Matricardi mused aloud. "They mean to trap everyone here. No helicopters. We probly can't drive outta here no more, either."

"How the hell are we getting out of here then!" one of the shooters asked.

"You thinking what I'm thinking, Joey?"

Tradittore looked back at his boss.

"I figure Smith will still keep his word, and he's got a plan."

"Yep," Frank said, nodding his head. "Smith's whole job was planning and he had the bank's money to do it. Figure he's got plan A through Z. Hell, he's probably only on D by now. And by now Oldryskya will be in there. He said he'd get us out as part of the Deal. Between her persuasion and his honor, it's still a done deal. Let's use his plan. Unless you got a better idea than 'let's try to get to the house in upstate,' Joey."

Behind the boss, another of the Cosa Nova shooters raised an eyebrow. Tradittore caught the man's expression and shook his head almost imperceptibly.

"Everyone back in the trucks."

Kaplan had made it down to the third-floor atrium with his people including Sergeant Copley. They were panting after their headlong gallop down nearly fifty flights of stairs. Copley paused by the exit door, counting heads. After a second scan he started looking around wildly.

"Where's Astroga?"

He turned to look back up the stairwell shaft and yelled, "Astroga!"

The elevator dinged and the doors slid open to reveal the smoke stained face of the indomitable specialist.

"I pushed for the elevator and by the time I turned around you guys had disappeared," she said, seeming puzzled. "Where'd you go?"

Copley was neither remotely amused nor understanding, and advanced menacingly to tower over the unawed soldier.

"I am going to bust you back to, back to..." He searched for a ranked destination far enough to match her crime.

Meanwhile, Durante exchanged a fist bump with Kaplan.

"No Rolex for you," he said.

"Yet, but keep it handy," the shorter man replied, eyeing the case that Kaplan gripped one-handed. "The stuff okay?"

"Should be, topped it off like Curry showed us."

A few others were exchanging back slaps and private asides.

Tom looked back from his crouched position where he was trying to discern the police movements outside. The tac teams had withdrawn out of sight.

"If all of you are quite through gassing, we need to identify the best exit," he stated briskly. "Or even *an* exit. The front is right out, they have at least two machine guns mounted to cover the street. Gravy take one man, check the garage side. Kapman, same thing but recon the rear fire exit and the connection to the subway passage."

As the two pelted off in different directions, Copley stopped glaring at the still-insouciant Astroga to ask Smith, "What can we do?"

"Find a spot where you can cover the doors from here in case they try a frontal rush," Tom replied. "Stay well back. Oldryskya, take your guy and get an angle on the coffee nook to the left. We hold hard here until we find a way out."

The remaining window glass began to blow inwards while the report of automatic fire rang through the lobby again.

The police machine gunner rapped out a long burst, traversing one side of the bank lobby.

"Deliberate fire," Dominguez said. "Take your time and conserve ammunition. We got all the time in the world."

The gunner didn't reply from his firing position behind another concrete planter. The thick, dirt-filled rectangles were ubiquitous in the downtown area due to their use for channeling vehicle traffic. Another machine gunner squatted a short distance away, awaiting his turn. The two largest remaining tac teams had been withdrawn half a block away, in order to put some hard cover between them and potential snipers inside the bank. He had a mixed team on perimeter security, chopping up the infected that were drawn to the sound of the shooting. So far, the largest group of zombies numbered less than half a dozen and most of the cops were reliable shots at close range. The number of dead zombies in view was gratifying, until you thought about them as victims.

And about how many were left.

Dominguez rubbed his eyes, which were irritated by the thin smoke that reached street level.

Above, flames were visible through the smoke that enveloped several upper floors.

"Sooner or later, they'll have to come out," he remarked for the benefit of his group. "Then we can collect another installment of payback."

"The garage is a no-go." Durante reported. "The armored roll-up door is shut, and it takes so long to open that by the time we emerge, they'll have shifted even more guns to cover it. Assuming we actually exit the garage in the BERT, we still can't drive very fast because we have to navigate the barricades. The MRAP is fifty meters past the entrance ramp—too big to fit inside the garage and too far for us to reach without getting most or all of us shot as we cross the open street."

Durante delivered his report to the group of survivors still huddling well back from the third-floor planters. He spoke over the fire that continued to probe the lobby area and adjacent floors. So far it had claimed three more victims.

Tom nodded and looked over at Kaplan.

"I went far enough to see that the basement level has zombies," the operator said with a shrug. "You can see them through the glass doors. Sixty, maybe more. Assuming we can clear those out, we still have to fight downwards to the platform level where, you know, the zombies are coming from. We could risk crossing under the street and coming up next door, but the cops are gonna have line of sight into every bottom floor. Hell, they could already be in the building waiting."

Tom nodded again.

"Why not stay here?" asked the MRAP driver. Tom hadn't even learned his name yet.

"Yeah!" Astroga said, piping up. "Now we'll get to confirm whether jet fuel actually can melt steel I-beams! Ouch!"

The last was in response to Copley's patented head smack bouncing off her helmet.

"Thanks, Sergeant," Tom said, trying for a withering glare, to which the young soldier seemed immune. "What she said; this building is on fire, plus what would we be waiting for? I can't think of anyone in a position to rescue us. So, we rescue ourselves. We need to evac to the RHIBs we stashed near Battery Park. We've got to break contact here and make it there far enough ahead of the cops that we can get the boats out of the shed and stay well outside of small arms range."

"And then what?" asked the MRAP driver.

"One thing at a time," Copley said. "What do we need now, sir?"

"Rope a dope. We're going to make a distraction in one direction and boogey out in the other."

"*Team two,*" one of the overwatch teams said on the radio. "*Movement on the garage door, north side.*"

"Let them come all the way out before you initiate," Dominguez radioed. He was a little relieved. The smoke was getting really thick. "Team Two, orient north and prepare to engage. Team One, stay on the front. I am en route to the garage side."

He would have more of Matricardi's people in his hands.

Finally.

∽ ◯ ๑

Joey Tradittore peeked around the corner. All the cops in view were looking towards the bank. He twitched his hand forward, and three Cosa Nova shooters took up staggered positions to his left.

He slowly raised his hand and the safeties on his men's weapons snicked off.

Stu Pegaso was a five-year veteran of the force when the Plague hit. After the precincts consolidated the second time, he ended up working directly for one of the spine-harvesting teams organized by OEM. It had been unpleasant work, but worth it to get the vaccine for Fran and their kids.

All of them were dead now.

He would die content if he could kill the fuckers that did it. The captain said it was the Jersey mob guys. He'd promised scalps.

That was good enough for Stu. They were on the side of the angels, weren't they?

Damn straight.

The BERT truck nosed out into the daylight as soon as the hood cleared the bottom of the armored garage door. It paused when the door reached the armored panel that had been lowered over the windshield, and then jerked forward again as soon as the door cleared the roof. The truck clumsily mounted the long exit ramp more slowly than a man could walk. The tac team watched it ascend and then, a hundred meters later, nose into a concrete bollard, failing to navigate the turn onto the street.

Pegaso pursed his lips. Something funny was going on.

Blocks behind him, he heard automatic fire start again. Even as he raised the radio to call Ding, he could tell that the sound of the firing was *different*. And there was more of it.

"Someone is shooting at the cops!" Kaplan reported.

The group had filtered through the pedestrian underpass to the adjacent building. They heard automatic fire start again. Several cops ran across their field of view, the last man being chopped into ribbons as they watched.

An Atlas truck lurched into the intersection to provide cover for the retreating cops, gun muzzles bristling from the firing ports. Before the occupants got more than a few rounds off, a series of very rapid overlapping booms sounded as the truck was covered in explosions. The cab roof of the black painted truck flew off under the jackhammer of explosions and the armored compartment collapsed inwards. The concussion of the explosions blew in the glass of their new building.

"The fuck?"

Tom couldn't hear Durante's surprised yell, but any experienced soldier could lip read that much.

"Grenade launcher," he hollered in Durante's ear. "Someone has brought a Mark 19 to the party. Friends of yours?" he asked Risky.

She shook her hair to get the debris out of it. A few pebbles of safety glass fell out. The formerly immaculate makeup was smudged with black, and her sleek dress was overlaid by her old plate carrier. The heels really set off the entire ensemble.

"Maybe," Risky said, then thought about it and shrugged. "Probably. We had one, but the standard of training in Matricardi's men is..."

She shrugged again.

Tom peeked about the corner of the now empty

window frame. He could see more than half a dozen black suited forms lying very still in the street. The grenadier had shifted targets to some other group out of line of sight, but the glass still danced on the floor from the vibration of rapid explosions.

"Grenade launcher. Fucking A!" Kaplan calmly shook the glass out of his hat. "I knew we forgot something from our shopping list."

"Quit bitching and pick your targets," Durante said grumpily.

"You're just wishing *you'd* thought to add it to the list, aren't you?" Kaplan replied, servicing targets.

The tarot card that Ding had been tapping against one fingernail crumpled in his fist.

"They've got a fucking grenade launcher," Team One radioed. "It's murdering us. The Four Unit is gone, just gone! Most of Tac Team One is down hard, the rest are out of the fight or pinned. I can see half a dozen shooters and two Suburbans. Looks like Cosa Nova."

Dominguez tightened his grip on the radio handset.

"Team Two, pivot back, the garage is a decoy," he said, squeezing his words past gritted teeth. "They're trying to pincer us from the west. Fire up anything that moves. Three Unit, engage the SUVs with the SAWs. Snipers, get that grenade launcher!"

He looked at his map. They had to kill the ambushers quickly and reestablish a cordon. Previously, he would have been content to allow the bank's people to escape however they might as long as he finished off Cosa Nova. But now, he knew that Smith was behind this, not just Matricardi. So be it. He would kill them all.

∾ ⊖ ∾

Tom felt the trip hammer of concussive tremors continue.

"The shooter's going to have to reload soon. The cops are reorienting now to face towards the attack. As soon as they look the other way, we hit them from the other direction and blow through the line. Get ready to move."

Pegaso had been pulling perimeter duty, dropping the occasional zombie while the remaining high-risk warrant teams assaulted the bank. He heard the staccato crash of explosives and the radio calls peter out as most of Tac Team One went down.

He heard orders to assault the hostile vehicles and responded by gathering up his immediate group and sprinting around the bank, collecting more of his people from perimeter duty along the way.

They sprinted down the street on the flank of the SUV with the grenade launcher and turned the corner in time to see the stubby barrel of the weapon pivot and orient on his group. He made out the features of the young gunner just as the muzzle of the weapon bloomed orange.

Thunder.

Darkness.

The young Cosa Nova shooter felt like a god.

He sat behind the tripod-mounted Mk 19, whose snout poked out of the back of the Suburban. He continued to obliterate anything that moved, chugging through grenades five and six at a time. He didn't know the difference, but his weapon fired dual purpose grenades. The "High Explosive—Dual Purpose" ammunition was designed both to defeat military armored personnel carriers and level entire buildings. Overlapping grenade bursts threw shrapnel for fifty meters, on one occasion reaching far enough back that he injured one of the Cosa Nova men.

Oops.

Despite the mishap, that particular burst was sufficient to critically damage a second police vehicle, this time a large white boxy truck resembling a fire rig.

Out of the corner of his eye he spied a group of cops pelting down the cross street. A quick twist of the launcher and he dropped another string of grenades in the center of the group. When the smoke cleared, he saw a few slowly crawling figures and lofted more rounds their way.

His own vehicle bucked with recoil as he neared the end of the ammunition belt. The last half dozen grenades splashed among another group of black garbed and armored cops sheltering behind the smoking wreckage of another Atlas truck. His fire tore through the boxy rig, and left the cops scattered across the sidewalk. He smiled as he lifted the feed tray and began the simple reload process, reaching for another heavy string of grenades.

He never heard the police sniper round that struck his temple, splashing his brains against the inside of the SUV.

"Center head."

The police sniper called his shot across the tactical radio link.

"I think that we dropped the grenadier, but we've lost a lot of men." The last FBI agent had lasted through the fight, and he huddled in the lee of the last police truck remaining in front of Bank of the Americas.

Captain Dominguez's voice replied right away.

"What is the status on the bank?"

Rounds cracked overhead and the FBI agent ducked. His liaison officer poked his head around the corner of the truck in time to catch a bullet between the running lights. More fire pocked the truck.

"They are bugging out, my way," the agent said. "Lots of fire."

"Hold till I get there." Dominguez's voice was insistent. "We got the grenadier. As soon as I clear the intersection I am sending some relief."

"No point," the agent answered. "This is all going to be over in a few minutes, either way. I hope this was worth it. I guess it doesn't matter."

The special agent set the radio down and once more tried to remember what his family looked like before he found their mutilated corpses. Then he took a deep breath and readied himself.

Tom led the diminishing knot of escapees down Stone Street, first away from the remaining sounds of combat, and then turned to circle the fighting. He'd lost the soldier who drove the MRAP and another of his security staff, and Kaplan was wearing a bloody head bandage.

Oldryskya trotted beside him. She looked at his face, which was drawn and tense.

Behind them the remainder stayed in a compact group. Durante brought up the rear.

Copley sped up and pulled abreast of Tom.

"What's the plan, sir?"

"I haven't heard the grenade launcher in a while," Smith said, looking both ways. "Unless Matricardi has more people than I expect, the cops that are left will take him for certain. He saved our ass, so we are going to return the favor. Then we E and E in whatever vehicle we can and head to the boats."

Kaplan cracked off a round, dropping an infected that was loping towards them.

"Damnit, noise discipline!" Tom snapped.

"You want maybe we let them take a few bites before we shoot, Boss?" Kaplan caroled back.

Tom took in the rest of this group without slackening his pace.

"Make sure you have a fresh mag in your weapon."

Ahead, the shooting slowed to a sporadic crackle and then ceased.

Tom halted the group and risked a look around the corner. There were at least half a dozen police officers oriented in his direction, hunkered down behind vehicles and inside doorways, effectively blocking their path. At least they had force parity, finally.

Sort of.

He gestured to Kaplan, pointing to the upper floors behind them and to the side. Kap nodded and tapped Oldryskya, who followed him back and upwards, to get an angle farther down the street.

Tom took in the rest of his people, composed of Durante, the roof security element and the two remaining guardsmen.

"Sergeant, detail Astroga to get our back," Tom instructed. "She keeps the cops from swinging behind us without us knowing. Hold off on infected unless they close. Then you take control of the fire element. As soon as you break cover, our top cover is going to burn through a magazine each on rapid fire, which they can only sustain for a few seconds, so don't dawdle. By then you need to be in fresh cover across the street and shooting. When I hear your base of fire pick up, Durante and I run the slot and flush the left side. By then the top cover is reloaded. Do that, and we can blow through this group."

Copley gave his head a single shake and circled up with the little group. Most were composed. A few were understandably pale. Astroga smacked the last Cosa Nova shooter on his butt and offered him a manic grin.

"Don't worry, we'll tell your ma' you died brave."

"Check out Rambette," Copley said, grinning. "Astro, you're an *admin clerk*, not Rambo."

"But I *wanted* to be infantry..."

Durante leaned in close.

"You figure we can rush them, just like that?" he said, his voice low. "This is bring your fobbit to work day, Boss."

The breeze, driven by the ocean that lay just out of sight, carried the smell of building fires, long since familiar. Tom looked up, but even though they hadn't moved very far from BotA's headquarters, his bank was out of sight, hidden by the serried ranks of skyscrapers. Looming far overhead the walls of buildings allowed the late afternoon sun to slant downwards at irregular intervals.

"Kapman knows what he is doing," Tom said, looking back at the team as they prepared. "The rest are just for noise. I figure that one of us should make it. Hell, we both might. But we've got to do this fast. If I let Dominguez consolidate, he'll pin us again. That means death, on this street, the next or the one after that—but we'll be done."

"That would be bad," Durante agreed. He looked down the narrow Manhattan road and then watched Tom roll his shoulder, settling his gear more comfortably. "You know, this reminds me of that job in Jordan, near Petra. Remember what you said?"

Ahead of them, the darkened street beckoned, a concrete and glass valley filled with deepening shadows.

"Yea, though I walk in the valley of the—?"

"No, no," Durante replied. "Not that old saw. You said, 'I sure wish we had a flight of two F-16s with JDAMs.' And then, like fucking magic, they showed up. You gonna pull another rabbit out of your hat or are Kapman and Risky all we got?"

"The second one," Tom answered. "They're just gonna have to be enough."

"When you have a clear headshot, give me a 'ready up' and I'll initiate," Kaplan said. "As soon as I do, take the shot, then put the rest of your magazine, single aimed rounds, as fast as you can into any cover that you see."

Oldryskya was tucked into the back of the room, invisible from the street. She picked out a man wearing the ruins of a suit, holding a radio.

"Ready up."

Despite expecting it, Tom still twitched when the first two shots cracked downrange, one right on top of the other. Immediately afterwards, his two designated marksmen began to fire one shot every half second. Before those two exhausted their magazines, the main group began firing rapidly, the sound of the rifles reverberating against the concrete and glass borders of the path that Tom and Durante would storm.

Tom waited until the firing reached a steady crescendo and then moved as fast as he could down the sidewalk, his rifle at the high ready. Moving briskly down the street with a rocking heel and toe stride, the pair moved faster than a walk, but slower than a trot. Tom kept every sense strained to the utmost, letting his combat instincts process the information faster than he could ever hope to do deliberately. His world was narrowed to the crystal clear focus on the red dot in the center of his optic and the somewhat fuzzier shapes of the cars and doorways that hid his targets.

Under severe stress, humans can begin to perceive time differently. Influenced by the changes in their neurochemistry, in turn brought on by the severe stresses of combat, even seasoned special forces soldiers were found to experience changes in how they processed sensory inputs and experienced time. Competitive shooters speak of being able to perceive the details of their pistol firing, the action operating and ejecting a case—something that happens in a fraction of second.

This is also true of how humans under stress can perceive sound. Sound is merely the movement of energy through matter via longitudinal waves. The human ear logarithmically parses sound impulses, allowing humans to both detect the quietest whisper and tolerate noise as loud as gunfire.

For values of the word tolerate.

Normally, a gunshot is heard as a single, overwhelmingly loud cracking sound. Persons without hearing protection will immediately perceive a high ringing in their ears as the cochlear cells respond to the painful amount of sound energy. This ringing, or tinnitus, overlays other auditory inputs, and severe enough tinnitus can blanket all other sounds, rendering a person functionally deaf. Even a single brief firefight can bring short-term deafness and varying levels of permanent hearing loss.

However, in a contained space, the effects of gunfire are even more profound. The glass and concrete surfaces of the buildings that lined the narrow canyons of the City were nearly perfect reflectors for sound energy. The reports of all the high-velocity weapons in use by both the banking team and the renegade police were bouncing not once or twice, but dozens of times per shot, and the combatants were exchanging hundreds of rounds. Each gunshot reverberated down the narrow street, the opposing sets of buildings reflecting it back and forth multiple times until the small battle generated a cacophony that approximated a full company in close combat.

Human speech was impossible. Rational thought was difficult, and even simple tasks became complicated. Combined with the effects of perceived time dilation, the sensation of combat was almost otherworldly for an operator like Smith. For the less experienced, it was shattering, leaving the former police at a considerable disadvantage.

Tom and Durante passed the friendly shooter line, and neither reacted as one of their own men folded over his belly, gut shot.

Ahead, a stranger in NYPD patrol blues pivoted onto the sidewalk, but Tom flicked the red dot across the rogue cop's chest even as he stroked the trigger three times, tumbling the target all the way to the ground. A head popped into view through a rear windshield and he punched rounds through that before moving on. Durante was a steady presence at his side, and Tom felt, rather than saw, his wingman pivot to add his fire to the target.

He felt a sting on his forearm but ignored the burning sensation, and sent several rounds through the ad hoc cover of an opened car door, dropping the shooter into a limp bundle between the curb and the squad car.

Another target, more rounds. He operated on reflex, reacting to each new input, servicing targets as fast as he could. Invisible fingers plucked at his pant leg. More movement. Target with body armor. Tom put his rounds through the neck and face. Next sight picture.

Tom's shooting was instinctive and rapid, the flash suppressor at the end of his gun barrel tracking precisely with every movement of his eyes.

The incessant echoes punished Tom's ears even more than the report of his own weapon, but even through the ferocious tinnitus that blanketed his world with a high-pitched, never-ending note, Tom heard the rate of fire begin to taper.

Durante was still moving close to his side, and Tom used his peripheral vision to watch as his wingman pivoted and sent a deliberate pair of shots into a corner display window, then one more. One leg flopped into view and was still.

Tom reached the end of the block and stacked on the edge of the corner building, changing his magazine and staying in concealment. Moments later Durante squeezed his shoulder and they turned simultaneously, one high and the other low. Empty, the street yawned at their theatrics.

Behind them several bodies leaked onto the sidewalk, but Tom couldn't muster any enthusiasm for shooting Dominguez's men. The best he could do was think about the next block.

There wasn't any firing now, just the moans of the dying.

Frank Matricardi stared at the black asphalt that was staining his slacks. The gunfight that had raged a few blocks away while he surrendered was over. His quiet radio and the lack of rescue made the outcome there pretty clear.

In the background, the cops exchanged comments as they policed the scene of their last firefight. Some chivvied their prisoners into a group.

A voice called out.

"Hey Ding, where do you want the guns?"

"Just dump them in the truck," the veteran cop answered. "We'll figure it out later."

The surviving Cosa Nova men were cuffed into a line of kneeling, bruised captives. Frank felt more than saw another person driven to their knees beside him.

Tradittore.

One of NYPD's former finest moved down the line, flex cuffing ankles and wrists. He heard hard, confident footfalls stomp up from behind.

"Well."

Frank craned his head one way, and finding the sunlight blinding his view of the speaker, he tried the other direction.

"Well."

Frank recognized the voice before he could discern the speaker's features.

Dominguez.

"I have dreamt of this moment."

"Well, this isn't exactly ho—" the Cosa Nova boss started to say but was silenced by an ungentle rifle butt to his kidney. A single shot rang out, and next to Frank, Tradittore jerked his head up in hope and fear, but it was only one of the cops dispatching an approaching infected.

"When I lost my wife, it was a warning," the tall police officer continued, ignoring the interruption, "that I had taken the wrong path. She left a message for me and I failed to heed it."

Matricardi heard the steps pace around him, slowly. Step. Step. Step.

"I stayed with the moneyed man, with the power-grasping bureaucrat, with you. Filth. Scum. Criminal."

Step. Step and turn.

Around the line of kneeling gangsters, a half moon of police gathered. They were breathing hard, almost panting.

"And I paid again. You left me a message. I found it, a perfect white flower in a field of red. Red blood. Blood of our children."

One of the vigilantes used his sniper rifle to muzzle-punch the last captive in the row.

"Our fucking kids, you motherfuckers!"

"Stop," Dominguez snapped. "Not yet."

Matricardi could hear his second muttering next to him, softly repeating a single syllable over and over.

"You represent the poison of this city." The top

cop resumed his litany. "I couldn't save my family. I didn't save my city—I destroyed it, with your help and your promises. So, you are going to watch us execute each of your animals, Frank Matricardi. And your last view will be of their pile of bodies. The wreckage of your evil, corrupt life. Then, I'll close your eyes forever on this island that you helped make into God damned hell."

Frank turned his head upwards, feeling the sun on his face for the last time.

"I didn't kill your family," he said, softly and calmly. "What kind of a fucking idiot would leave a fucking calling card for something like that, huh, *porco*? But you know what? I could give a shit, *coglione*!" He spat the words. "Your *porca dio* means nothing to me—so enough with your self-righteous monologue. Get this done. I don't got all day."

Sicilian wasn't Spanish, but Dominguez got the message. His face contorted in a silent snarl and he raised his pistol to the gangster's head.

"In a hurry, Frank? Then you can go first."

A shot rang out.

Tom recognized Dominguez even as the latter extended his pistol to shoot the kneeling man, but there was no time for a warning. Tom followed his first aimed shot with several more, keeping his rifle on the center of the form as it crumpled all the way to the ground.

Behind him, the others delivered rapid aimed fire. Caught looking the wrong way, the cops dropped in twos and threes from the unexpected fusillade. One put a burst of fire into the two closest gangsters before rounds from Copley and Durante scissored across his body.

A few cops, farther away, broke and ran.

Astroga and Kaplan jogged a short distance to get a firing angle on the fleeing figures, but Tom raised his hand to halt them. He chopped his hand at the far end of the gangsters, some starting to squirm to a seated position.

"Risky, Sergeant, let these guys loose. Kapman, Gravy, police the area and then get me a guns and ammo count. See what we can salvage. Astroga, check if that truck will start."

Tom walked up on Dominguez's still, facedown figure. If shooting the other cops left him somewhat remorseful, shooting Dominguez had left him empty. The cop hadn't been all bad though, it wasn't . . .

"What are you gonna do, close his fucking eyes?" Matricardi asked, squinting at Tom. "Very sweet. How about a little help, first?" He wiggled a bit, tried to get to his feet, then twitched his bound wrists. "Cut this off wouldja? I can't talk for shit with my hands cuffed."

CHAPTER 18

UNCLAS//
OPERATIONAL IMMEDIATE
I 270355Z AUG 27
FROM COMNORTHCOM
TO NAVSTA KINGSBAY KITSAP MAYPORT NEWLON
NORFOLK SANDIEGO PEARLHARBOR
INFO CJCCSWASHDC COMDTCOGARD C2FLT C3FLT
C5FLT C7FLT COMSTRATCOM COMSOUTHCOM
NARR/ REF A IS TELCON BETWEEN CJCCS00
SECNAV00, OPNAV00, NORTHCOM00
RMKS/1. H7D3 INFECTED INDIVIDUALS
CONFIRMED ABOARD NAVY VESSELS.
2. EFFORTS TO QUARANTINE H7D3 OUTSIDE
NAVAL INSTALLATIONS INEFFECTIVE.
3. CONOPS DEVELOPED REF A FOLLOW
4. ALCON IMMEDIATELY LAND INFECTED
PERSONNEL ASHORE. ISOLATE SHIPS CREW
ABOARD.
5. ALL SHIPS CAPABLE OF GETTING UNDERWAY
ARE TO SORTIE UPON RECEIPT.
6. REPORT TO SENIOR OFFICER PRESENT AFLOAT
WHEN OUTSIDE TWELVE MILE LIMIT.
7. THIS IS NOT A DRILL.
8. SORTIE SORTIE SORTIE.
I
BT//

—U.S. Navy Sortie Order

From: *Collected Radio Transmissions of the Fall*
University of the South Press 2053

The combined party of survivors was forted up in the lee of the least damaged Suburban. Tradittore was cooperating with Oldryskya and Copley as they triaged and provided first aid to the injured Cosa Nova team. The hale Jersey-ites and the remainder of Tom's little band pulled security.

Matricardi and Tom had begun to talk when Kaplan and Durante returned, seeking decisions on which salvage Tom wanted to retain.

"What do we got?" Tom asked his two partners in crime.

"We lost seven on the roof and in the building, four after we bugged out," Durante said with a sigh. "Apart from that, no wounds that are disabling. Well, for our people. The wops have two that are hurt pretty bad and two more that are pretty dinged up."

Smith looked down for a moment, then back up at the second man.

"Well, you already know what we brought to the party," Kaplan continued. "We're nearly out of subsonic rounds for the suppressed stuff. I scavenged thirty or so cop ARs and maybe a hundred magazines for them. Another couple of crates of five-five-six in the back of that Atlas that I haven't finished looting. A dozen subguns, all in nine mil, not much ammo for those. A lot of pistols, mostly Glocks and all of them are in nine mil too. Several bolt guns, varying calibers and limited ammo for those. Then there are these babies."

Kaplan gestured to the collection of fully automatic weapons. Tom looked the pile over. He recognized two military spec M60 variants, a Belgian designed SAW and four Russian pattern RPKs which could accept AK magazines, extended magazines or even drums. At the end of the line was the MK19, which still had a few blood smears on the feed tray cover.

"Ammo for the 19?" he asked.

"Not much," Kaplan answered. "Two cans of thirty-two rounds each. We got a bunch of radios, batteries and some car chargers. Also, some decent trauma gear from one of their big trucks. Are these things running?" He gestured to the Suburbans.

None of the vehicles were in ideal running condition. Matricardi's two SUVs had been riddled by police bullets, and the police vehicles had damage ranging from been blown apart by grenades to multiple flats and broken glass.

Tom's musing was interrupted.

"This is your plan?" Matricardi emphasized his words by poking the air in front of Tom's chest. "I thought that you college boys would have something better than let's haul ass out of the city and figure it out as we go."

The banker looked over.

"Last time I checked, you were still breathing despite the best effort of NYPD's finest."

There was a rattle of fire nearby and both men looked over as a couple members of the party spotted a trio of infected. Their fresh kills bled out in the street.

"But to answer your question, yeah, we have a plan. We take your trucks, we get to Battery Park and we get out in my boats."

Matricardi was incredulous.

"You want to motorboat all the way to the refuge?"

"Not particularly." Tom regarded him steadily as Tradittore walked up behind his boss. "You made it possible for us to break out, so I returned the favor. If you want to come, great. If you don't..."

Tom gestured broadly, taking in all of New York City.

"Mr. Matricardi, a moment?" Tradittore interrupted.

Matricardi eyed Smith, and then turned to his aide. Tradittore waited until the banker walked away.

"Close call, Boss." His voice didn't quite shake, but his hands trembled as he removed his sunglasses.

The older man looked at Joey, noting the tone and the hands. Kid was shook.

Matricardi grunted and shrugged one shoulder.

"We all got problems. So, what?" went unspoken.

"This deal is getting pretty thin," Tradittore continued. "We're right at the limit. We lose more men, we can't flip this thing. We get to Smith's base where we are outnumbered, we can't flip this thing. Any more people, we can't all fit. We just lost Stevie and Big Sam isn't gonna last. Any guesses on who dies next? More of our people."

More rifle fire interrupted their conversation. Then still more. The infected presence was getting distinctly heavier.

The new specialist was uncomfortably squeezed into a corner of the third-row bench seat. Despite that, she was writing on her ranger notepad.

"Number thirty-three: Must not remind scaredy-cat bankers that jet fuel does in fact melt steel I-beams when we are standing inside New York City burning building. Number thirty-four: Ass slaps for encouragement still count as sexual harassment. Number thirty-five: Even in combat. Number thirty—"

Astroga glanced up after an especially heavy thump

shook the lead Suburban and made her pencil slide across the page.

"Are you *intentionally* aiming for the biggest groups of zombies, Kap?"

Outside the little convoy, dozens of zombies were in view, partially clogging the street, but by maintaining a steady twenty-five miles per hour, Kaplan had successfully maintained headway while preventing catastrophic damage to their vehicle from the repeated impacts. The zombies showed only modest interest in personal survival, running at the car and bouncing off. Most caromed off the fenders to land in the street before fighting to their feet again. A few left bloody red smears on the windows. Those that fell under the bumpers as often as not were serving as impromptu buffets for their fellows, who fed on still living, struggling flesh.

Despite zombie fratricide, the trucks still pulled a growing comet tail of infected.

Tom looked ahead and considered the problem, then he tapped Kaplan.

"We're going to need some space in order to get to the boats before our noisy hungry friends gather in numbers. Need you to beat them there by a bit more."

Kaplan scanned the street, judging the partial roadblocks of abandoned vehicles.

"Gotcha."

He put his foot down and accelerated. Despite his efforts to avoid infected, the thumps and crashes against the trucks mounted in frequency and violence. That was all right, the truck only had to last another klick or two.

As long as the boats were there.

The truck shuddered again, shouldering aside an especially dense clot of infected.

Next to Copley, Astroga groused.

"Great. Now I can't write anything at all. Ouch!"

In the very back of the trail car, one of Matricardi's men banged his head on the roof liner as the heavy SUV rolled over infected knocked down by the first truck.

"Ouch!" He added some Sicilian phrases, probably for his boss's benefit.

The basic bitch thug wasn't even Sicilian born and his idiom was a little...poseur quality. Oldryskya wasn't fluent, but she had been around Matricardi enough to know the difference. She could see her erstwhile boss's face. He didn't need to speak for his eye roll to be understood.

Kids these days.

She saw the Cosa Nova leader tighten his grip on the chicken handle built into the SUV's dash as the truck rolled over another clot of bodies. She listened in on his next question to Durante.

"Why are we speeding up?"

"Tom figured out that we need to gain some distance from the mob behind us if we are going to do this safely," Durante answered without lifting his eyes from the road. "Well, safe-ish. The RHIBs are in a boathouse that looks like a shitty floating tool barge. We're gonna need a few minutes to embark."

Oldryskya was in the middle of the second bench seat, keeping pressure on a bandage she had put on one of the Cosa Nova shooters. Their body armor kept the second-row passengers from feeling the tight quarters as much as they would have otherwise. On her other side, Tradittore's leg unavoidably pressed against her bare thigh. Although he didn't seem to be paying attention to her, she still worked at not shuddering and kept her rifle propped between her legs, muzzle down.

She focused on Durante's words.

"Once we stop, we have to unload people and gear, unlock and prep the boats and meanwhile hold off dozens and eventually hundreds of zombies until we get underway," the contractor explained. "I bet the boss has some of us jock up in the zombie gear from the CEO rescue, if there is time. There is a steel fence at the head of the docks, but enough bodies can push it over. We want to be gone by then."

Risky craned her head, imitating Matricardi as he looked forward while they traversed Battery Park. Landscaping crunched and scratched at the bodywork as they motored towards the gate. Once they left the trucks, they were committed, since the vehicles would soon be overrun. The group could shoot their way through, for a while, if they didn't mind using up ammunition. Risky knew that Matricardi wasn't a soldier, but logistics was his business.

Judging from his expression, this business looked bad, but they ought to make it.

Then some civilians dodged across their path and Durante swore as he jerked the wheel and then fought to keep the heavy truck upright as it threatened to roll.

"Fuck, fuck, fuck, fuck, bloody fucking HELLFIRE!" Tom said, finally at long last losing his patience with the situation. "JUST BLOODY FOOKING *ONCE* COULD ONE *FOOKING* THING WORK WITHOUT A FOOKING COMPLICATION?"

The civilians were a group of students in school uniforms, mixed boys and girls, probably middle school at a guess, with a couple of equally terrified adults. The cluster was making a beeline for whatever looked like safety while being chased by a pack of rabid infected.

They were also blocking the locked gates to the boatshed.

"DEPLOY!" he screamed, yanking open the vehicle's passenger door. "Just fucking *once . . .*"

Wedged into a triangular patch of water between the Staten Island Ferry and the Battery Maritime building was a single narrow pier that the bank had leased. Formerly owned by a tour operator, it had come available on the cheap, following a profound post-Plague drop-off in midsummer tourist custom. A large but decrepit tool barge floated alongside with some sort of machinery covered by a stained tarp.

"Durante, Kaplan," Tom said as they cleared the gate. "Hold off our friends and get the gates shut. Guard," he continued, pointing to the barge, "get that cover off."

"Astroga, dockside," Copley said. "You, Numbnuts . . ."

"They call him Lugnut," Astroga said helpfully.

"Lugnut, fine, whatever," replied Copley, pointing at one of the remaining Cosa Nova goons. "Cross over there and grab the tarp. I'll take this end."

There was a platform on the landward side of the barge Copley stood on as Lugnut crossed to the narrow bulwark on the water side to undo the ties of the tarp while Astroga worked on the ties on the pier side. When they had them off they helped Copley pull the tarp to the rear.

The "machinery" turned out to be the two ten-meter RHIBs with inboard-outboard motors, the same ones that the bank had been operating during the collapse. The barge had already been partially flooded with the boats floating in the cargo space moored to the aft platform.

"Fucking cool," Lugnut said, balancing on the narrow bulwark. "But hows we get the boats outta da barge?"

"What's this?" Astroga asked. Right by her feet was a red lever. So, naturally, she pulled it.

The barge began to rapidly sink. Unfortunately, the gangster was standing on the water-side about midships.

"What the shit, Army!" he shouted, waving his arms. "The fuck do I do now?"

"Swim for it?" Astroga asked, jumping onto the pier.

The barge stopped sinking as it hit the shallow bottom, leaving the goon standing knee-deep in the water. The aft platform was just above the waterline, making for easy entry to the boats.

"Or, you know, walk to the platform?" Astroga said.

"Carefully," Copley pointed out. "Since, you know, you can't see your footing."

"Why's the torch and the crown on the Statue still lit?" Astroga asked, looking east towards the monument.

"Talk about non sequiturs," Copley said as Lugnut started to cautiously make his way to the rear of the barge. "Most of the lights are powered off the grid, Specialist. Those are the only lights on Liberty Island that have internal generators that still have fuel."

He might have just learned that last night, but no

sergeant ever misses an opportunity to prove their superior knowledge to an overpaid private, *promotion* be damned.

"Is it just me or does the head shed appear seriously pissed?" Astroga asked.

"God, you ask a lot of questions," Copley said, looking over at the cluster of Smith and the Mafia dudes. "But, no, it's not just you."

Lugnut looked up too.

"Those little boats?" Tradittore blurted angrily. "How are we going to fit everyone into those things! How far are we gonna get?"

Matricardi waved him to silence, one hand palm down.

"I was expecting something a little more substantial," Matricardi said, looking at Tom. "How far are we gonna go in those things, Smith?"

Distracted, Tom looked up at the dockhead, gauging the number of zombies beginning to accumulate outside the fence. He waved at Durante and vigorously pointed at the entrance. The tall operator looked, then gathered his remaining team as he trotted back towards the steel gate that barred entry. At the boats, Kaplan was trying to start the second RHIB. Copley had the black nonskid-coated engine covers off, following Kaplan's directions. The rest of the party was passing gear towards the first boat, whose engines idled, spreading acrid gray exhaust across the harbor chop. Matricardi's wounded were already aboard.

Tom's mind was racing, weighing the variables. He tuned out the not so quiet asides between the

376 John Ringo & Mike Massa

two mobsters. He spoke as he watched Kaplan's arm emerge from the engine compartment and wave urgently for a tool.

"Far enough," Smith said. "And we run south."

"South!" Tradittore didn't quite squawk. "There ain't nothing south. The closest Site is north, right up the fucking Hudson. The next closest site is even further north, in fucking Maine."

Matricardi raised his hand, as if to slap his subordinate, but held it. Tradittore barely flinched, but his eyes blazed.

"Shut up, Joey. We know that. Let him speak. He has a plan. So maybe take the time to explain, because like my excited associate pointed out, south isn't exactly what we were thinking."

A shot sounded by the gate, but Durante's calm voice followed right after.

"No problem, just giving them a little something to eat. But hurry, would you?"

Tom jerked his head back from the gate and focused on the Sicilian pair.

"Ask me for anything but time," Tom muttered, then turned to face the mobster. "Nationwide failures of the power grid are cascading as we speak. The last and biggest movement of refugees has started. The Hudson narrows past West Point. Every Tom, Dick and Harry is going to be tear assing out to sea in the opposite direction and those that haven't will do anything to take a boat. Do you *really* think we can motor upriver, just like that?" Tom snapped his fingers. "We go south, a couple miles offshore. We get clear of the worst of the Boston to D.C. gridlock. Then we head for Site Blue."

Tom watched Frank Matricardi's calculating eyes as Tradittore began to argue.

"We have enough guns to blow right upriver!" Tradittore shook his fist. "We just speed up and use the belt-feds and the grenade launcher!"

"No," Tom said, shaking his head and holding Matricardi's gaze. "You're ignoring logistics. Ours is limited—both shooters and ammo." Over Matricardi's shoulder, he saw Oldryskya approaching. Even torn, even under a plate carrier, that dress was still distracting as hell.

"The Boston–Washington corridor is fifty *million* people—more than ten times the population density in most of this country." He lowered his voice a little, making his point to Matricardi. "This is about logistics. Anywhere we go upriver, we hit people. *Lots* of people. First from here, then Albany, then Schenectady, then the crossovers from Boston. We would never find a place to get off the river safely before we were overwhelmed with the refugee traffic from the densest population belt in the country. We head south, out to sea, all we hit is waves and yachts punching out to sea. We'll be better armed, faster than what we encounter and risk fewer incidents. Upriver...we're fucked."

Matricardi put his hand on the shoulder of the still-expostulating younger man, but he nodded at the little group of civilians that they had narrowly dodged on the last dash across the park, and then pulled inside the fence to safety. Tom followed his gaze to a forlorn tangle of middle school kids in some kind of maroon parochial school uniform and a couple of adult females, probably the minders.

"And them?" Matricardi asked.

"*Everyone* gets out," Tom said levelly. "No discussion."

Matricardi looked at Tom, back at the refugees and then glanced up at the gate where more zombies were intermittently visible through the gaps in the fence. Durante and two others were pushing against the gate, keeping it closed. He shook his head, first side to side, then paused and looked upwards.

Tom waited a long count, but didn't break the silence. Matricardi shifted his gaze to Tom's face and then out at the water. Shaking his head in the affirmative, he spoke.

"*Va bene*. Everyone goes south." He shrugged and turned to look at his second. "Joey, what we are gonna do i—"

Joey Tradittore calmly and smoothly produced a pistol and shot Matricardi in the face. As Smith began to react, Tradittore shot at someone past him, then sidestepped behind Oldryskya and socketed the pistol in her neck. Several shots sounded, including a short burst of automatic fire. Tom froze, his hand on the pistol still in the holster high on his hip. A loud splash made him look over his shoulder.

One of Matricardi's hale goons was competently holding the RPK, aiming at a little group of bank staff. Astroga was floating facedown in the dirty green harbor water. Kaplan wasn't in view, but blood was visible on the RHIB sponson. The kids were screaming hysterically.

"Nothing personal, Smith," Tradittore said, his tight grin showing clenched teeth. "Just changing the business plan. We'll take one boat, and Frank Matricardi's wayward little lamb, and just evacuate ourselves."

Other than moving his head, Tom had frozen, his hand still on the holstered SIG. Despite his watchful stillness, the gangster could see the imminent threat.

"Nuh-uh-uh, Smith. Not even a quiver. I know you are a badass, but are you good enough to drop me and all of them before either I put one into your girlfriend or my boy shoots every mother's son?"

Backing away, Tradittore continued to drag Risky towards the boats. She placed her hands on the arm around her neck, but otherwise shuffled backwards too. Her violet eyes were locked on Tom's.

Durante was still shoving against the gate, yelling, his voice full of strain.

"*Boss?*"

Tom spoke for the first time since Matricardi fell. "Hold what you got, Gravy."

"That's right, *Gravy*," Tradittore said, his confidence growing. "Do what the big man says, and you all can leave, after we are clear. All you assholes at the gate should keep that thing closed. Sure hate for this to turn into a gunfight, what with my man already aiming at those zombies behind you with his AK."

Oldryskya snorted in derision, then choked as Tradittore squeezed her neck between his bicep and forearm.

"Shut it, bitch." His eyes flickered in constant motion. The gate, Smith, the girl, the Army guy, back to the gate. "When I want your fucking opinion I'll give it to you!"

His eyes jerked left and right. He kicked a dropped AR off the dock. It plopped into the water satisfactorily. Behind him, the remaining two upright Cosa Nova men joined their wounded in the idling boat.

Tom kept watching, weighing the odds and measuring the angles. No combination of friendly shooters and timing would keep Risky and other members of his dwindling group from getting shot, perhaps multiple times.

"Take her," Tradittore called over his shoulder once he reached the boat. The Cosa Nova gangster at the coxswain's console grabbed her hand and spun her into the rear of boat, where she landed roughly, scraping on the nonskid. She cried out, but quickly subsided, leaning against the sponson and clutching her knees. She looked at Tom a last time and then turned her head away, shoulders shaking.

Tradittore unwound the painter from the dock cleat and hopped aboard, then called to his man holding the heavier automatic weapon. That man stepped aboard and took a position just behind the coxswain, maintaining a clear field of fire landwards.

"Now, I'm gonna go my way, Smith." Tradittore explained. "Don't follow me. Next time I see you, you're all dead. And just to keep you honest..."

The new mob boss emptied his pistol into the sponson and console of the remaining RHIB.

"That's fixable, but you'll be a little delayed." Tradittore clumsily reloaded his pistol, fumbling the empty magazine onto one of the wounded covering the foredeck. He rapped the center console to signal the driver. The goon with the machine gun kept the dock covered from the rear deck as the boat smoothly accelerated away.

Tom watched the boat for a few moments, then yelled to Durante.

"Find something to wedge the gate and come help

me, Gravy!" Without waiting for an answer, he dove into the water to grab Astroga.

Risky listened to Joey's little soliloquy. She twitched as he shot his pistol. She kept her face turned away as her carefully metered shaking continued, but ignored the lacerations on her knee and shin, courtesy of the ungentle push onto the nonskid decking of the RHB. Joey was talking to his two upright thugs. She couldn't make out all the words over the increasing roar of the dual Volvo-Penta engines, but the triumphant tone was unmistakable. Someone nudged her exposed thigh with a scuffed combat boot and laughed. She heard the conversation more clearly now.

"Hey Mikey, you can ignore the silly bitch," Tradittore said. "Help Lugnut with the wounded. I'll drive us out to mid channel so we can get situated."

The speed created a strong breeze, pulling her hair over her face. She shook a little more, folding her arms on the sponson and surreptitiously ducked her head enough to get a view of the gangsters' feet.

Lying flat, the bipod folded, the RPK was not even a long reach away. Beyond it she could see Tradittore's heels where he balanced against the motion of the boat. Glancing back up she could see the Staten Island ferry terminal recede as the RHIB continued to smoothly curve towards the middle of the river. If she was going to act, it would have to be soon, before the odds against her increased. She had an ugly feeling about her ultimate value for Matricardi's former lieutenant. She'd been down that path before. She'd do it again as an absolute last resort. Maybe. But not if she had any chance at all to avoid it.

Oldryskya carefully turned back to face the interior of the boat. Unnoticed, she gathered her legs under her, measuring the distance to the machine gun. Back on the dock, she had snorted because the weapon wasn't an AK, as Tradittore had said; it was an updated RPK, the modern version of the venerable Russian fire-support weapon with a slightly higher rate of fire and a much larger magazine. Neither a talent for organization nor a wide streak of sadism was quite the same thing as proficiency with weapons.

As she was about to demonstrate to the new head of the Cosa Nova.

The basic controls probably hadn't changed in fifty years. They certainly hadn't changed in the fifteen years since she first learned on a Kalashnikov.

Still seated, she made a long arm, drew the gun to her, and shouldered the heavy weapon.

Tradittore might have caught the motion or maybe his sixth sense warned him. He turned just in time to see Risky click the safety downwards. Violet eyes slitted against the wind met his wide brown gaze for a long second.

Then she fired a continuous burst, striking him in the groin and riding the recoil as the point of aim climbed above his suddenly ruined face. Big Mikey turned and gaped, then dove for her. She fired into his center of mass, and his lunge became a clumsy fall. Bleeding, his corpse dropped onto the black nonskid.

She looked up and met the eyes of the original coxswain who unhesitatingly dove over the side.

Good instincts, that one.

The boat continued to motor on, so she shrugged the RPK's sling around her neck and used a handrail to haul herself up. The weapon rewarded her by rapping both shins. Wincing, she retarded the boat's throttles. In the front of the craft, the two wounded Cosa Nova men lay on their back, all eyes.

Risky's hands were steady as she swiftly pulled a fresh magazine from a pouch on the deck and rocked it into the RPK. She stood, swaying slightly, and covered the unmoving men. She looked shoreward, and then back at the bloody tangle that she had created.

Right. *First things first.*

The two short bursts of fire were clearly audible several hundred yards away.

Tom yanked his head up from the rescue breathing he and Copley were using on Astroga. The little specialist's plate carrier had been good enough to stop the nine mil rounds, as advertised, but she had been stunned and dropped face-first into the water. Durante was judiciously using his remaining ammunition to discourage the zombies, despite the noise that surely attracted even more.

Kaplan, his bandage missing and his head wound seeping blood, grimaced as he twisted the crane on his tourniquet, tightening it even further on his thigh.

"If it doesn't hurt . . ." he strained through gritted teeth, "then . . . you aren't . . . doing it . . . right."

Previously ignored in the urgency-filled moments following its departure, the stolen BotA boat was still in plain view less than a half mile away.

The shots drew all the survivors' attention. In the receding boat, motion was visible. A body went over the side. After a longish pause the RHIB slowed. More motion was visible as another body was dumped over the side. Another long pause and another plunked into the mild chop.

What the hell?

"Copley, Kap, arm up," Tom rapped out. "Durante, leave the gate, get ready in case they come back." Tom leaned back to continue rescue breathing, just in time to catch a mouthful of ejecta from Astroga, who convulsed weakly as she coughed.

Using her gear, he rolled her onto her side, then puked himself. Rising to hands and knees, he looked up and mentally shook himself. The boat was getting underway again.

A single figure stood upright. Long dark brown hair streamed backwards from the coxswain and then disappeared as the bow turned back to the dock, foreshortening the perspective.

Less than a minute later, Tom watched as Risky pulled the throttles all the way back. Coasting the final yards, the RHIB stopped as the rubber bow sponson absorbed the slight impact of docking. The tall brunette was poised like a big-game hunter, the RPK perched on her hip. Forward, the last two Cosa Nova gangsters in the world lay one on top of the other, carefully *not* moving.

"Despite Joey's objection, I gave him my opinion anyway," Risky said with a grin, keeping one eye slanted towards her prisoners. "I decided that he didn't deserve a ride in my boat. These two are spare parts."

As the flotilla cleared Sandy Point, Tom Smith spared but a single look over his shoulder for the burning city they left behind. New York was mostly invisible, but several large buildings were silhouetted against the wreath of smoke, illuminated from underneath by the dancing orange and yellow flames consuming the city. The wind-ruffled water was bisected by the arrow-straight wakes of the RHIBs.

In the forward well of his boat and under his watchful eye lay the two wounded Cosa Nova gun men, securely bound. After Tom insisted on bringing them out, Kaplan had methodically used a half roll of duct tape to immobilize them for the journey, helpfully arranging them head to foot.

Astroga had assisted him and rolled them rather ungently against the gunnel, eliciting a grunt of discomfort.

"Oh, did that hurt?" she had asked solicitously. "My bad. Coordination is off since, you know, your asshole friend *shot* me." She'd snugged the goons safely into place against the inner hull with a few judicious knee strikes.

Smith glanced at his watch and solved the time and distance equation in his head, estimating the length of the water transit. He swayed slightly as the hull met the swells just offshore, lifting and falling in a rhythm that had ignored men for millennia. The shooting glasses he appropriated from Kaplan kept most of the windburn from his eyes, and the amber lenses brightened the path ahead for a time, but eventually yielded to the deepening nautical twilight.

For the first time in what felt like a long time, there wasn't anything that he had to attend to right *now*. No emergency, no phone calls . . . there was just the boat, the sea, the journey. A glance at the afterdeck revealed that the passengers were mostly sleeping.

His glance lingered on the bundle of blankets that covered Risky before he resumed his scan.

Tom felt alert, alive, and the helm was rock steady. In his wake, Durante cox'd the second RHIB. The offshore wind from the river brought the smell of things not meant to burn.

Waves reflected sullen red as the boats quit the memory of man for the cover of night.

Behind the boats, the torch and crown of Liberty continued to burn until, in the darkness, they flickered, lit one last time, and were extinguished.

NEXT STOP? THE WILD, HAUNTED WORLD OF

TIM POWERS
DON'T MISS YOUR EXIT

An ex-Secret Servant agent. A woman haunted by the ghosts of California's highways. And the government conspiracy that ties them all together.

ALTERNATE ROUTES
HC: 978-1-4814-8340-7 • $25.00 US / $34.00 CAN
PB: 978-1-4814-8427-5 • $7.99 US / $10.99 CAN
A fast-paced supernatural adventure story that sweeps from the sun-blinded streets of LA to the horrifying labyrinth of Greek mythology. Sebastian Vickery and Ingrid Castine must learn to abandon old loyalties and learn loyalty to each other if they hope to survive in a world gone mad.

FORCED PERSPECTIVES
HC: 978-1-9821-2440-3 • $25.00 US / $34.00 CAN
Pursued by a Silicon Valley giant hungry for their souls, fugitive ex-Secret Service agent Sebastian Vickery and his companion Ingrid Castine throw themselves deep into the haunted world that lurks just beneath the surface of sunny California.

"Powers writes in a clean, elegant style that illuminates without slowing down the tale. . . . [He] promises marvels and horrors, and delivers them all."   —Orson Scott Card

"Other writers tell tales of magic in the twentieth century, but no one does it like Powers."   —*The Orlando Sentinel*